From Science to Emancipation

The Bhaskar Series

From Science to Emancipation

Alienation and the Actuality of Enlightenment

ROY BHASKAR

Sage Publications

New Delhi/Thousand Oaks/London

First published in 2002 by

Sage Publications India Pvt Ltd
M-32 Market, Greater Kailash-I
New Delhi 110 048

Sage Publications Inc.   **Sage Publications Ltd**
2455 Teller Road   6 Bonhill Street
Thousand Oaks, California 91320   London EC2A 4PU

Published by Tejeshwar Singh for Sage Publications India Pvt Ltd, typeset in 10.5/12.5 Galliard BT by Tulika Print Communication Services Pvt Ltd, New Delhi, and printed at Chaman Enterprises, Delhi.

Library of Congress Cataloging-in-Publication Data Available

ISBN: 0-7619-9716-4 (US-Hb)   81-7829-198-3 (India-Hb)
        0-7619-9717-2 (US-Pb)   81-7829-199-1 (India-Pb)

Sage Production Team: N.K. Negi, P.J. Mathew, Vamanan Namboodiri, Rajib Chatterjee and Santosh Rawat.

Contents

From Science to Emancipation
Manifesto of meta-Reality

eta-Reality is a new philosophical position devised by Roy Bhaskar, originator of the influential, international and multi-disciplinary philosophy of critical realism. It accepts but goes beyond critical realism, in so far as it pinpoints the reality of non-dual states and phases of being, showing how they underpin and sustain the totality of all forms of human, and indeed all, life. Understanding *meta-Reality* is to realise the limitations of the world of duality.

Critical realism already understands reality as structured and differentiated, as in process and changing, as a totality or whole and as containing human, potentially self-conscious, transformative agency. The world that humankind has made and which we currently inhabit is a world of duality: of unhappiness, oppression and strife—more especially, it is a world in which we are alienated from ourselves, each other, the activities in which we engage and the natural world we inhabit, currently hurtling into crisis and self-destruction.

The philosophy of *meta-Reality* describes the way in which this very world nevertheless depends upon, that is, is ultimately sustained by and exists only in virtue of the free, loving, creative, intelligent energy and activity of non-dual states of our being and phases of our activity. In becoming aware of this we begin the process of transforming and overthrowing the totality of structures of oppression, alienation, mystification and misery we have produced; and the vision opens up of a balanced world and of a society in which the free development and flourishing of each unique human being is understood to be the condition, as it is also the consequence, of the free development and flourishing of all.

In developing this vision the philosophy of *meta-Reality* confirms and re-presents many aspects of the vision of the great philosophical traditions of the past, but does so in a radically new way, apt for contemporary times. We begin this process of becoming free, that is, of expanding the zone of non-duality within our lives, by becoming aware of all the elements that currently constitute them and throwing off all those elements which are inconsistent with our free, creative, loving natures. In this process we come to realise that the very world of misery and destitution we have created itself contains and is sustained by the seeds of a society of abundance, peace and fulfilment, in which we are all free to express and fulfil our essential natures.

Preface

This book describes my journey from my presentations of critical realism in 1997, when I was already interested in and working on spiritual and transcendental questions, trying at once to relate them to my philosophical explorations and at the same time to the weaknesses and failures of socialist and more generally Left wing politics in the west; through to the position which I called transcendental dialectical critical realism, which I articulated in my book *From East to West*,[1] published in April 2000. And then the journey from that position, my first systematic attempt to integrate spirituality into the philosophical framework of critical realism, to the position which I now hold, which I have elaborated as the philosophy of meta-Reality.

The main difference between the philosophy of meta-Reality and critical realism, in all its forms, including the transcendental dialectical critical realist system articulated in *From East to West*, is that critical realism has been founded on the principle of non-identity, and as such reflects the limitations of the world of duality; whereas the philosophy of meta-Reality stresses identity, identification and unity; and the ubiquity and centrality of

---

[1] Routledge, London and New York, 2000.

non-dual states and phases of being in our social life. The philosophy of meta-Reality accepts critical realism, as hitherto developed, as being the best account of the *dual* world of relative reality. That is a world which is at present (as it has been, as far as we can tell, in most recorded history) dominated by the *dualistic* world of demi-reality, in which the dualities of the world of relative reality sharpen into antagonistic, oppositional splits, proliferating into gaping contradictions and producing profound alienation at all the planes of social being.

Critical realism possesses a huge advantage over irrealist philosophies, whether of an orthodox (which would include empiricism, neo-positivism, neo-Kantianism, hermeneutics, structuralism, post-structuralism, including ethnomethodology and discourse theory) or a heterodox sort (ranging from various Marxist to various postmodernist positions, including ones which have been generated in the wake of the rise of the new social movements, particularly feminism, ecology and the peace movement). The advantage of critical realism is this: that for the most part and to the greater extent, these irrealist philosophies merely reflect the surface structure of relative reality, the world of demi-real duality and the alienations, contradictions, reifications and dualisms of that world, which they merely replicate or elaborate in theory. Critical realism, in virtue of its commitment to the explicit thematisation of being and its understanding of the stratification of being and its development of the ideas of being as in process, as a totality and as incorporating transformative agency and reflexivity (as well as, in its latest, most contentious phase, a spiritual aspect) can show the possibilities of a non-dualistic world of duality, from which the structures which presently oppress us are shorn.

The deep structures which critical realism theorises are still however structures of duality, founded on principles of non-identity; and so they cannot penetrate through to the non-dual basis which underpins the whole world of duality, including the structures of oppression and alienation which currently dominate not only the world of duality but its non-dual basis or ground.

There are three ways in which the world of non-duality underpins the world of duality:

1. It underpins it in a very quotidian, ordinary way as being essential to the constitution, that is the reproduction and transformation, of everyday life. Let me go into this a little bit here. Most philosophers who have talked about non-dual or transcendence/transcendental experiences have regarded them as being something very extraordinary, only achieved in special places or moments of communion with the divine or in nature or in some other way consisting in a bliss, peak and very unusual experience. Moreover, normally the other term in the experience of union or identity is left mysterious. On the contrary, I argue, in developing the philosophy of meta-Reality that non-dual, including transcendental, experiences are essential for any form of communication between human beings, and ultimately any perception; and also for any act at all. For when you understand or even listen to what I say then in that moment of understanding or listening you are in a non-dual state of transcendental identification with me. Similarly, in order to act at all there must be something, at some level, which you do not do by thinking about how to do it, but which you just do, spontaneously, unconditionally, normally pretty effortlessly, and unless you acted in that non-dual way, you could never do anything at all. Moreover, in the case of communication, perception and action, the terms identified are clear enough: we are at one with another being or our action, and though we are not split or in duality, the terms which are identified are clearly defined, entities like you or me. In its most basic sense, transcendental identification is just unity with a context and there need be nothing mysterious about that.

In genealogical terms, elaboration of this moment of non-duality occurred to me by reflection of the way in which there was a non-algorithmic moment in any scientific revolution, discovery or even ordinary learning, that is a moment of pure creativity which could not be derived by induction or deduction or any mechanical formula. And it seemed clear to me that this was a very obvious paradigm of transcendence, with analogies to transcendence experiences in religion, art and other forms of life; but it was one, defining a moment of absolute transcendence in the movement of relative transcendence to a more totalising scientific or practical position, which was absolutely essential for the understanding of (among other activities) science, the paradigmatic human activity for western philosophy from Descartes if not indeed Aristotle. An obvious question arose: what were the terms in the union when we had a moment of scientific or any other creativity, for in as much as it was a breakthrough, it was also a moment of emergence out of the blue. I came to see that this epistemological transcendence was quite consistent with ontological immanence. But in making full sense of this, I had to develop the idea of the moment of creativity, discovery or even simple learning (or re-creativity) as involving the union between something already enfolded within the discovering agent, brought up to consciousness by a moment of Platonic anamnesis or recall, with the alethic self-revelation of the being known, existing outside him. And this is of course, in all its terms—that of the subjective condition, the objective result and the union between the two—is a very radical theory of discovery, one applicable, however, to all spheres of learning and, *a fortiori*, to all human life.

So this is the first way in which the world of non-duality underpins the structures of duality, including dualism.

2. The second way in which non-duality underpins the world of duality depends on a feature of the stratification of being which critical realism should find it particularly easy to situate. Science reveals a hierarchy of strata in being; and such stratification is a very characteristic feature of all forms of activity and being. Theories of emancipation, whether secular or religious, have always posited a level of human nature or potential which, in some way, either man himself, or his existing social order, inhibits, stunts, suppresses or even altogether screens or occludes. The task of emancipation has characteristically been conceived as involving the throwing off of this emergent oppressive level which reposes on the primary, foundational but suppressed level. Christianity, Buddhism, Marxism, Western liberalism all involve the idea of human nature, which would usher in a better world, if only the structures which fetter it could be thrown off.

Now there is a crucial strengthening of this position which I would like to register. And that is that this level which actually underpins and sustains the world which we know must already contain all, but not necessarily only, what we need to realise the utopian ideal. Thus we must assume that human nature, as it is constituted now, must be capable of sustaining a communist society in which, in Marx's vision of it, 'the free development of each is a condition of the free development of all', could be realised. And similarly, that human beings even now must be capable of being able to evaluate the realisation of all other beings in the universe as highly as their own, as in the ideal of the Bodhisattva. These are not utopian ideals. Rather, they point to or indicate a level which is an actual and continually efficacious condition of possibility for all states of being and systems of social order. This level of an essential human nature is actualised everywhere as a necessary condition for everything we do, it is a condition of the world which oppresses us and in which we oppress ourselves. Thus consider the phenomenon of war. This phenomenon, in a way the epitome of human hatred, is sustained only through the selfless solidarity of soldiers fighting at the front and the support they receive from their sisters, daughters and mothers at home.

This idea developed from an argument which made use of a concept I had already introduced in as early as *Dialectic: The Pulse of Freedom*,[2] namely that of an ultimatum, an ultimate or basic level of the universe which would have to be ingredient or immanent in all other levels of the universe emergent from it. This idea of an ultimatum is developed in the philosophy of meta-Reality into the idea of all beings having a *ground state*, which both embodies the qualities necessary to bind the universe together as a whole and at the same time is always specifically differentiated in the species or being concerned. Thus every species, and every being within a species, will in principle have a different ground state, but they will be united with every other ground state through, and at the level of the ultimatum, what I call the *cosmic envelope*. The ground state qualities of human beings consist *inter alia* in their energy, intelligence, creativity, love, capacity for right-action and the fulfilment of their intentionality or will in their objectifications in the natural and social world. It is the energy, intentionality and qualities of the ground state which are

---

[2] Verso, London and New York, 1993.

everywhere used and abused in the world of the emergent orders which they sustain, and which constitute the hidden or dominated basis or ground of all our alienation, suffering and ills.

This then is the second mode in which non-duality is central to social life and human agency. It is that level without which no other level could exist and have the particular properties they do, no matter how horrendous they are.

3. There is a third level, only slightly more recondite, in virtue of which non-duality can be said to underpin the world of duality and dualism. This is the sense in which if you go deeply enough into any aspect of being you will find buried in its fine structure or deep interior qualities which can only be described in terms of such quasi-metaphorical language as emptiness (*sunyata*), suchness (*tathata*), the void or the Buddha-nature, pure unbounded love or *sat-chit-anand*, that is the bliss consciousness of being which, whether you want to argue it possesses a teleological dynamic, in the sense that in some actual or metaphorical way all things strive for it (so that it would then be the fundamental driving force of evolution) it nevertheless, certainly constitutes, in interiorised form, the ground state of every moment of all being, the 'quiddity' of everything which is.

Whereas the first two modes of non-duality can be shown by relatively simple transcendental *arguments*, this third mode has to be *experienced*, and pertains to the experience of mystics and poets throughout the ages. However, these three modes are also inter-related. For if you go deeply enough into any non-dual state you are in, or into any being or object you have achieved transcendental identification with, ultimately you will come to *that* mystical experience, and when you do, you will be at one with *its* ground state in *your* ground state. At this point, we have, if you like, the unity or transcendental identification of two ground states.

These are not the only ways in which the philosophy of meta-Reality differentiates itself from existing critical realism. But this is not the place to articulate those further differences. My *Reflections on meta-Reality*[3] does that; and they have been system-

---

[3] Sage Publications, New Delhi, Thousand Oaks, London, April 2002.

atically set out in *The Philosophy of meta-Reality*,[4] where I show how we need to add two additional levels of ontology to the existing five of critical realism. The first, which I call the sixth realm (6R) of *re-enchantment*; and the second which I call the seventh zone or awakening (7Z/A) of *non-duality*, underpin the existing five levels which I rehearse in Chapter 1 of this book. Moreover these issues come up systematically throughout the book, and in the interview in Chapter 10 with Mervyn Hartwig, the differences between critical realism and meta-Reality are specifically thematised. It is also just worth mentioning here that this book has a companion, consisting in a sustained series of dialogues, *Fathoming the Depths of Reality: Savita Singh in Conversation With Roy Bhaskar*,[5] which retraces, in great detail the development of these ideas from their first seeds in the late 1960s and early 70s through to the present.

This book is based on talks given in Europe, Asia and America over the years 1997–2002. The most basic acknowledgement I need to make is that of my appreciation of and thanks to the organisers of the meetings, projects or programmes in which they were held, all voluntary contributions by people dedicated to the cause of free debate and discussion of these issues. Without such unconditional commitment none of these talks could have taken place. During the initial stages of the period covered by the talks in this book, my colleagues in the Centre for Critical Realism, and its sister organisation the International Association of Critical Realism, played a very important role. In particular I must mention Andrew Collier, Margaret Archer, Doug Porpora, Tony Lawson, Alan Norrie, Nick Hostettler, Sean Vertigan and Mervyn Hartwig. I was at one point intending to write a book with the first three of these, and a discussion which took place around some propositions which I had formulated on the basis of the discussions the four of us had had, is recorded in the interlude between Chapters 5 and 6. It will be apparent then that, though we were all committed to the importance of the philosophical discussion of issues

---

[4] *The Philosophy of meta-Reality Volume I: Creativity, Love and Freedom*, Sage Publications, New Delhi, Thousand Oaks, London, forthcoming.
[5] Sage Publications, New Delhi, Thousand Oaks, London, forthcoming.

to do with spirituality and religion, and to the idea of their compatibility with a this-worldly approach oriented to transformative political practices, there were, even then, differences in the ways we were going; so that the book we intended to write together, they are now pursuing, with my best wishes, on their own.

My lecture and workshop tours in America, and possibly even more so in India, played a decisive role in stimulating the formation of the ideas which the philosophy of meta-Reality articulates. To my friends and organisers in America, especially Hans Despain, Howard Engelskirchen, Hans Ehrbar, Doug Porpora, Charlie Smith (but many more could be mentioned and are gratefully remembered), go my very special thanks. It seems even more gratuitous to single out a few people in India, when there are so many people who have done so much; but it would be extremely unfair of me not to record my very special appreciation of the unstinting work put in by Manindra Thakur, Savita Singh, Nirmalya Chakraborty and Madhucchanda Sen, and Lakshmi Kumar. However, I am only too aware of how much I owe to all those throughout the world whom I haven't specifically mentioned here.

Now is perhaps the time to say that, in a way, my greatest debt of all has been to my audiences, without their presence and attention, without the stimulus of their debate and questions, these ideas would not have been sharpened into their present form. Then I would like to thank my British-based organisers, who no less than their non-British counterparts played an absolutely indispensable role—among them are Juliet Nusser and Pauline Hadley. All these transcripts were superbly typed by Jenny Cobner, with great speed and accuracy, backed up with good philosophical acumen, and she also put the final touches to much of the editing work. Then I must thank my publisher, Tejeshwar Singh and all at Sage, especially Omita Goyal, for her extraordinary efficiency, industry and commitment. Andrew Neal also helped in the final stages in an administrative capacity; and finally I must express, not for the first time, my warmest appreciation to Elaine Parker for her unique qualities and commitment.

10 June 2002   Roy Bhaskar

Part One

The Development of Critical Realism

Chapter One

From a Philosophy of Science to a Philosophy of Universal Self-realisation[*]

Part I: From Science to Freedom

It is a real pleasure to be here with you in Mumbai and to be the guest of this institute. What I want to do is to talk this morning and tomorrow about the progressive development of critical realism starting out from a concern with science, through various stages, to a concern with questions of human realisation and ultimately universal self-realisation. There are five stages, as I understand it, in the development of critical realism. It started out as a philosophy of science, a critique of positivism but also of neo-Kantianism and radical philosophers of science like Kuhn and Feyerabend who said many shocking things which have also been resumed in postmodernist discourse today. That I call *transcendental realism*. Then it moved on to *critical naturalism* and concerned itself with the dispute between naturalists and anti-naturalists, between positivism and hermeneutics, and it tried to resolve this dispute. Basically it was oriented against the dualisms that beset social theory in the mid- to late 1970s

* Tata Institute of Social Sciences, Mumbai, 1 December 2000.

and still to a large extent do today. Those are the two things that I will concentrate on today, that is problems in the philosophy and methodology of science, but particularly leading on to social science. Tomorrow I will go through the next three phases of critical realism, which I will briefly mention today. The third stage in critical realism broke down one particular dichotomy, characteristic of the dualisms of social science, which was very popular and insistent particularly in western thought: that one could not move from a factual statement or any set of factual statements to a value judgement. This prohibition was called Hume's law, and I argued that one could move from facts to values. And I did this through what I called the *theory of explanatory critique*. This then provided the lynchpin by means of which I moved from a concern with science to a concern with questions of values and human freedom and emancipation. The fourth stage of the development was a dialectical one in which I developed a system which I called *dialectical critical realism,* which went into dialectical notions such as absence, totality, negativity and so on. In the latest stage of my work I have gone on to questions of the convergence of east and west liberatory thought around what could be loosely called a spiritual dimension. This I have called *transcendental dialectical critical realism.* Those later stages, particularly the dialectical and the spiritual turns within critical realism, I will be dealing with later. Here I will mainly be talking about science and social science.

So how did critical realism start off? It started off really as an account of science which critiqued the seeming incapacity of philosophies of science to really say anything about the world. As Professor Singh has mentioned I was initially a practical economist and I wanted to do a thesis on the relevance of economic theory to underdeveloped countries. And it seemed to me to be very difficult to do this in a rational manner because most philosophy as we have it today embodied presuppositions about the nature of the world which were so obviously false that we have no guidelines for any sort of assessment of the relevance of economic theory to the problems of developing countries. So I had to go back to what was probably my first love, intellectually, that was philosophy. What I found was that existing philosophy of science, in the mid- and late 60s, when I started work on the movement of thought which eventually became critical realism, really pivoted on a central theory, that was the Humean theory of causal laws. This was a theory that the natural world was governed by causal laws which were understood as empirical regularities, that was as constant conjunctions of events. This theory underpinned the very fashionable Popper/Hempel model of explanation. I think you are probably all familiar with this, this is still the orthodoxy. It is called the deductive nomological model of explanation and it says that to explain an event you subsume it under a set of initial conditions and a set of covering laws; that is how you effect explanation. Now those covering laws are empirical regularities, constant conjunctions of events, Humean empirical regularities. This pivotal Humean theory of causal laws finds it way into very radical approaches to social science. For example Habermas, in describing in his theory of our three constitutive interests in knowledge, our knowledge-constitutive interest in prediction and control, presupposes a world which can be described and explained in a Popperian/Hempelian way. That account of reality informs his understanding of nature. Even without going to Habermas' standard anti-naturalist account of social science the dominant hermeneutical accounts of the 70s and 80s all took a very broad contrast and argued for the categorial differentiation of social science, the absolute differentiation of social science from natural science, because they believed that the natural world was described by constant conjunctions of events.

We can see this if we take what was a very influential text book in the 70s which was Winch's, *Idea of a Social Science*. His argument was that social phenomena could not be understood in the same way as natural phenomena but instead had to be understood in terms of the rule-governed linguistic paradigm that Wittgenstein had enunciated in his *Philosophical Investigations*. This led to two things, and there are essentially only two main arguments in his book. One is that constant conjunctions of events, that is empirical regularities, were neither necessary, as Weber had argued, nor sufficient for understanding social life. This was achieved in an entirely different way, namely by the discovery of intelligible links in its subject matter. You could certainly say that that is what we are concerned to do in social science, namely to discover intelligible links. But of course the idea that natural science is just concerned with the search for constant conjunctions is completely false, as I will go on to show in a moment. But it was tacitly presupposed and it provided the grounds for Winch's contrast. His second argument for the specificity of the social and the categorial differentiation of the social and natural sciences turned on the fact that social things, as distinct from physical things, have no existence apart from our conceptualisation of them. That of course is quite true, and that marks, at least in the first instance, a major difference between social and natural scientific methodology. But when he came to give his positive account of how social science was done we find there the displacement of themes from positivist philosophy of science. Thus rules function as a normative displacement of empirical regularities and the assumption is that conceptualisations which are ordered in a rule-like way completely exhaust the subject mater of social science and that they are more or less incorrigible. So there is nothing for social science other than investigating the way that agents understand their own subject matter as intelligible, and furthermore, that social science must accept the way that the social agents interpret their own subject matter as incorrigible. Those were assumptions or theses that I want to take issue with. So that is really why I felt that it was very important to come to terms with the Humean theory of causality.

So what we do in philosophy is that we start from phenomena, as in any other subject matter. You cannot just say something is false, you cannot just juxtapose in philosophy your idea of the world with something like the world. What you have to do is engage in an immanent critique of some existing conceptualisation or theory of the world. You have to engage in a reassessment of something which your protagonist thinks is pivotal and which you can show he has given a wrong account of.

Now there was one thing that positivism and positivists, empiricists and neo-Kantians all agreed was crucial to science, and that was experience. Experience, and more particularly experimental activity, is the heart of the empiricists' account of science.

Actually I did not disagree with this, but whether I did or did not, on the method of immanent critique that had to be my starting point. What I did was try to show that experimental activity actually presupposes a different ontology or account of the world. So let us see how this would work out. What the experimental scientist does in the laboratory is to artificially generate a closure of what is essentially an open system, in order to identify the working of a single generative mechanism or causal complex, a single process,[1] or complex, totality or field, whatever the object of study, in isolation from the influence of other factors. Only when he has affected that closure experimentally can he identify an empirical invariance. This means that what he is looking for, the object of scientific investigation, is not a surface pattern of events, because the surface pattern of events in natural life is chaotic. We do not actually find empirical invariances anywhere in the world happening spontaneously. The whole point of experimental activity is to generate an empirical invariance. Now if it is artificially produced, then we have to ask: is it that all man is doing in the experimental laboratory is discovering something he himself produced? The answer is of course not. Because what he or she is trying to do is isolate a structure, a causal complex, a process which will work independently of that closure, independently of whether he artificially closes the system or not. In virtue of that he can then apply it to the open systemic world where it will act in co-determination with a multiplicity of other factors, a multiplicity of other mechanisms, a multiplicity of other agencies. To give you an example, the law of gravity is operating on me now but I am not falling to the ground, it is operating tendentially, it is one of the factors that go to explain why I am sitting relatively stationary. It is actually not operating empirically, it is operating at a supra-empirical level, what I call *transfactually*, as one of the tendencies which are operating on me now. If you wanted to do a test of the law of gravity we would have to set up a laboratory situation and then measure the rate at which a heavy object falls to the ground. That we can only do in a few special contexts.

---

[1] I entirely agree with Professor Singh in wanting to accentuate process.

This had a very important implication because it does mean that what the scientist is doing is searching for something *behind* the pattern of events which generates them, whether or not we have a closure of that system of events—irrespective of the human activity which discovers it. So what I did was to argue that the field or the domain of the real is greater, more encompassing than the field of the actual, which describes the pattern of events; and that in turn is greater than the field of the empirical, which describes the pattern of events that we actually apprehend. Because clearly there would be things, and there would be events, actual phenomena, even if humanity was not here to observe it, even if one particular agent was not here to observe it, or there was no agent to observe it—there would still be patterns in the world. The differentiation between the real, the actual and the empirical was a big break with empiricist ontology. As was the view of causal laws as the workings of generative structures, causal mechanisms and processes; that is, as being tendencies, tendencies which could be possessed without being exercised, which could be exercised without being realised, which could be realised without being manifest in a one to one way with any set of phenomena, and which also could be manifest without being detected or identified by men, that is by humanity. This was a radically new account of causality and it led to a completely different ontology.

It led to a view of the world as being stratified, as being differentiated and as being changing, as distinct from the implicit, Humean empirical realist ontology which informed almost all philosophy of science since at least the days of Hume. It was there in Kant, also in Hegel in his account of nature, but probably goes back far longer than Hume, perhaps back to Aristotle in the west, and it was certainly there as the general assumption of philosophers of science in the 60s and 70s. So we had—through this analysis of experimental activity and a similar analysis of the conditions of possibility of applied activity, that is, of what happens when we apply science in the open systemic world where we find that exactly the same categorial distinctions are presumed— a radically different account of the world.

However, at a meta-level it was very difficult to say this, because Hume and more especially Kant had declared a taboo on ontology. To use Wittgenstein's words, all we could do in philosophy was talk about what he called the net, the net of language, the network, the framework—not what the network described. In other words we could not talk directly about the world. Now it seemed to me pretty obvious that any claim about knowledge must tacitly presuppose something about the objects of knowledge. But that is not in itself a very strong argument so what our transcendental argument from experimental activity had done was to actually ask the Kantian question: what must be the case for sense experience, in its specific form of experimental activity, to be possible? But it had come to a radically non-Kantian conclusion that the <u>world</u> must be structured. Kant, you will remember, had talked about the structure within us and the way in which we, as scientists, imposed the categories and schematisms on the empirical manifold. So there was structure inside, but of what there was outside us, we could not say anything at all. The best we could say was that there was a thing in itself.

This taboo on ontology is still very strong. I call that taboo the epistemic fallacy. Let us look at some of its manifestations today. In postmodernism in discourse theory there is a general assumption that all you can do is talk about talk. It is most clearly explicit in the work of discourse theorists like Ernesto Laclau, but it is there in Derrida in a slightly different form, it is there in others associated with poststructuralism and postmodernism. So discourse becomes a kind of intertextuality, a kind of relating of one text to another text or talk. But what you have to do is ask what is the status of that talk: *is the talk real or not?* If the talk is not real then it can have no causal effect, then you have to ask what is the point of the talk at all. If the talk is admitted to be real, then you can re-refer to it; if the talk is to be intelligible it must be possible for that talk, that statement, that discourse, to become an object of a subsequent act of reference. We must be able to refer to what we have said again, and if we can refer to what we have said again, then there is at least one real object in the world. That is talk. So that is the thin edge of the wedge:

because once you accept the reality of discourse, of talk, then you can accept the reality of a referent for any discourse, just a straight first order of referent. So when I am talking about a table or when I am talking about culture, there is a referent in the real world which is that which I talk about. In the language of semiotics, what we have is not only the signifier, the talk and the signified, the meaning or the concept, but we have the referent, the thing or object talked about by the word or words, and so we have the *semiotic triangle*. What the postmodernists and many structuralists and post-structuralists did was to leave out the referent. What realists tried to do was to put back the referent in.

This mistake of discourse theory is sometimes corrected by saying, well of course we admit there is the thing in itself, but there is no way to describe or get at it except by talk. So what is the point of having an ontology, because after all anything that you know you know under a particular description. That is fine. There are two ways to take this line of thought further. The first is this—it has often been said to me, by postmodernists and discourse theorists: of course we do not deny that there are things in themselves, and nor would I deny that there are things like stones, because you do not need to conceptualise them. But then I said to them, well, if you accept the reality of stones then why will you not accept the reality of the molecules and atoms that constitute them, why won't you accept the reality of the universe that englobes them. The thin edge of the wedge has already been made, once you can say anything about the world then you are into ontology. The question then is not whether or not to do ontology. The question is whether your ontology is correct or not, which means whether it is adequate to your subject matter.

Another line that postmodernists and discourse theorists, contemporary deniers of ontology, will take is the more classical Kantian response, which is to say well, this is all just anthropic, something which is happening subjectively within myself. So let us look at Kant from that standpoint. Kant as you know had a view, contrary to Hume, that our knowledge was structured, and actually the neo-Kantians of the late 60s and 70s like Popper, Hanson, Harre, Hesse and so on (as did the more radical post-

Kantians, Feyerabend and Kuhn) also had the same view as being structured. Now in it's classical, Kantian form the structuration of knowledge occurs through the imposition of the categories. Now what was it that applied the categories to the empirical manifold sensed in sense experience, what was it that did the schematisms that made empirical science possible as a structured totality? It was the transcendental ego. And what was the status of the transcendental ego? For Kant it was unknowable: it was a thing in itself. But surely, if knowledge was real then that which made the knowledge had to be real. So that is the great aporia, that was the great weakness, the great problem with Kantianism is the fact that it hangs on an unknowable thing in itself *inside*. Not only is there an unknowable thing in itself outside, the whole system is posited on a transcendental ego or self which is the unknowable synthesiser of the empirical manifold. So ultimately the structure collapses in on itself. And something like that tendency of thought happens within all forms of neo-Kantianism and all systems of thought which take their lead from Kant.

Now let us revert to the main thread of my argument. There were many philosophers of science around that time who were having problems with orthodox philosophy of science. They were saying it leaves something out, it leaves out the way in which reality is pictured in the scientific imagination, the creative imagination of the scientists. So that certainly empirical invariances cannot be *sufficient* for a scientific theory. But what I was arguing was not only was it not sufficient, but it was not even *necessary*, because it was in fact false. It was false that the world was constituted by constant conjunctions of events—false, because they did not actually occur. This was a much more radical break and it gave us a structured world *out there* and a structured world *in here*, in the scientific community, knowledge was structured and that reflected in some way the stratification of the world.

Thus, one of the first and most fundamental theorems of transcendental realism, after the categorial distinctiveness of the real, the actual and the empirical, and the analysis of laws as tendencies, was the distinction between what I called then the intransitive dimension and the transitive dimension. More simply between ontology and epistemology, between the world and knowledge. And what I argued for was that ontological realism was quite compatible with epistemological relativism, pluralism, diversity and indeed fallibalism. This is what neo-Kantians have got right: knowledge was a social process, but it was a social process which was designed to capture the ever deeper stratification of the world.

To show the sort of problem that philosophers of science in those days got into because they did not have a concept of the world, let us take Kuhn and Feyerabend. They formulated what was known as the problem of incommensurability. What was this problem? What they noted was that Newtonian theory and Einsteinian theory were so radically different in their conceptual structures that they shared no meanings in common. If they shared no meanings in common there was no way to compare them. So that is why they said they were 'incommensurable'. This seemed to make science a process of irrational breaks or splits—that was actually how Kuhn formulated it, though he did it in a sociologically sophisticated way. Now let us see how a critical realist might approach this phenomenon of incommensurability. The critical realist does not deny the phenomenon at all, but by adding to that level of *epistemological relativism*, the level of *ontological realism* and *judgmental rationalism*, the second and third levels of what we could call the holy trinity of transcendental realism as an account of science, it resolves the problem. First of all, the very formulation of the problem of incommensurability presupposes common referentiality, that there is an object world in common. No one bothers to say that physics and cricket are incommensurable or that Newtonian theory is incommensurable with classical music. Why? Because they are not describing the same world; intuitively you know that Newton and Einstein are describing the same world, describing the same phenomena. The problem however still remains that the way they describe it is radically different. So is it the case then that we have no grounds for preferring Einsteinian theory to Newtonian theory? No. What we can do is formulate a very simple criterion. We can say that Einsteinian theory is superior to Newtonian theory because Einsteinian theory can explain in *its* descriptions almost all or all the phenomena that Newtonian theory can explain under *its* descriptions *plus* some phenomena that Newtonian theory cannot explain. That is actually the case. There are very few phenomena that we actually know, only about eight or nine test situations in which Newtonian theory comes unstuck in its terms. But Einsteinian theory can explain them in its terms. So we have a purely quantitative criterion for preferring Einsteinian to Newtonian theory.

This goes against something which is a very widespread assumption of western thought, which is that basically we do not really have any grounds for anything in life. Any grounds for belief. This is something which is resumed, though in a more sophisticated way, by postmodernists and others. Let us take a classic formulation of it. Hume said we have no grounds for preferring the destruction of the world to my little finger. That is extraordinary. If it is the case that there are no grounds for preferring the destruction of the whole world to my little finger then there must be something very wrong with philosophy. But there was certainly something wrong with Hume's example because the little finger is of course included within the whole world. So he could have saved the rest of his body by preferring the destruction of his little finger. What he was tacitly doing was detotalising, extruding himself from the rest of the world, alienating himself from the rest of the world, setting himself off against the rest of the world. This is a categorial tendency in philosophy which we will come to tomorrow. Another example of this, he said really, when you think of it, there are no grounds for leaving a building by the ground floor door rather than by the second floor window. But of course we do have very good grounds. Once we know the Newtonian theory of gravity we know why it is we fall to the ground, other things being equal. Even common sense and experience give us inductive grounds for that belief. This trinity of ontological realism, epistemological relativism and judgmental rationalism allows us to sustain say the postmodernists' grasp on difference, the processual, the geo-historical diversity and change, all of which are quite true, with ontological realism, that is, a belief in the existence of a reality which does not depend on our subjective interpretations of it and with judgmental rationality, that is, with the idea that we have better or worse grounds for belief or action. So we begin to sustain, through the concepts of objectivity and truth, the possibility of better or worse grounds for beliefs and social practices, and hence we can eventually sustain the possibility of the project of human emancipation.

Transcendental realism had marked out a dialectic of scientific discovery, in which at each moment of time, science was seen as a kind of snapshot of what is essentially a process in motion. The nature of this process was always moving from the description of a domain of phenomena, a level of reality, to the underlying structures, mechanisms or processes which would explain it. This scientists did by the creative imagination of models, structures which, *if* they existed and acted in the way they imagined, would explain the phenomena which occurred. By rigorous empirical controls and tests they eventually eliminated all but one structure or causal complex. When they got to the point where they could actually empirically identify and describe that structure or complex, they then moved on to discover the deeper structure, field or totality that explained it. Thus we saw science as a process in motion, of reaching out to ever deeper levels of reality and building ever greater totalities. It gave us a different account of science, as engaged in the search for ever deeper structures or wider totalities which were relatively or absolutely independent of them, which would help to explain the phenomena they observed at some more superficial level.

One interesting consequence of the analysis of causal laws and the objects of scientific thought as tendencies of structures, was that we had to accept that powers, tendencies, liabilities, fields, capacities and so on were all real. Ontologically, epistemologically and logically this meant the possible was real and more important to science than the actual. So it reversed, as it were, the priorities between the possible and the actual. That is what I called *dispositional realism*. But another consequence of it was also very important and this I called *categorial realism*. It is obviously part of the logic of transcendental realism that the world is really there outside, transfactually efficaciously operating independently of the working scientist, or relatively independently, as we have to say when we come to domains like quantum physics. Now if it is the case, then what are we to say about causality, or about space, time, process, totality? Are they real or not? The philosophers really from Aristotle, but particularly Kant and more recently Popper, have thought of categories as subjective classifications of the mind imposed on the phenomena or the empirical manifold. But transcendental realism said categories were real, they were out there, for example the world really was tensed, well, the social world was at least. Causality was really there, part of the general furniture of the world. So we had a categorial realism. It is obviously absurd, when you think of it, not to accept categorial realism. Because what would be the point of saying that Ohm's law and all the other laws known to physics and chemistry are real but not lawfulness as such. That would be like saying, OK, we have knives, forks and spoons but we do not have cutlery because cutlery is a higher order concept. Or it would be like saying we have rupee notes, 10, 20, 50, 100 rupee notes, but we do not have the money system as such because money is a category.

Now if you regard philosophy as having as its subject matter the categories, then this means that philosophy becomes important. And if you are a working scientist and you are working with, thinking reality in terms of an inadequate categorial framework, sooner or later if not necessarily you, then someone who is applying your work, will fall into a theory practice inconsistency. Let us assume that you understand in your practice that laws are transfactual, that they are not empirical regularities, but you still have in your mind the idea that they are empirical regularities, then you are really going to have a false account of what you do. This is theory–practice inconsistency or what some writers have called performative contradiction.

Now we come to what I think is the most general criterion of philosophy, that is *reflexivity*, the capacity of an account to adequately situate and sustain itself. Typically most philosophers themselves fall into theory–practice inconsistency. Let us go back to the working scientist; what he is actually doing in his practice is to presuppose something that, in his intellectual theory, he is denying. That gives us a very interesting figure, the figure of, if you like, ideology or false consciousness going along with right practice. What I want to say, and to show, is that even if you deny ontology, you are still implicitly assuming it, you are implicitly assuming the truth of ontology. If you were an empiricist you were still a realist, you were an empirical realist. This is what I called the TINA aspect (TINA standing for There Is No Alternative); there is no alternative to ontology, there is no alternative to realism. Even more so, we see from the example of the working scientist there is no alternative to an assumption of the world as transfactually efficacious. That is, there is no alternative to tacitly presupposing the nature of reality as it is. There is no alternative to the truth, at whatever level it informs your practice, if your practice is to be efficacious. So this is a very important figure that we have hit upon now. This figure of the necessary presupposition by what is false of something that is true, for it to have causal efficacy. It plays a great role in the idea of social science and philosophy as having liberatory or emancipatory powers. Because one way a philosophy or a social science can be liberatory is by getting rid of that illusion, that false account, and so result in greater consistency and great reflexivity. If you have a theory–practice inconsistency then you are sooner or later going to fall into error. That is why it is important; and this is how philosophy can come to inform science and social science. That is really all I want to say about the philosophy of science—except to say that in my first book, *A Realist Theory of Science*,[2] I did ask: but how do you explain all this? Ultimately, I hinted, that you had to explain it in terms of the dominance of certain paradigms. Certainly the Cartesian paradigm of action by contact. Then also in terms of the celestial closures that Newtonian physics had achieved, though these were geo-historically locally specific closed contexts. And finally in terms of an underlying model of man. This underlying model of man was essentially a very superficial one, which I will come on to talk about tomorrow. Because I want to argue for a very different conception of man, a deep, more essentialist conception of man in which the subjectivity of man himself, not just the world out there, is structured, differentiated and changing.

---

[2] Leeds 1975, London 1997.

Let us see how we can apply this understanding of science to methodological issues and debates within the social sciences. When I first started to go into the philosophy of social science I found that it was rife with disputes and dichotomies. The biggest dichotomy was definitely that between naturalism and anti-naturalism, between positivism and hermeneutics, but there was also a dichotomy between individualists and holists, a dichotomy between the proponents of structure and the proponents of agency, there was dichotomy between mind and body, there was dichotomy between reason and cause, there was a dichotomy between fact and value, and also between theory and practice.

The main question in the dispute between naturalists and anti-naturalists was about understanding social phenomena. Do we understand them in the same way as natural phenomena? Now the critical naturalist argument was that of course social phenomena would be different, but there would be no difference in principle in that we would still have the essential movement of science from a superficial phenomenon that you have identified to a deeper understanding or explanation of it. But this would have to be grounded in what was *emergent* in society and man from nature. Because it is clear that we are material things, so we are still governed by the laws of physics and chemistry and biology, but there are also emergent properties of human beings and social phenomena. Let us take the idea of the structure or a causal mechanism or a process. What we have to ask is: what are the distinguishing features of these structures or structure-analogues in the social world?

One thing is that obviously they are very dependent on human activity, very immediately, in a way in which they are not in the natural world, unless we go to very deep physics. So they are *activity dependent*. Secondly they are obviously *concept dependent*; these structures do not exist without some sort of conception that the agents have. This does not mean they have to have a concept of the structure, because they may know nothing about the structure but the structure could not operate without the agent's activity, and the agent's activity would not be a human activity unless it was also conceptualised. So conceptuality is clearly a distinguishing feature like (and derivative from) intentional activity dependence in the subject matter of social science. But contrary to the claims of the hermeneutical tradition, that conceptuality did not exhaust the subject matter of the social sciences. Everything in the social world was concept dependent but not everything in the social world was a concept. Nor did something else follow from what was generally taken to be the anti-naturalist stance. It did not follow that the agents necessarily had the correct conceptualisation of the social world. Now the third thing that distinguishes the social sciences, or seemed to distinguish their subject matter, was their greater *space–time specificity*, their greater speed, their greater locality. This is only a relative difference because natural phenomena themselves were always in motion, they are in space and time like social phenomena, but the social world seemed faster, more transient. The fourth difference, which I also called the fourth limit on naturalism, was what I called the *critical limit* on naturalism.

This is very important because if we start from the conceptualisations that agents have of the activities in which we are engaged then we have the basis for something which is like a social scientific analogue of transcendental argument. Understanding the necessity for hermeneutical moments in social science gives you a basis for building up theories which answer analogous questions to the transcendental question, what must be the case for these activities, as conceptualised in the experience of the agents whose activities they are, to be possible? And this sort of transcendental argument is very common in social theory, at least in high level social theory. You can find it in Marx's work and Weber's work and Durkheims's work, all the great social theorists. But of course what you have to do when you have understood this hermeneutical moment is to empirically test the theories that you produce through this method of argumentation against empirical data.

Here we come up against a big problem. In the social sciences we do not have decisive test situations, we cannot really do true analogues of natural scientific experiments and we do not find, except in very rare cases, closed systems spontaneously occurring. So this means that the apparent symmetry between explanation and prediction in the natural sciences has no analogue here. I say it is only apparent because it is only at the superficial level, of the analysis of laws as empirical invariances, that it works. But that apparent symmetry breaks down. The empirical criterion in social science can only be *explanatory*. So we judge one theory better than another theory because it can explain more, not necessarily because it is a better predictor. Now the best predictor, I am talking now from experience in England, the best predictor of the weather tomorrow is that it will be the same as today. But everyone knows the weather in England is always changing. Nevertheless the prediction 'same as today' is better than most meteorological forecasts. Econometricians have a terrible record at predicting economic phenomena but nevertheless few people would say that economics cannot throw light on to tendencies that work in the social world. Very few people, even if they are very critical of neo-classical economics, would not say that when a price rises, other things being equal, there will be a tendency for demand to fall. Other things being equal people will buy a cheaper good of the same quality rather than a more expensive good. That is only a tendency. So unless we have this kind of understanding of laws then you are not going to find any intelligibility in social science. You are going to throw out the baby with the bath water. This then was the essence of my critique of hermeneutics and what I tried to do was provide a more general account of social science which could do justice to both the hermeneutical and the empirical moments and reconcile them in a broader, more totalising theory.

Let me just go through how this approach resolved a few of the other dichotomies which beset the social sciences and still do so to a large extent today. In contrast to the dichotomy between individualism and holism or collectivism I argued for a view of the subject matter of the social sciences as being essentially relational. That is we were not really concerned with individual human beings or collectivities. I was not denying that human beings or that collectivities existed. But the collectivities that the methodological holists at the time talked about were very uninteresting. They were things like crowds at football matches and so on. We can see that they had a very limited conception of true holism. What I argued for was a relational view of the subject matter of social science which took as their paradigms things like the relationship between husbands and wives, between employers and employed, between coloniser and colonised, between capitalists and workers. On the basis of these relational accounts you could actually start to define more interesting collectivities. To be in the social world is to be the bearer of a relation. It is to be related. This is the *relational* account of the subject matter of social science.

A third major and still ongoing dispute is between the protagonists of structure and the protagonists of agency. There are those philosophers and social scientists who wanted to explain everything in terms of the human agent. This was taken to an extreme in the work of some ethnomethodologists who believed that what basically happens is that when we wake up in the morning we recreate society. When we go to sleep we put society to sleep. Everything is just a result of our own spontaneous action. That is an extreme voluntarism but this voluntaristic tendency is there in the work of Weber and in the work of such social theorists as Rom Harre and Tony Giddens with whom I have a lot in common. What I argued was, against voluntarism, that we never create the social structure, we never create the social circumstances into which we are born. We never create it from scratch, it always pre-exists us. Therefore we must acknowledge the presence of the past, we must acknowledge the presence of the structures which we inherit. We can reproduce and change them as radically as we want or as conditions allow us, but they pre-exist us and that legacy of the past must be acknowledged. At the same time, against those who commit the opposite error to voluntarism, that of reification, these social structures would not be ongoing unless we reproduced them or transformed them in our conscious intentional activity. So we have a view of the social structure pre-existing humanity, but existing only in virtue of our ongoing human activity. This was the basis of the *transformational model of social activity.*

The mind–body problem was a classic case of what happened when a totality—such as ourselves as embodied human beings constituted neither simply by brute matter, nor simply by consciousness but as embodied consciousness and actually not just mind and body but also feelings, thus as embodied feeling consciousness—is split up into different parts. What I argued for here was what I called *synchronic emergent powers materialism*, that was a view of mind and the other properties irreducible to the laws of physics, chemistry and biology as a genuinely emergent level, a genuinely emergent stratum of reality. This leads on to a fifth dichotomy, which is immediately related to the mind–body one, the reason–cause dispute. Here the general view was that reasons and causes describe different language games. They belong to what Waismann, in the spirit of Wittgenstein, called different language strata. So when we appeal to a reason and the cause we are playing two different games. In that case how can we make sense of any human action? Supposing I turn to Bridget over there and say Bridget, could you raise your hand. She has raised her hand, my speech action gave her a reason for performing a material change. Someone is nodding over there. I have given him a reason for nodding. If you analyse any human action of any sort it involves some sort of mediation by consciousness which has a material effect in the world. So we have to come to terms with the causality of ideas, the causality of reasons. I did this through the theory of *intentional causality*.

Turning to the fact–value dichotomy I have already argued that you can actually derive values from facts and will tomorrow expand on the way we do this. The fact–value dichotomy is also immediately related to the theory–practice dichotomy, the split between theory and practice. We have seen that is something that the social scientist has to overcome by putting himself in the picture he paints. In other words, social science is part of the greater totality it describes, it cannot be excluded from it. I go on in my later works to argue for a systematic view of it being part of the manifesto, part of the charter of social science to actually orient itself to the project of human emancipation. Human emancipation is something that cannot be imposed from without; so it has to be self-emancipation. Social science and science generally, can play a great role in that project. In my dialectical works, such as *Dialectic: The Pulse of Freedom* or *Plato Etc.*, I deepened the transformational model of social activity a bit. The transformational model of social activity was that conception which allowed us to reconcile structure and agency by seeing how structure pre-existed but continued to exist, or was perpetuated, only in virtue of intentional agency. So now in my dialectical works I have argued that we had to understand social being in terms of four dimensionalities, each of which was necessary for a full understanding of any social event. These were the stratification of the subject or self; our transactions with others, our interpersonal relations; our relationship to the social structure; and our material transactions with nature. These four levels were necessary for the location of any act. And here I talked about *four-planar social being.*

Now what I do believe is that we are profoundly alienated at all four levels of our social being. We are alienated from ourselves, we are alienated from each other, we are alienated from the social structures and we are alienated form the material world. Our alienation from the material world can be witnessed in the ecological problems that humanity is suffering. These ecological problems are so great, and also coupled onto our economic ones, that the very survival of the human species on this planet is at stake. We have all become aware of how globally interconnected we are, the fact that what happens here in Mumbai will effect what is happening in Tokyo and that will effect what happens in Rio de Janeiro. We are one world, a single world. So this dealienation, I am going to argue tomorrow and in the discussions we have today, this dealienation must be a *universal* one. And in thinking of this dealienation we also have to think very profoundly of our own role in that alienation. Because each and every one of us in what we do can make a difference. But we can only make a difference if in some way we are not alienated from ourselves. What I am going to argue tomorrow is that the *self-alienation* of man does not exhaust, but is the root cause of all the other ills that we have.

Now what I argued in my work was that because we were all part of a totality, the same totality, so inevitably, logically, we were all committing ourselves through what I call *dialectical universality,* to the project of universal human emancipation.

Let us see how this might go. Suppose you have a desire and you find that desire constrained. Then inexorably you want to get rid of your constraint. So you must be committed to getting rid of the constraint for all dialectically similar agents. Then you will move to a position in which you want to get rid of all constraints as such in virtue of their dialectical similarity as constraints on the flourishing of human powers, potentialities and possibilities. And this will mean that we are committed, in our action, willy-nilly, just by the merest want or desire (however you start up), purely logically, to the project of removing all social ills. And this in virtue of any human act that we do.

This is a very strong position, and it is one the basic meaning of which can be put as follows: that what we do when we act—this is the strong claim—is to tacitly presuppose (through this logic I have begun to sketch) a society in which, to quote Marx's words here because I believe that the vision would commend itself to everyone and practically commit ourselves to a society and to a world, in which the free development of each is a condition of the free development of all. Of course that was not observed and practiced by those who have tried to produce a communist society, but that vision, that very inspired vision of a society, a world in which the free development of each would be a condition for the free development of all, stresses, places at the heart of the problem, the issue of the *concrete singularity*, the freedom, the respect that we must all give to each other, but also preserves, indeed accentuates, the element of *universalisability*. And what I will argue tomorrow is that self-realisation implies action which is spontaneously oriented to a good society, the removal of all social injustices and ills, and the totality of what I called *master–slave type* or oppressive *relationships*. And moreover, that in fact that starting from the most ordinary desire we end up with a position in which we are committed to the realisation of every being in the cosmos.

* * * *

Part II: From Truth to Self-realisation*

Today will really be a continuation of yesterday so I will presuppose most of what I said yesterday, but we will be recapitulating, as we go through the subjects to be discussed today, some of the themes that we developed yesterday. So I hope that people who are here today but weren't yesterday will be able to pick things up.

Briefly to remind you, in these talks I am situating the whole topic of the progressive movement of critical realism from a philosophy of science primarily concerned with knowledge to a philosophy of freedom, human emancipation and ultimately universal self-realisation in the context of the development of critical realism. I mentioned five stages in its development: as a philosophy of science which I called transcendental realism; and a philosophy of social science which I called critical naturalism; then there is a theory of explanatory critique, concerned with the derivation of values from facts. These were the topics we discussed yesterday. Today I will concentrate on the fourth and fifth stages. The fourth stage was a theory of dialectic, in fact a dialectical system, called dialectical critical realism, which I elaborated especially in my book *Dialectic: The Pulse of Freedom* and recapitulated in *Plato Etc.* Then there is the fifth stage, this is a spiritual turn within critical realism, in the development of a system or an approach which I have called transcendental dialectical critical realism. It sounds a bit of a mouthful but it is basically applying transcendental realism to the self.

What I will be doing today is talking about the dialectical and the spiritual deepening of critical realism and I will do it really by first of all elaborating the general structure of dialectical critical realism and showing how the latest stage, the fifth stage in the development of critical realism, deepens that system of dialectical critical realism, which already further deepens the levels of critical realism we were discussing yesterday. So the whole development of critical realism basically moves according to a

---

* Tata Institute of Social Sciences, Mumbai, 2000.

single logic, which is dialectical, and basically oriented to the norms of truth and freedom. What is this logic? This is a logic in which we are looking at a subject matter and this subject matter finds itself with an absence, an incompleteness. There is something a little bit wrong with it, it is leaving something out, leaving a dimension of reality out. And that *incompleteness* ultimately reaches a point where it generates *contradictions* either externally with the totality, the discourse, the knowledge systems outside and/or internally within the discourse of critical realism itself—actually it will always be both—and those contradictions must be remedied by taking into account in theory and practice the missing levels of reality. Let me just focus on the aspect of theory–practice inconsistency. Suppose one acts dialectically but one thinks according to the canons of non-dialectical deductive logic, then sooner or later that inconsistency will lead to error and a variety of other ills unless remedied by resort to a greater totality. So the dialectical process is a continuing movement, of deepening of greater totalisation leading to greater reflexivity, ultimately that is the unity of theory and practice. At some point or other critical realism would have to come to terms with the processual nature of life which is what is thematised in dialectic and the spiritual dimension to life which of course has been talked about by lots of philosophers and sages before, but which was then a taboo subject within western philosophy.

To make things very simple and clear what I want to do is outline the four stages, moments or levels of dialectical critical realism, what they are, give them a name, and for ease of memory, I will call it MELD. The M stands for the *first moment*, 1M, of the system of dialectical critical realism, ontology. So there we will be recapitulating some of the themes of transcendental realism and in fact the whole dialectical and spiritual turn within critical realism can be seen as a deepening within ontology. That is what the M stands for in MELD. The E stands for the *second edge*, 2E, that is the second dimension or stadium of dialectical critical realism and that is the edge of negativity, of absence, of dialectic itself. The great absence that dialectical critical realism pinpoints in hitherto existing western thought was the absence of the concept of absence. This is in a way the key moment within dialectical critical realism. That is what the E stands for. The *third level*, 3L, that is the level of concern with issues of totality. The fourth stadium or stage of that system, the *fourth dimension*, 4D, which is where the D comes in, is the dimension of transformative praxis and reflexivity. Let us call the fifth stage of development, a *fifth aspect*, 5A, or a fifth turn within critical realism, then MELD becomes MELDA and the A stands for the fifth aspect.

Let me just summarise what I am going to say by saying that at the level of 1M, that is ontology, the spiritual turn or transcendental dialectical critical realism thematises issues to do with the ultimate nature of reality, including issues to do with god. That is the big topic there, god. The second edge thematises issues to do with transcendence. The third level thematises issues to do with love and emotions, particularly love which is the primary totalising agency (or so I want to say) in the social world. The fourth dimension deals with questions of right-action and also of enhanced reflexivity which ultimately entails what has been called cosmic consciousness or what is more popularly known as enlightenment, that is individual self-realisation. This I want to argue actually presupposes and entails universal self-realisation and without universal self-realisation you cannot ultimately have the unity of theory and practice.

Yesterday I argued that we had in contemporary society a profound alienation of the four dimensions in terms of which social being had to be understood. We were alienated from ourselves; we were alienated from each other; we were alienated from the social structures which we reproduced or transformed but which we had never created; and we were alienated from the material world, the natural world which we inhabit. This last is a very profound alienation which is taking the form of an oncoming global crisis. The root of all these alienations was self-alienation, that is alienation from ourselves. This is a position which brings together the most profound theorists, philosophers and indeed practitioners of emancipatory thought in east and west alike. They all presuppose that in some way we are essentially at some level far greater, far nobler, far more creative, far more loving, essentially free, even perhaps divine, unique (unified but unique) individuals with powers and possibilities which are in some way blocked or constrained by a superstructure in terms of which we live our lives. So that deep reality is in some way occluded from ourselves and systematically at all those four levels of social being. These thinkers—and this is the line that I will be arguing—actually presuppose a very noble and great view of humanity. Equally at the same time, therefore, a thorough critique of what happens in actuality, including the actuality of alienated man. This whole turn really is a reversal of much of the interest of western philosophy. You will remember Kant talked about two things which he thought were fundamental. One was the starry heavens above, the other was the moral law within. We in the west have investigated thoroughly the starry heavens above, but we have not explored this moral law within. So what I am doing today is looking at how we set about exploring it. That is the deeper, essential self that is actually tacitly presupposed by all our practices and in which oppression, unhappiness and other ills feed as parasites because they could not live without it. They could not live without this more basic substratum but certainly we could live here without those ills and oppressions which are parasites on us.

Let me resume some of the themes of ontology, that is the first stadium 1M of ontology. Yesterday I argued for the inexorability and irreducibility of ontology. And I also argued for the necessity of an ontology of a specific kind, that is for a view of the world as being structured, differentiated and changing against the flat, undifferentiated, unchanging view of orthodox western philosophy—particularly as encapsulated in theories like the Humean theory of causal laws which I argued was actually the lynchpin of most western epistemology. Then I looked at how someone who had a wrong theory in practice, say a working scientist, could nevertheless do good science, produce good results (as it will inevitably be the case that scientists and ordinary people do succeed in finding out about the world, just as they succeed in being loving, creative, spontaneous etc.). And we saw that a scientist to do science had to work with an idea of the transfactuality of reality. This was a tacit presupposition of his practice. He had to assume that causal laws and the other objects of scientific investigation existed and acted at a deeper level than that of the pattern of events. So if in his philosophical consciousness he thought of himself as merely passively recording empirical regularities then he would be in theory–practice contradiction. And this gave rise to the figure of what I called the TINA formation. That is the way in which a truth or a level of reality is necessarily presupposed in practice for any causal efficacy whether it is denied in theory or not. TINA, it will be remembered, stood for *there is no alternative.* So if something is true and we are operating at that level, whether or not we are aware of it, we must act in a way which is in accordance with that truth. And no engineer who is investigating a train crash, or trying to launch a rocket or trying just to mend his car, fridge or washing machine, will for a moment assume that the laws of nature that he is employing are merely describing the pattern of events, because the pattern of events is idiosyncratically chaotic. So he assumes that there are mechanisms really at work operating behind and irrespective of what is going on at the surface level where he is practically engaged. And that figure of thought, of a false theory nevertheless presupposing for its causal efficacy a truth, is a very important one. We can see in it parallels to Marx's critique of a political economy where he argues that the whole surface appearance of capitalism describes but nevertheless depends on a deeper reality which it occludes. He called that reality exploitation, because it consisted of the extraction of surplus value through unpaid labour, a mechanism necessarily screened for the effective functioning of a capitalist economy. But nevertheless a level of reality, which was there, without which nothing else could go on. That superficial level of reality actually dominated as well as occluded the level of reality on which it was parasitic. We looked at a comparison there with the Vedic concept of *maya,* the world of illusion, actually presupposing the world of spirit or the absolute or Brahman or whatever on which it reposes. But it reposes as a kind of veil until we force our way through the veil. And the everyday world of illusion, or to use Marxian terms, ideology, in which we live is the dominant world in our everyday life, or so it seems at a theoretical level.

Then I want to argue that though it actually is the dominant world, at least in our conscious activity, nothing at that dominant level could happen <u>without</u> the tacit presupposition of the more basic level on which it is dependent. There is an asymmetry, a unilateral dependency of the false or mystifying, dominant level on the true, more basic, underlying but suppressed and screened level. We can take an example here from Chomsky. Chomsky argues that in virtue of our innate capacity to acquire a language we are capable, in principle, at birth of generating an infinite number of sentences, including sentences that we will never generate, including languages that we will never learn. There is an essential creativity which lies behind our specific uses of a specific language. We have that innate possibility of the infinite. Rousseau put this point of view very well when he said that man is born free but is everywhere in chains. So what we are trying to do in the project of universal self-realisation or emancipation is throw off the chains. This immediately gives rise to a general definition of emancipation or liberation as the shedding or disemergence of unwanted and unnecessary determinations. That much we covered yesterday under the general rubric of ontology.

We also talked about dispositional realism, the reality of powers, possibilities, tendencies. We talked about categorial realism, the way in which you had to be a realist not just about specific laws but about lawfulness, causality, space, time, process —all the basic categories in terms of which philosophy thinks the world. There was one thing which I did not go into yesterday and that was the concept of truth. I will briefly discuss this now before talking about what is perhaps the most troubling aspect for many minds, the aspect of this deepening of ontology at the first moment of dialectical critical realism, namely the topic of god. So let us discuss truth for a little bit first.

Now we could do a semantic analysis of truth, which applied to all reality. When we say that something is true there are four levels at which this statement or assertion must be understood. The first level is when you say 'that is true'. This is the fiduciary aspect, you are saying trust me, act on it, I give you my word, if I was you I would do it. It is like a social bond, it is a commitment, a promise, that is true as fiduciary. The second level of the analysis of the concept of truth is the epistemological level, in which when you say that something is true you are saying you have good grounds for believing it to be so. This is warrantedly justified, this is epistemically assertable. This is the level of analysis of truth on which most philosophers have fastened. The third level to the analysis of truth, in this progressive deepening of the concept, is invoked when in saying something is true you are making a categorial claim about the world, you are saying this is how things are in the world. If I say grass is green I am saying that is the way it is in the world. If I say the structure of water is given by the formula H_2O (leaving aside a few complications), I am saying that is the way the world is. That is truth as expressive. So we have truth as fiduciary, truth as epistemic, truth as expressive of the world. Then the fourth level of truth is truth as alethic. This is that level of truth in which when we talk about the truth of something we are talking about the reality which grounds, explains or causes it. If I wanted to say the truth of the statement that water boils at 100 degrees centigrade is the molecular structure of water (plus some other laws of physics), then that would be the alethic or real truth of it. Once I know the crystalline structure of a particular stone then I know why it reflects light of a certain wavelength in a particular way. Once I know the crystalline structure of emeralds I know why they must manifest themselves to us as green. This is truth as the real reason or underlying ground for phenomena. So it is important for our topic today because what I am arguing is that there is an alethic truth to man, which is his deep, hidden, occluded self which is nevertheless a necessary condition for everything that happens in the superficial, ordinary world of events. And that deep alethic truth has been buried not only in theory but in practice. The task of liberation is to free it, to realise it. I will be saying more about this when I come to the fourth dimension of practice after moving through the second dimension of negativity, dialectical reasoning and the third level of totality.

I have to say something about ultimata, the absolute which we briefly discussed yesterday and I am going to say a little bit about god. Now I do not believe that a belief in god is a necessary condition for being a good man, or anything like that. Quite the contrary. There are so many bad people who believe in god that no sort of equation like that can be made. Secondly, most,

but not all, of what I say is susceptible to purely secular interpretation. Thirdly, what I am really concerned about is the re-
emphasis of spirituality in life and right-action, rather than theology. Nevertheless I do believe that we can rationally discuss the
topic of god. So let me enunciate seven propositions on god.
Seven statements that I think are true or would be true about
god if god existed. And they may give you grounds in some way
for a belief in god's existence.

So the **first** point is that ontological realism about god,
that is a belief in the reality or existence of god, is quite consistent with epistemological relativism. That is with the idea that
god manifests himself or herself or itself in a variety of different
ways or is accessed by different people in different traditions in a
plurality of different ways. This is exactly on a par with any scientific object. We know that scientific realism, ontological realism
in science is compatible with, indeed necessitates, a view of the
cognitive process in science as being relative, as being a social
product, as being transformable. So the content of the experience of god should not be expected to be the same from one
region of space time to another, from one person to another. So
that is the first very important point; and nothing else is consistent with the transcendental realism that I have been developing
in these talks.

The second thing to note is that the compatibility of ontological realism and epistemological relativism also entails judgmental rationalism. That is to say we can have better or worse
grounds for adopting some particular god-oriented, some particular spiritual practice, and this means also that our claims to
knowledge of god are fallible like anything else. Just because you
claim to have a knowledge of god, it does not mean that you do.
Fallibilism and all our rational faculties remain intact. I said 'if
god exists, if god is real'. There are two senses to ontological
realism about god. The first is just to make god in principle something which could or could not exist. This is the first step in
realism. The second step of course is to say, yes, god does exist.
It is important to see that you can be ontologically realist about
god in the first sense and be an atheist in the second, that is deny
that god exists. This is opposed to a widespread view in the west

today, among many priests and bishops but also Christian theologians, who say we do not have to ask questions about god's existence. God is just a convenient metaphor, a convenient way of redescribing certain religious practices. That is their position, and it is probably the dominant position in western theology, that we can abstain from any view on whether god is real or not. This in fact is a kind of cop out. Because whilst it is fine to say that you do not know whether god exists or not, to invoke god in some way as a metaphor in a religious practice without considering it's truth or reality to be a legitimate topic for discussion is absurd. For this is something which is actually believed or disbelieved by religious practitioners; for instance in prayer the person who is praying is praying because he believes that god exists, is listening to him and in some sense cares.

All these moments are very important and they all imply certain things which are wrong about contemporary theology. Obviously once you accept epistemological relativism you must accept tolerance and pluralism. Obviously once you accept judgmental rationalism you must accept your own fallibilism and the fallibilism of your tradition to any claim to knowledge of the absolute or the divine. So that is the first proposition, namely, ontological realism, epistemological relativism and judgmental rationalism are all compatible and they all must be applied to the topic of god.

The **second proposition** I want to assert is that ontological immanence, that is the view that god is immanent within being, is consistent with epistemic transcendence—either in the sense of being unknown, god could be real even if we do not know it, or in the sense of being knowable in a way which is not susceptible to the normal canons of our discursive intellect. That is, knowable in some sort of way, through some sort of experience, in which the normal subject–object division, distinction or duality, that is the terms of the categories in which we normally think the non-theological and the non-spiritual, as I will go on to argue later, breaks down. Typically in this moment of transcendence people feel infused. This parallels what happens in science when there is a breakthrough, a moment of inspiration. Or while we are listening to music, or when we are going for a walk in nature and we have an experience of transcendence, in which we become engulfed by, that is, overawed by the object, phenomenon or experience. In this moment you become one with what you experience; and this is the characteristic of transcendental experiences. The subject–object duality, in terms of which we normally apprehend and think the world, collapses. There are two ways in which god could be epistemically transcendent, one is that he is not known at all, the other is that he is not known through the discursive intellect.

The **third proposition** I want to affirm about god is that the ontological ingredience, that is immanence within being of god, the ingredience of god within man, if god is truly a kind of envelope which sustains and binds everything, then god, in a certain way, must be ingredient within us. If you accept that there is a level of the divine which binds everything, which sustains everything, then it must also sustain or in some way be the ontological basis of man himself. To talk about the ontological ingredience of god in man is not to say that man exhausts god, because god will always be transcendent with respect to man and this is implied by the non-anthropocentricity and the non-egocentricity that I argued for yesterday. God will always be transcendent with respect to man because god, in this view, is the envelope which must be present in other beings to some extent or other, but of course in a different form. And secondly, because he is a bigger and wider totality he will always be something which is in part beyond man. There will always be a 'beyondness' about god, even if he is ingredient in man. This actually defines within religious practices and traditions a spectrum of immanence and transcendence, what I will call the immanence/transcendence spectrum. For some religious traditions, for example Islam or Judaism, god is transcendent, that is we cannot actually access him or we can only access him indirectly through the mediation of a holy text like the Koran or in a particular practice like prayer. For other traditions, particularly Hinduism and Buddhism, if it sustains the concept of god at all, which I believe it does, god is immanent, ingredient in man. So you can actually look at religious practices and traditions in terms of how much they stress immanence and how much they stress transcendence. Now if god is ingredient in man, he does not exhaust man. Thus, not only is he not exhausted by man, he does not exhaust man, because man has free will and so we have the possibility of error, evil and what has been called 'structural sin', that is the proliferation of ills, evils at all those four planes of social being at which alienation occurs. And from all this it follows that god is the alethic ground, the ultimate essential ingredient within man. God would be, in some sense, the truth in man. That is to say the ingredient within man which we are trying to liberate would be divine. Not the whole of divinity but at least have a claim to be called divine.

The final aspect of this third theorem that I am discussing involves the distinction I made yesterday between the domains of the real and the actual and the empirical. Remember the real includes as a proper sub-set the actual, which in turn includes as a proper sub-set the empirical. God or the divine is present in man at all three levels. First at the level of the real, as I am talking now about god as the essential ingredient, god is there as real as an infinite field of possibilities. That is the deep, ingredient, essential self that we want to liberate. Secondly god, or this divine aspect within man, is present as actual, as the presupposition of everything we do. I once gave the example of the dependence of the violence of war on love. Oppression actually presupposes free, creative, loving human beings. The totality of what I have called master–slave relationships depends entirely on the creativity of slaves. All these things depend on innate, free, and great and noble capacities which are present there in man in actuality. So we have god not just as a field of possibilities, but as actuality. Thirdly, this divine ingredient within us can be experienced in at least two different ways. First of all it can be accessed through practices or in moments of what one might call deep or bliss or transcendent experiences. But secondly it is manifest spontaneously, or so I want to argue, in every genuine human act. For instance there is an element of creation *de novo* in all truly transformative acts. Creation out of the blue, creation which seems to come from nowhere, is an element of all genuine emergence, all genuine novelty and therefore all genuine transformation in the social world. In this sense man, in his human activity, recapitulates in some way the idea of gods' creation of the world. This was however not only *de novo*, but *ex nihilo*, completely out of the blue, from the void, out of nothing and logically god must in some way create himself out of the void—a very difficult concept for dualistic, or indeed any other kind of thought.

When we have these transcendental experiences they typically slip between thoughts, they occur in moments when thought is suspended. Of course they only occur to people like our hard working scientist when the ground is immanently well prepared by rigorous discursive thought. So when Newton had the idea of gravity the sublating concept came to him when he saw the apple fall. It came only to him, because only his mind had been so prepared that he was capable of getting this burst from nowhere. But it is also important to note that it only came to him because he was not thinking, because his mind was at rest. You might say this burst from nowhere is actually the kind of alethic self-revelation of some deeper being that knows it all—or just is the reality he is investigating, or that it is already present, implicit in him, waiting to be explicated in his conscious experience. Actually I would probably want to say all of these things (suitably qualified), but we need not go into this now. What the case was that in that moment he touched or accessed a deeper level of reality, in virtue of his own deeper, essential self, which slid through the space or gap, in that moment between thoughts which was the occasion of his inspiration. This moment is typically of silence, of rest, of relaxation in which we recharge ourselves. When we talk about social transformation we must not forget the moment of play, of idleness, of silence, of sleep, of stillness, of peace, of calm.

Now very quickly on to the other propositions that I want to affirm about god; and then we will move on to the other moments of dialectical critical realism and the spiritual turn within them. The **fourth proposition** is that the proof of god's existence can only be experiential and practical. No one can prove to you that god exists. This can only come from your experience and practice, it can only come from experience within. The **fifth proposition** is that if you accept this view of god as an all-sustaining envelope ingredient in man but not only in man, an envelope, a sort of cosmic envelope, which sustains, creates and plays a significant role in transforming man and the rest of the world, then this gives a certain view of what man's role is. Man's role may be called, appropriating a term used by medieval theologians in the west, 'theosis'. This means the maximisation of the presence of god or the divine on earth: then firstly in himself through the liberation of this essential ingredient, this (if you like) divine spark; and secondly, through the project of universal self-realisation, that is liberation of all beings everywhere. **Sixth,** the transcendent and transcendence are not unusual phenomena. I want to argue that the experience of transcendence is not just exceptional but a part of the normal process of science; it is not only saying there is something there which transcends our experiences, but that in scientific innovation we have an experience which is transcendental in the sense of collapsing subject–object duality. Transcendence then is something which is vital for scientific discovery and growth, which is never mechanical nor algorithmic, always involves a moment of inspirational creation on the basis of that hard prepared ground. Moreover, all dialectics of dealienation, like this general project of theosis or universal self-realisation, will depend essentially on love, the great expanding, liberating force in the social world and arguably the universe. Even as a scientist you will never discover something new about your subject matter unless you, in some way, love it: Aristotle, Darwin, Newton, Marx, Freud are all cases in point. That then was the sixth proposition.

The **seventh** and final proposition that I want to assert about god (and remember I am really talking mainly here about the god within) is that there is a relationship of unilateral, one-way dependency. What has been called a fallen world, a world characterised by evil, oppression, sin, alienation, whatever categories you want to use, could not exist without that essential ingredient, that is without our noble, higher selves. But we could certainly do fine without them. Concretely this means that if we are emergent from god or the divine then we could not exist without that. If there is a bit of god within us, then this puts a different aspect or perspective on things. Just as Krishna told Arjuna in the Bhagavad Gita, your soul is immortal so do not worry about whether you die or not, that soul will exist independently of your death, so you could say that if there was a higher essential aspect to humanity, it could survive and flourish without all the ills that beset us on this planet. But certainly those ills that beset us on this planet could not survive without that deeper essential creative, loving self. We cannot carry on as we are. Rosa Luxembourg declared at the beginning of the twentieth century that the alternatives were between socialism and barbarism. We can say at the beginning of the twenty-first century that the alternatives are between self-realisation, ultimately universal self-realisation, or the decimation of the species, the mortal coil in which our immortal divinity is embodied within us. We could exist without those ills which are threatening the very survival of the species on the planet. I have said a lot about god, because it is a topic which has been rather taboo in western philosophy and because I wanted to air the subject. Not, as I said, because I want to convert any of you to a belief in gods' existence. For what I believe is truly essential to rescue in human life is this element of spirituality which I will come to when I talk about right-action.

First a little bit about the second edge of negativity. This is the domain of absence. Absence is an absolutely crucial concept. Absence is necessary for the intelligibility of any being at all. It would be impossible for you to hear me unless there was a space, a gap between my words and indeed unless there was actually a physical gap between us through which that sound could travel. Absence is necessary to any phenomena. Most importantly absence is necessary for change. Because change and process is always the absenting of what was present and the presenting of what was absent. So there is this duality of absence and presence. But since the time of Parmenides western philosophy has had a taboo on absence. Parmenides said you cannot speak of what is not. Even the very greatest dialectician in western thought, Hegel, actually eliminated absence as soon as he could. At the beginning of the logic, his famous *Science of Logic*, starting from the category of being he moves quickly from being to nothing and in fact nothing is the last negative category we hear of. The next category is becoming and then everything else takes place on a purely positive plane.

The kind of absence I am arguing for is not indeterminate absence like nothing; it is *determinate absence*, absence as experienced as lack, as need, as want. It is the absence which prompts a hungry man to search for his dinner. It is the absence of water, the absence of fresh air which is what pollution causes. That absence is in fact a vital motor of change in social life. This brings out what I think Marx meant when he talked about Hegelian dialectic having a rational kernel which was shrouded by the mystical shell. So what I want us to do is say a little bit about what that kernel is.

The rational kernel of dialectic is as a learning or developmental process driven by absence. For instance in science we have a theory which is incomplete in some way, this incompleteness, betokening absence will generate contradictions, inconsistencies, anomalies which will pile up to a point at which they will become unbearable. Then we will have the moment of transcendence to a greater totality and that transcendence to a greater totality will remedy the initial generative absence; and in that remedying of the absence will restore consistency within the theoretical field. That is the dialectic of science; and that is also the dialectic of all developmental learning processes. It is driven by absence and it is also remedied by absence; because in this transcendence to a new concept, in this moment of scientific creation, this new concept which is going to do all the work leading to a new theoretical edifice, a greater scientific construction, that concept cannot be mechanically or algorithmically induced or deduced from the preexisting data. It is not something which is given by the data. It is something which is genuinely novel, which comes from the creative imagination. So within this moment of transcendence to a new concept there is a moment of transcendence itself—a moment of transcendence in the process of transcendence to a greater totality. It is in this moment that the new concept comes, from nowhere or anyway from an experience in which subject–object duality breaks down. That is the rational kernel in Hegelian dialectic. There is no time here to go on to talk about the mystical shell which is briefly the absenting of the concept of absence and its other features, but we will do that some other time.

I go on to two very important things which are implied by the dialectical view of the world at this second edge. The first is that analytical reasoning is limited: this is the dialectical critique of analytical reasoning. Every process of thought, every process of development breaks at some point or other the strict laws of deductive logic. Deductive logic has a role to play within science but what is happening when we are doing creative science or creative philosophy is that we are always teasing concepts, stretching our imagination. For instance, to give an example which I have used already, when initially in critical realism the subject of ontology was opened up, that is of a real world of being existing relatively independently of our beliefs, then it seemed like ontology, or being and our beliefs were being counterposed. But, upon reflection, of course those beliefs had to be situated within ontology itself. So knowledge became part of reality. Epistemology properly understood was not only opposed to, but a part of ontology: beliefs were in the same world as the objects they were about. In any movement to a greater totality concepts are always going to be stretched, so that the process is always going to appear slightly shocking and to violate strict deductive logic.

What then is the role of deductive logic? What happens then is that when a scientist has successfully described a field of data, and this is true of all practitioners, they will stretch their concepts, build creative models in order to capture a reality deeper than or wider than the data. The creative scientist is a bricoleur. The bricolage is the junk in a builder's yard, which is the Heideggerian ready-to-hand, the material a scientist must use if he is to capture in words or in materialised phenomena something new. This will always involve tinkering around, folding one concept in there, another in there, generating a lot of superficial inconsistencies until he gets to a point where he has built up a theory which can be rigorously tested, in the empirical moment of science, against that new deeper reality, which generated the more superficial one he was initially at. Then he can write it all up in a nice research paper and everything will follow from the premises to the conclusions, everything can be set out in strict deductive logic. That is what I have called the Leibnitzian hour, that is the final test of a theory. It is not the starting point, but an ending point. An ending point which is purely provisional. It is certainly not the end of science, but a bouncing off point for a new round of scientific discovery. For once you get to that point the scientist will then move on to discover a deeper, or wider totality which will explain *that level.* So science must be viewed as a process in motion continually, incessantly. Development in a science, in thought, in intellectual life, in culture, in society, must be viewed in an organic processual way. Our model should be the development of an acorn into an oak. It cannot be the derivation of our conclusions from premises. That plays only a limited role within thought. What most creative scientific thought is trying to do is to stretch itself, trying to stretch our concepts until it is able to appropriate discursively something new.

As I have touched upon transcendence, I just want to add that once you have a moment of transcendence, even though the subject–object duality may have broken down, this does not mean that it cannot be described *retrospectively* in a discursive way. It just means that the transcendental experience is not equivalent to its discursive description. So we not only have thought which does not satisfy the canons of deductive logic, but experiences which do not satisfy the canons of the discursive intellect; and both play a part in science as well as in ordinary life. The non-discursive experience can be described discursively, but that discourse is not the same as the experience. I may be talking about prayer or meditation but that talking is not the prayer or meditation it is about. It is also worth noting that both deductive logic and the discursive (as distinct from the intuitive) intellect are closely intertwined with a society which systematically privileges the digital, sentential, binary, oppositional, sequential, 'masculine' left brain over the analogical, iconic, holistic, synthetic, fuzzy, intuitive, convergent, 'feminine' right brain—that is conditionality, calculation, contract and control over unconditionality, immediacy, spontaneity and freedom.

The final point I want to make turns on the critique of the notion of the fixity of the subject in the subject–predicate form. Western philosophy always assumes that if there is any change, it will be at the level of the predicate. You know the standard form of a proposition is: a subject is such and such. Pauline is happy. If there is any change it is going to come at the level of the predicate, what attributes she has. It is not going to come at the level of herself. And then the subject, Pauline, is assumed to be fixed. Only her happiness is changeable. Now this is a completely wrong view of change. What we have to do is understand that the subjects themselves are processes in motion. We cannot reify them in the way in which analytical logic has typically done. We can also note that no coherent account of change can be produced unless change is attributed to a subject—for what is it in the predicate that changes, that too must surely be a subject? Any change is a change in the thing; as such, always presupposes an Aristotelian material cause. Moreover, it is essential to place change within the subject, because I am going to argue (as I suggested yesterday) that not only is self-alienation the root of all ills, but that all emancipation is self-emancipation, that real emancipation, self-transformation can only come from within; it can never be imposed from without. And that self-change, self-transformation, which naturally will usher in change at all other levels of social being; and that self-transformation is the heart of the process of the project of universal self-realisation. So that is why the critique of the fixity of the subject in the subject–predicate form is so important.

The third level of totality. Totality includes concepts such as interconnection, objectivity, subjectivity, internal relationality, but above all universality and universalisability. Just as I argued for dialectical reasoning, which subsumed analytical reasoning as a special case, I want to argue for dialectical and developmental universalisability. Analytical universalisability is just the subsumption of an event or a thing under a universal without any mediation and this is characteristic not only of western philosophical thought but also the social systems in which we live. Thus, on the Humean theory of causal laws which we discussed yesterday, reality is seen as being empirical invariances. This means that everything can be subsumed under a universal covering law, seen as actualistically describing what the phenomena are. Everything is just subsumed immediately under that empirical invariance. In Kant's categorical imperative the maxim is this: what you do you should be able to universalise. In other words test whether you can tell a lie. Is it the case that you want lying to be universalised? no. So you cannot tell a lie, therefore you must never tell a lie. Now this is very counter-intuitive because obviously we all know there are lies and lies, and some white lies are good. Similarly if I give Pauline some advice, this may not be the right advice to give to Bridget over there. What is right for one person is not necessarily right for another. These are the intuitions we have. What this means is that we have to think universalisability and universality in terms not just of analytical universality which covers everything in a blanket way, but in terms of specific differentiations and in terms of geo-historical trajectories, and then in terms of the uniqueness of that individual or phenomena. No two human beings are ever going to be the same, no two instances of an event, nor will the same phenomena ever be *exactly* the same.

The logic of uniformity, the logic of analytical universalisability is written into the logic of the capitalist mode of production; and I must add (because this is not a political point) that it was written into the practice of the so-called actually existing socialist states, and it is written into the practice of many political parties. It helps to explain the postmodernist reaction. The post-modernist reaction is to stress difference, diversity. The post-modernist is saying in his or her politics of identity, no we are not the same, we may be members of the same political party, but some of us are women, others of us are men. We women, we will be feminists, we will be different. You well know this form of reaction which stresses difference, diversity and change and that is a very salutary reaction. It goes wrong only when it leaves out the whole idea of universality itself. So it is fine for women, feminists to say we women are different, or for Indian women to say we Indian women are different, if they therefore do not split themselves off and perpetuate their own alienation by dividing themselves off from their essential unity as human beings with men or with other women who are not Indian. So that underlying unity is what is lost in the politics of identity. This politics has other forms besides postmodernism such as communalism and fundamentalism, forms which are fear-based reactions which reproduce the alienation they are a symptom of. Counterposed to fear is love. Love unites, binds, totalises, heals. Fear divides, ruptures, alienates, splits. I cannot say anything more here about the third level of totality.

We now turn to the fourth domain of agency. What we have to do is, as Krishna did in the Bhagavad Gita, resolve the problem of action by an expanded conception of the self. The Leninist question 'what is to be done?' has to be resolved by asking the transcendental question 'who am I?' or 'what is the self?' Once we have a deeper conception of human being then we have a better conception of action. I want to enunciate five theorems or necessary truths about action, because it is very important to be clear about this.

Five theorems. Firstly the irreducibility of intentionality, action is always mediated by consciousness. This entails the critique of all materialism, but also a critique of dualistic disembodiment, we are embodied; and understanding consciousness and ideas are causally efficacious and also causally explicable, which means that reasons must be causes. We are against an artificial dualism there. That is the irreducibility of intentionality. Secondly there is the irreducibility of agency. The fact is we must act. This is a critique then of what Hegel called the 'beautiful soul'. For example the yogi who disengages himself from action, or the would-be yogi, not the true yogi, because yoga as you know means union therefore it must mean delineation everywhere. The would-be yogi disengages from action but exists as a parasite on society, actually tacitly presupposing it. So this gives a model of engaged but unattached activity. That is what we are seeking. The moment of engagement is stressed by western philosophers. The moment of unattachment has been stressed by mystics in east and west alike. Thirdly, agency is geo-historically processual, always social, always has these four dimensions I talked about earlier.

Finally, agency ultimately, at some point, must be spontaneous. That is to say at some point a practical syllogism, as Aristotle understood, must issue in an action. We cannot just go on thinking; at some point thought must issue in an action. I may think about how to tilt this microphone and I may think well, should I do it this way, should I do it that way, but at some point I just have to do it, at some point we always just have to perform an action. At some point thought must pass into action. There is a direct link then between thought and action. My argument is that the deeper the level of our selves from which we act, the more our actions will be complete, coherent and in this way spontaneously right. When we know how to drive a car, we do not have to think about it, we just do it. When we know how to speak, we do not need to think how to formulate a sentence, we just formulate it. So the deeper we go into ourselves the more spontaneously right our action will be. If everything depends on action and action is ultimately spontaneous or basic in the sense coined by the western philosopher Danto, then all the actions we do at all the levels of social being must ultimately come from the self. This therefore immediately prioritises self-change and self-transformation as the key moment in remedying the alienation at all those four levels of social being. So we prioritise self-change to social change. But there are three points to notice here. Firstly, and this is the fifth theorem about agency, I cannot act myself without simultaneously acting at all four planes or levels of social being. That is to say anything I do, coming from me, will be (or involve) an effect at the level of the stratification of my personality, but will also involve material exchanges with nature, social interactions with other human beings and impact in some way on the social structure. So though all action comes from the self, necessarily, at the same time all action is always potentially or actually efficacious at all other planes of social being. The second point to note is that we cannot be free as individuals unless and until that freedom issues in and is coupled with the self-realisation of all. Finally, more specifically, there is a dialectic between self-change and social change.

We can show this briefly through dialectics of inaction and dialectics of action. What we have to do is access our higher self; then—and this is the really important point—we have to shed everything which we are essentially not; then we have to fully embody it in the totality of our being; then we have to witness this higher self in every moment of our action and stabilise it in our daily life. These *dialectics of inaction* will automatically—in virtue of the fact that we must act, we cannot just be (this is what I have called the axiological imperative)—result in *dialectics of action*. These are briefly the more fully in touch with ourselves we are, the more we will spontaneously do what is right, the more compassionate, loving, caring, our action will be. So we have dialectics of love and solidarity. You will recall the dialectic of desire to freedom which I sketched earlier, the dialectic in which logically, once we have a desire, we are driven to the abolition of constraints on that desire; and then to the abolition of all dialectically similar constraints; and then to the abolition of all constraints, in virtue of their dialectical similarity as constraints on the realisation of human freedom. That dialectic can be given a further twist, by seeing that it entails a state in which one has no desires. First, subjectively because any desire will itself be a constraint, a limitation on our freedom. And secondly because objectively one is living in a world of abundance, one is living in a world in which, to use Marx's words, the free development of each is the condition but also the reality of the free development of all. Then we have the dialectic of recapitulation, for, as Freud put it, what we cannot remember we are bound to repeat. So we must thoroughly come to terms with, understand and then shed, that is let go of the past, the presence of the past. That will include the totality of attachments, and among our attachments are of course our aversions. Finally we have philosophical dialectics which include understanding and changing reality in accordance with the level of it's deepest, most comprehensive categories, and rooting out everything which is inconsistent with it. From this perspective we can see alienation as actually a category mistake in reality.

Seven properties of right-action. Firstly, it will be spontaneous, coherent and compassionate. Secondly, it must be in the present, in the moment, we must not live in the past, we must let go of the past, let go of our attachments. This involves the idea, if you like, of ceasing to be bound *karmically* and acting from the *dharmic* standpoint. Nor can we live in the future, we should not worry, we should not project our ideals into the future; our ideals are here, in the present even if they are actually hidden, occluded or prevented from being realised. So we live in the present but we can only act from where we are, on our own particular axiological world-line. So we must not act in a voluntaristic way. We can only do what we can do with the resources we have got. So this universal new beginning I am arguing for must be a chipping away with the resources that we actually have. We have to understand how we are actually, and not just ideally, constituted. This means that we have to take on board the negativity, the limitations and the conditionalities that we have inside ourselves; if you think you can be immediately and spontaneously free then that is a recipe for disaster. Fourthly, this action will be orientated to the installation of social justice, the abolition of the totality of master–slave relationships, the ending of all reified, voluntaristic modes of thought and behaviour. The ending of all conditionalities. What is normally called love is an exchange, what is true love is unconditional, is a giving.

Fifth, this must be fully integrated and balanced. Mind and body will be linked but we must also include the great missing element, emotion; we need to understand the tri-unity or trinity of mind, body and emotion. We will not have the dualism that leaves out emotions (including the negative emotions as well as the positive emotion of love). And right-action will be action under the inspiration of that essential ingredient which is spirit. Sixth, we move beyond dualism to the synthesis of opposites and their transcendence in higher totalities; to the elimination as far as is possible of all strife, to living in peace and harmony in the world, to the ending of alienation at all those four levels of being. Seventh, this will result in a simpler, purer society but also a richer and deeper one. It may be easier to create than we think. Because once we let go of false modes of thought and being, once we begin to access our higher selves, we can begin to see that really the problem is not so much of evil. Or not only of evil. For there is also, at least philosophically, a problem of good. Because how extraordinary it is that there is so much goodness and love in the world. Just think about it, let us focus on that, that love, goodness, nobility, courage, these are displayed everywhere in the perpetuation of social ills. Once we can tap through to that level then we may find it easier to build a world that we already (but not only) have inside us and universalise it everywhere.

Part Two

Debates within and about Critical Realism

Chapter Two

Critical Realism and Marxism[*]

Four recent turns in social thought that put dialectic back on the agenda

The core of this paper will be on dialectic, but I am going to approach it in a slightly roundabout way by listing four recent turns in social thought that put dialectic back on the agenda, in fact make it an urgent priority for us to come to terms with dialectic, and in particular with what was right and what was wrong in Hegelian dialectic which, as Marx quite rightly said, but did not really sufficiently elaborate and explain, is the core of all, at least western, dialectic. I want to situate in the context of these four recent developments in social thought, which make these times, contrary to surface appearances, actually quite dialectical. Secondly, I want to relate these four categories of changes in recent social thought to the four-dimensional schema which I have outlined in my book *Dialectic: The Pulse of Freedom,* articulating the system of dialectical critical realism. This tries to bring out Marx's intuition about dialectic and provide for us a

* ULU, London, 20 March 1997.

materialist but transformatively oriented dialectic. Then I want to take up the question of exactly the structure of Hegelian dialectic, what it is, what is the rational kernel, what is the mystical shell, and I want to argue that in addition to the rational kernel and the mystical shell, there is what I call the 'golden nugget', and then there is a fourth item: a platinum plate. So this paper will be a trio of quartets.

Turn towards realism

Let us talk about changes which have put dialectic back on the scene. The first movement in cultural and social thought has been a turn towards realism, an understanding to deny the reality of anything is self-defeating. What is it that you are denying the reality of? It is quite obvious that the category of reality must include everything. It must include logical contradictions, inconsistencies, mistakes, and reality is a totality which defines the limits of our reason, and therefore, not to be a realist in the appropriate sense is pretty well impossible. Even if you are an idealist, I want to argue, you will end up by being an implicit realist. That is the first turn; it is a turn towards realism of a particular sort.

Processual turn in the natural sciences

The second is a processual turn, an interest in questions of geo-history in all the sciences, particularly in the natural sciences; in the social sciences it seems to have been eclipsed but that is only a surface illusion. But in biology, in physics, questions of space and time and causality and geo-history are there and increasingly coming to the fore.

The inter-connectedness of things

The third turn is perhaps the one which is most familiar to all of us, it is the holistic, ecological turn. Analytical thought cannot come to terms with the inter-connectedness of things which has been brought into sharp focus by issues of environmental and related crises. For, is virtue of its atomism and commitment to existentionalist definition, it disconnects things from each other, affectively treating them as separate and independent issues.

Reflexivity

The fourth turn is in a way the oldest turn, and it is a turn to reflexivity, and it is in fact very important. It was initiated by Descartes in modern philosophy, and then radicalised by Kant, Hegel and Marx, moving through the other so called 'masters of suspicion' Freud and Nietzsche into the twentieth century. It took a preoccupation with a concern with language as a means and medium of knowledge. This was very salutary, but in fact it is much more general than that. The criterion of reflexivity means that any philosophy which can not sustain the intelligibility of its own content and production must be categorially ruled out; we can say straight away that it is false. A truly reflexive philosophy, I want to argue, will be totalising, it will thematise ontology, and it will reassert concepts of negation and negativity.

Critical realist component

Let me now turn to the critical realist component. Corresponding to the realist turn in recent thought, critical realism thematises ontology. I am going to argue that all these categories, the four categories I am going to discuss, are the categories of ontology, of absence, of totality and reflexivity; and I am also going to talk about transformative practices. These categories are essential for understanding dialectic. Let me go through the categories as thematised by dialectical critical realism: **ontology,** or the **theory of being**; absence as crucial to all transformation and to **dialectic** itself and to concepts of **negativity and negation**; the third concept is that of **totality**, which is an absolutely critical concept because typically in science, when we have an inconsistency, this means that there is an absence in our epistemic or thought field and we remedy this by a resort to greater totality; alongside totality, we have the **absence of totality** which is split, alienation, dualism, fragmentation, dichotomy.

When I am discussing these categories, I will also be discussing their inverses, which are so characteristic of analytical thought. The fourth category which I am going to highlight is the reflexive criterion of philosophy, but I am going to relate this to the possibility of a philosophy which would be truly transformative, which would relate theory to practice, and which would act as an underlabourer to the real processes which are going on and which are seeking to overturn the way in which capitalism is systematically spoiling the natural, social, subjective, and relational conditions of production. This is a philosophy which is really pro-active, but also a pro-activity which is not a hypostatising, but something that vitally concerns all of us as human beings and citizens.

What is the contribution of critical realism to the first turn, the turn to the thematisation of reality? It is the re-thematisation of ontology, of being, which was systematically denied by the whole tradition of contemporary philosophy from Descartes in favour of knowledge. I quote from Wittgenstein: 'It is sufficient to talk only of the network, not what the network describes'. A lot of people think that as philosophers all we have to do is talk about language or knowledge and we do not have to speak about that of which language or knowledge speaks about. But that position is evidently self-undermining, because what is the status of the discourse which enunciates that? I mean, is it real or not? Clearly, the discursive act has to be understood as being real and has conditions, real conditions and a real content, or an imaginary content, either way we can not avoid questions of reality. It is quite obvious when you are studying the classical traditions of empiricism and rationalism that all these philosophers had an implicit ontology.

What was the implicit ontology in Humean positivism? It was a world which was constituted by atomistic individuals, possibly gendered man, cut off from their fellows and who sensed constant conjunctions of regularities thrown out by nature. The form of natural laws was taken to be this, therefore that. Two implications of this are very important.

The first is that reality is on the surface, there is no depth to it. The second is, if these conjunctions are regular and constant, they are also eternal, so reality can not be changed, whatever is must be. Wittgenstein again brought this out when he said that 'philosophy in the end leaves everything as it is'. This is quite the opposite of my view. In fact philosophy either reinforces or undermines the status quo, it is either conservative with a little 'c' or radical with a big '**R**'.

Let me say why this account of laws and this account of nature is false. If I go to the laboratory and attempt to test the law of gravity, what I have to do is to set up a specifically constructive environment in which I can appreciate the way in which a body falls to the ground. This does not mean to say that the law of gravity is not operating outside the experimentally closed conditions; the law of gravity is operating on us when we are sitting here, it is just counter-acted by real tendencies which are preventing the natural disposition of objects to fall to the ground. What in fact **Humeanism** does, or **positivism** does, is that it **undermines the human praxis or labour that goes into establishing our knowledge of laws of nature and at the same time it undermines the depth of understanding that scientific knowledge can bring to us, the way in which it shows us a deeper level of reality.** You can see it from the position into which classical philosophy got itself in the case of someone like Hume who argued that there was no good reason to not go out of a building by the window on the second floor rather than the door.

That is true in terms of the surface appearances, but we have a scientific understanding and also practical understanding informed by science and common sense: if we go out of the building by the window on the second floor we will fall to the ground and there won't be very much of us left, whereas if we go out by the door then we will, other things being equal, make a relatively trouble free exit. **This failure to think through, this failure of philosophy, is extraordinary**. I just take another case, because what critical realism does is that it says that knowledge is very important, and that in addition to knowledge, the overencompassing knowledge is being; it also says that value is very important, and value was something else that tended to get eliminated by the positivists and a traditional account of science. You can see the sort of absurdity into which modern philosophy falls when Hume can come out and say 'It is not irrational to prefer the destruction of the world to my little finger'. If this is a result of modern philosophy, then it is a *reductio ad absurdum*. It is not even true on its own terms because it is clearly more rational for him to prefer the destruction of his little finger to that of all the world. Why? Because the whole world includes his little finger. He was detotalising himself, he was excluding himself from the system of which he is a part.

And this is why the criterion of **reflexivity**, the capacity of a philosopher (or of a philosophy) to sustain his own content and conditions of production is so important. Once you establish that reality has a certain depth to it, then you can also ask questions about the conditions under which reality might be changed, which is also obscured by the failure to thematise being. That would take us very neatly to the second category of absence, but first I want to explore two consequences of the **thematisation of ontology**. The first consequence is a categorial realism. People have a misunderstanding of the nature of categories, they think like Kant that categories are things we impose on reality; but to the critical realist, the transcendental realist, the **categories**, if they are real, **are constitutive of reality itself**. That is, causality is no schema we impose on reality, it is actually out there.

The subject matter of philosophy, therefore, traditionally defined as being the understanding of categories, is **reality**, is **being**. This becomes very important when we move we move to the social world because we can then argue: reality is pre-categorised, but in the social world the way in which reality may be categorised may be false. Social reality is conceptually dependent; the categories in terms of which we understand social reality may be systematically false, illusory, or misleading, and that is the clue to the concept of ideology. Ideology is a categorially confused reality. It is real but it is false. This is a possibility and an actualised possibility in social reality. The true nature of social reality is there.

Let us suppose, as I actually believe, that Marx got the fundamental structures of the capitalist mode of production absolutely right. This does not mean that there isn't a lot of work to be done. There we have a correct description of the categories of the economy, but part of this description shows the way in which reality appears to its agents as being categorially confused in virtue of the concept-dependent nature of the categories in terms of which they live their life; they live it in terms of illusion, they live it in terms of what I would call a '**demi-reality**', a half-light reality. **The task of social science is to penetrate that demi-reality through to the underlying reality** and situate the conditions of possibility of the removal of illusion, of systematically false being. This systematically false being is also systematically oppressive, paralysing, related to irrealist categorial structures and, I argue in **Dialectic: The Pulse of Freedom**, master–slave relationships, instrumental reasoning, analytical thought, analytical as distinct from dialectical universalisability, money and lots of other profoundly important phenomena. No one would argue money was just a category, but money in our present society takes the form of categorial error; it depends upon categorial error. These are the implications of a categorial realism.

The second kind of realism is a **dispositional realism**. In critical realism we are talking about and concerned with the powers, the possibilities, the tendencies of things, which things possess even if they are not exercised. Why is this radical? Why should this interest a Marxist society? Clearly, if people had the capacity to organise a decent system of transport in London, they are not capable to do so, these are very important data, isn't it? The idea that we have tendencies, a child has a tendency to become a good musician, or possesses the power to acquire a range of skills, possesses the need, which is a closely related capacity, for adequate food, housing, health care, etc., these powers, possibilities, dispositions and needs are not satisfied, then they do not cease to exist; but the Humean actualist, collapsing reality, the domain of the real to the domain of what is actualised, does not allow for that possibility.

Critical realism asserts the absolute priority of the possible over the actual. The possible is ontologically, epistemologically and logically prior to the actual, and the possible is real. In addition to these tendencies and powers being possessed without being exercised, they may be exercised without being realised, in the way in which the law of gravity is operating on us now, or, to take an example from political economy, there is a tendency for the rate of profit to fall, as a result of the rise in the organic composition of capital without it being realised as a result of offsetting tendencies which may be internally related to the mechanism which explains the tendency, its exercise and its non-realisation. We get an **idea of reality as being stratified, as being complex, as being deep, transformable**, and we situate such things in the social sciences as the possibility of a more satisfactory true to human nature, emancipated, freer mode of being, socially and individually; a dichotomy of which we should be very critical in its term, but I just use it as a temporary place-holder. The key set of categories for dialectic are categories of **negativity turning on the concept of absence**.

This is the time for me to say what I think of **Hegelian dialectic**, and how absence features in its rational kernel. What I think Hegel did, and this is the rational kernel of dialectic, is that he produced a **general theory of all learning processes**, which is very simple. It applies to science, to social phenomena, and it goes like this: you have an incomplete totality, there is an absence, the **absence generates inconsistencies, splits, incompleteness, tensions**. This is resolved by transcendence towards a greater totality which incorporates the split-off element, the absented element as a part of the greater, more inclusive, totality. So, we can work our way towards a general definition of dialectic as a theory of the experience of the processes of a stratification and differentiation of phenomena.

Let me refer concretely to science in illustration of this general theory of learning processes. Everyone is familiar with the work of Kuhn; what happens before the scientific revolution is that the scientists are going along in a paradigm, there may be anomalies, these anomalies are satisfactorily explained and resolved, but sooner or later an anomaly becomes really problematic; that is the moment of inconsistency. From a dialectical point of view this signifies that the totality with which the scientist is working is incomplete, there is an absence. Error, although it is not the same as, always depends upon, absence. What happens is that the scientist has to have a **reconceptualisation** of the field, he has to introduce new phenomena, a deeper or wider level of reality, or a more inclusive totality. When s/he has done that, then the inconsistency is resolved and we have a greater totality, a wider totality and ultimately, when we incorporate the social scientist itself, that totality, which of course exists in reality, should be capable of reflexively situating the scientist itself. The schema is really very simple. It is incompleteness or absence generating inconsistency which is resolved by resort to transcendence, by a higher or more inclusive totality, including a greater or deeper one. That I think is the **rational kernel of dialectic** and it applies not only to science, but also to art and to all processes which change in human and, by a slight extension of the argument, in the non-human world. It was a great innovation for Hegel to bring out this logical structure which is nothing other than the dialectic of progress when it occurs.

What is the **mystical shell in Hegel?** The mystical shell in Hegel is his endism, his triumphalism and his failure to see that the dialectic will carry on; his commitment to what I call **ontological monovalence**, which is a purely positive account of being. What Hegel does is, when he was completed his system, he absents the very crucial notion of absence itself, he absences absence. It is true to say that he is an apologist for the Prussian state of his time. I think that the Left Hegelians were right.

We see philosophers such as **Fukuyama** writing in 1989 celebrating the end of history, echoed by philosophers such as **Rorty**. The idea that the dialectic is going to stop, the idea that no more change is possible. Together with this endism goes triumphalism. Hegel, also committed the **epistemic fallacy**, that is the fallacy of reducing ontology to epistemology, because he thought the dialectic occurred only on the level of knowledge. Ultimately everything was subsumed by the absolute concept, the concept of absolute knowledge. We will see also that Hegel is detotalising and unreflexive, so he fails to satisfy all the categorial criteria that I have set up.

One thing is very interesting about this dialectical schema, and that is this: if we have a problematic situation, it can not be resolved from within, the resolution is always by resort to what is left out, to what is transcendent with respect to the level of the experience concerned. It may be something that is split off, something that has been forgotten, or denied, or it may be something that operates at a higher level of reality. So the moment of **transcendence** in terms of which science or any other learning process; so society moves to higher or more inclusive level of reality, is itself informed by a moment of transcendence. There is a transcendent element within the moment of transcendence and you can see that it is quite obviously the case that science is not algorithmic. If the solution is already there then there is no problem. You need something else. This points to the role of the **scientific imagination**, and in ethics the role of what I call 'concrete utopianism'. Using imagination to build models of a better society. That is the rational kernel and the mystical shell.

What is the **golden nugget**? The golden nugget in Hegel's theory is that he shows the way in which **two things which cannot possibly be true together can be transmuted into negative sub-contraries**, two things which can both be true together. If you understand the working class or the bourgeoisie correctly, then you change your description of them and then in social science, to use again Marx's example, we have a coherence description of the social totality. If you stick with the nations and the bourgeoisie from Marx's point of view. Then you are going to have incoherent totality. The golden nugget is just **this dialectic by which two things which can not possibly be true together are transmuted by enriching their description and conceptualisation**. And remember, we are talking about practical totalities in the practical field, that is by transforming them in a very literal sense, changing them, just as we are changing their descriptions, and changing their descriptions is also changing something real, so I am not artificially juxtaposing epistemology to ontology.

Epistemology can be contrasted with ontology but only within a concept of ontology which embraces them both. In other words, the knowledge of an object can be contrasted to that object but only within a concept of objectivity which embraces the knowledge itself. That is I think the golden nugget, which products what I call a dialectics of co-presence. One of the things we have come to learn in the context of Marxist historiography and economic theory is the way in which capitalism develops by eating up, as it were, other modes of production. Up to now there has always been a co-presence of modes of production, but we are getting to the point at which capitalism is becoming itself totalising. And we are living in a world in which capitalism, in particular I think **finance capitalism**, that is money, is becoming the all-dominating, hegemonic and all-consuming power biting and exhausting everything. That is a true and very frightening totality in which we live, in which there appears to most people to be no plausible alternatives to capitalism. Because it is very difficult to point to any actually existing alternatives to capitalism. Prior to 1989 one could argue that the Soviet Union was there, the Soviet empire was there, it might be, so to speak, wrong, and it might in many respects mimic capitalism, but at least it provided an alternative, in terms of which in the space of two you had the possibility of a third or a fourth, or the possibility of transforming one or the other. But now **our polity is suffocated**, this is an illusion, because something is going on underneath, but it is a very frightening illusion. If you look, it is not just a question of economics; post-structuralists and lots of so-called non-realists are very interested in things like the media, but if you turn on the television you get the same programme in India . . . today as you would in Cyprus or in America. **This dialectics of co-presence and the apparent elimination of alternatives today** is the so-called golden nugget in the Hegelian dialectic.

What I call the '**platinum plate**' was something which Marx was very keen on, although he did not call it that, and this was the way in which Hegelian dialectic and in fact thought forms in general reflect, provide a diagnostic key to the reality to which they are a part. He talks about **abstraction not being a figment of Hegel's imagination but a feature of the state which Hegel describes**, the state itself abstracts, money itself abstracts from the needs and possibilities of the individuals who exchange it. This is dialectic as a platinum plate.

Why is the concept of absence so important, and why has philosophy denied it? What are the consequences of it? Nothing which is purely positive is possible, and anything which contains an absence contains the possibility of change. I will give a well-known example. If you consider a sentence, the spaces, the absences in it, make it one sentence rather than another, whether it is a written or a spoken sentence. We would be indistinguishable as people without the spaces, the absences that mark our particular physiognomy. Absence is a truly vital concept, and I think it is not possible to have a purely positive account of being, it is not possible to have a purely positive world. Where does this illusion come from? Historically, it comes from **the Parmenidian distinction of being and non-being**, the suffusion of non-being by being, which Plato took over in terms of his analysis of negation and change in terms of difference; he said, well obviously things are different, but there is no real negativity, there is no real change, there is no not. As early as Parmenides and Plato, philosophy's ideological role as a reifier, a reinforcer of the status quo, was already there. **What is the consequence of eliminating absence?** Of eliminating something which is categorially necessary?

What would happen is that implicit totality would be formed, and we would have the split. If I argue that absence itself is categorically necessary, then its denial will produce an inconsistency or a split, and so we have the problem of induction in epistemology; how can we guarantee that the laws of nature will continue as they are? Because the absence of ontological depth is a present one has to resort to a fideistic account, because either one says: there is no ground to the laws of nature continuing, or one says: god by a miraculous move will keep, by resort to a transcendent ground, these laws of nature going. If you ask: Why do you believe this? **then it is just a question of faith, which was essentially Kant's answer.** You have the split between fact and value, and, most important of all, the split between mind and body. Other splits go along with it: the split between theory and practice, the split between philosophy and knowledge and reality. All these splits are symptoms of the absence, and there, I want to argue, is the primordial mistake of philosophy.

In fact, **without absence you can not sustain difference** and unless you can sustain difference, then philosophy will consume everything, so you will not be able to distinguish the reality within philosophy from the realities which are science, from the realities which are human needs or survival, from the realities which are the needs of other species on our planet. That is what is so important about absence. What happens when you eliminate absence? If absence is categorially necessary, it is an implicit totality rather than an explicit totality. If something is categorially necessary, it will appear. Let me give you some example of this. The famous pragmatic philosopher Richard Rorty argues for a form of eliminative materialism in Part I of his **Philosophy and the Mirror of Nature**, basically arguing that the world consists just of atoms and the void. So, what is the status of his own discourse? We have a revealing incapacity of the philosopher to situate himself; if his own discourse is categorially necessary, then it will appear some way or other, and of course, he does in Part III of his book, where he argues that the task of philosophy is conversational hermeneutics. How do you reduce conversational hermeneutics to atoms and the void? You had crude reductionist materialism with an hyper-idealism sitting hand in hand.

Instead, what I would argue for is **an emergent powers materialism**, which would situate the discourse of philosophers as one level of reality within a stratified reality which contains of course atoms and the void and things far beneath atoms and the void and contains much else besides conversational hermeneutics. This particular polarity, variant of the mind–body dualism is very popular in philosophy today. Philosophers like to think of themselves and the academic community as being sort of language, and everything else is kind of body, crude body. It is not a caricature. These splits reveal **the absence of coherent philosophy within a lot of contemporary thought**. What I and my colleagues as critical realists are trying to do is point to these absences and reconstitute an explicit and well-thematised totality.

That is, engage that transformation which I called the 'golden nugget', the **transformation of positive contraries into negative sub-contraries**, by situating both, say, atoms and the void, and conversational hermeneutics within a wider, broader totality, and ultimately, situate our own discourse itself as philosophers. I would like to end up by saying that I want to argue that dialectical critical realism or dialectic and critical realism and everything else which is necessary for an adequate ontology and philosophical sociology is a package. **You can not select some items of it and reject other items of it.** If you do not embrace something like critical realism in its dialectical form, then you are going to end up as being a solipsist, you are going to deny: . . . he could not sustain the reality of other objects, he could not sustain the reality of causality, then the question is: What was the status of himself? The person who could not sustain all these other things, the self disappeared. He could not sustain the link between two impressions. It was an extraordinary *reductio ad absurdum* of his own philosophy, and instead of questioning his premises, it has been accepted as a textbook example of good philosophy since his day. Instead it is a caricature.

Philosophy must be consistent with itself, and to be consistent with itself it must be consistent with its context, and to be consistent with its context it must be consistent with the whole of reality. What I want to argue is that something like dialectical critical realism, and I would want to add now further moments or elements to it, is a package, and that irrealism is a package likewise, and that irrealism is deeply intricated into the categorial structures, the demi-reality of societies which are characterised by master–slave or oppressive relationships. And in fact, I think I can show that any society characterised by master–slave relationships or the existence of money or instrumental modes of reasoning, will have an irrealist categorial structure. So, it is not just an oddity that all these philosophers have come up with such absurd theories. **These absurd theories are rooted in structures of oppression** and it is our task as philosophers to give social scientist and ordinary people and tools to eliminate these structures of oppression, what I call master–slave relationships, these modes of manipulative and instrumental reasoning, these abstract universals and narrow particulars that inform social reality, these vested interests, these reifications, these alianations.

It is our job to give ordinary people and social scientists the critical tools to bring about a society in which something like dialectical critical realism would be the common sense of the day, because it would reflect the categorial structures at work in that society. This is really to throw everything open for discussion now, and leave it to everyone to have a go at me.

* * * *

Question: Ontology seems to be only descriptive and not radical enough in postmodernism. I was wondering if you have noticed that tendency?

Roy: There is that tendency. Let us talk about post-structuralism. The main problem with a lot of post-structuralism is that it does not thematise ontology. Heidegger in a certain sense is an exception to this, but it thematised it in a way which can be valuable from a point of view of common sense, but it is not adequate from a point of view of understanding science. The extraordinary thing about contemporary philosophers who are renowned on the Left, I just name three: Derrida, Habermas and Althusser, is that they all denied ontology. Derrida perhaps less than Habermas, but Habermas, if you mention the word ontology to him he goes berserk. What happens in the case of these authors is that they implicitly inherit an implicit ontology, which is the positivist ontology, the epistemology of which they reject, so that you get a super-idealism, you get a post-structuralist and the kind of trendy epistemology but on the basis of an implicit positivist ontology, because of their failure to thematise ontology. I think there is a lack of ontological depth in Derrida's work. I think Derrida is a great philosopher, I think Habermas is too. I think in **Foucault's** work again the failure to coherently thematise ontology and thematise the different ontologies that we know, the ontology of science, the ontology of the social world, results ultimately in an ontology of chance, of contingency, of accident. This denies the deep structures which are so important in explaining the oppression and the misery, these deep but demi-realities, because they are structures constituted by false consciousness, but real, denies these deep-realities which explain the ills of humanity.

I believe the thing about **Althusser** is that he did not clearly thematise ontology. This is the first point that I would object to. The first thing you have got to do is to bring out the absent concept, the concept which is missing. The second thing about Althusser is a failure to situate a coherent totality. Because you have the problem of science and of ideology, science becomes eternal ideology, becomes a-historical, eternal. Where is the motor, where is the generative mechanism? If you situate ontology you have a chance of employing notions like generative structures, transformative change, you have a notion of ontological depth and of transformative praxis within a totality that we constitute.

He had the moment of structure all right, but these structures were disconnected, he was still imbued with purely positivist, extentionalist thinking. There is so much one could say about dialectic that I have gone into in my book. It is a very radical and holistic way of thinking. It literally shatters the foundations of statistics thoroughly enough. It is not surprising that a great Marxist epistemologist like him did not get to the secret of dialectic. You need all these concepts to get to the secrets of dialectic. He basically detotalises and partialises the social totality into discrete elements, he does not show mechanisms of change, and dislocates structures from the praxis, which reproduces or transforms them. I think this is the problem with Althusser, and you can see this in the *Conundrum of Science and Ideology*. What he does is science, what other people have done is ideology, there is no connection between the two. That is a classic stance of an absurd philosophy which is inherited.

* * * *

The question concerns the platinum plate, and the thesis that links idealist or irrealist philosophies with societies characterised by master–slave relationships. These terms seem very general, and the question revolves around the problem of what sort of things we can do today in a more specific way, differently from someone like Rorty who makes those very similar general errors. Is there something more specific?

Roy: I think one can see in Rorty's work huge splits. What is not mentioned, post-structuralist mention. So, questions of class and exploitation, to use classical Marxist terms, are detotalised; Eastern philosophy is not mentioned, the North–South divide is not mentioned, so they are detotalised; women are sort of added on as a fragment at the end, he becomes interested in women. It becomes a sort of compromise formation. What you see in the platinum plate analogy is a split between intellectuals and the world, the disconnection. He says the world consists of atoms and the void, which is an absurd ontology; the world is so rich, so deep, so multilayered, so highly differentiated, so variegated, containing so many interesting and complex and horrible, but also exciting, and joyous phenomena, that to attempt to situate them all using the concept of atoms and the world is absurd. And then we philosophers engage in conversational hermeneutics, which means polite discourse, and then other social scientists presumably do the same. It means that he and his friends are somehow in a sort of Platonic realm above and disconnected from the world.

This is surely how **academic life** represents itself. If you did a critique of the demi-reality, the half-light reality, the twilight reality of academic life, that is the sort of way you would start. Humanity is in crisis, how many academics actually talk about the crisis of humanity, what are the causes of this crisis? How many academics see themselves as part of the crisis of humanity? See their own role in the reproduction of thought systems, which go to reify or voluntarise that reality? (Both of them equally bad mistakes.) It is equally mistaken to think that social reality is independent of human beings as to think that a single human being can wake up one morning and change it himself or herself. That is the sort of thing we should be doing.

We should certainly be looking at the output of academic discourse and we should be using that as a tool to situate that academic discourse, those academics, ourselves, reflexively within it. Because we are not immune to these irrealist categorial structures, and there is no question of infallibilism here, so they may affect critical realism itself. But, to follow that up, I would say that **critical realism is part of a progressive dialectical learning process, which can begin to correct itself like the sciences**, but we situate all this in the context of a totality which explains it. What is crucial here is the concept of ideology, I think, and I would like to see three kinds of criteria firmly established. Ideologies are systems and practices and realities which are false, which can be explained by the critique of ideology which involves the retroductive argument characteristic of science, the transcendental argument characteristic of philosophy, and a lot of social science in virtue of the hermeneutical moment in social science and the dialectical argument characteristic of ideology critique. Dialectical argument is just a form of the general kind of scientific reasoning in which the reality we identify is false, real but false, and we describe that false reality as correctly as we can. So see how we need an all-embracing notion of totality, an ontology, which allows us to make these distinctions. Ideologies are false realities, they are explicable in terms of ideology critique, which involves dialectical argumentation and category mistakes. This is where the philosopher has a distinctive role, the philosopher whether as social scientist or whether as 'professional philosopher'. I think you can see these demi-realities at work in a lot of social scientific discourse: the Weberian concept of an iron cage in which we are trapped and we are motivated us in ever increasingly rationalize ourselves. So many deep social scientist and philosophers, as Hume was and as Wittgenstein was, ended up in tragic positions.

* * * *

Question regarding Roy's work and its relation to Habermas's Work.

Roy: I think that **Habermas** is an immensely important theorist, I think that his early theories, speech action, and his later theory of discourse, actually presuppose a realist account of language, something like Chomsky's realism. He actually presupposes for his rational reconstructions of a linguistic capacity, that they are capacities, that they are real, that there are generative structures, the ideal speech situation and the other constructs that he uses normatively presuppose real possibilities of consensual discourse. All that involves ontology, and I think the contradictory intentions there derive from his failure to thematise ontology. When he tries to rationally reconstruct Marxism he would be able to understand and criticise Marx's theory much better if he had a notion of ontological depth. That is my feeling about Habermas. What I say about the value side is that we both believe that speech action presupposes emancipation. I show how, through the logic of dialectical universalisability the ideal society presupposes human emancipation. That is a presupposition of speech action. But he has no mechanism to show how we can get from the facts of social life to a better society in a rational way. Because he does not have the other side of the ethical argument which is the entailment of values by facts. One of the things I tried to show is that understanding misery or error or categorial error leads, of necessity, to make a negative evaluation on that error and to attempt to build a positive theory of the conditions under which it is transformed. In other words, I argue that it is possible to go from facts to values. We both agree that speech action presupposes the good, or a good and freer society, presupposes human emancipation, but I have an argument to the effect that we can move naturalistically in that way, from fact to value, that values need not be question of arbitrary choice.

* * * *

Question.

Roy: Underneath the capitalist is forced to observe the laws of Marxian political economy. These demi-realities are sustained by realities, which are there. If you like, what we have got to do is throw the chains of illusion. These categorial structures are there and Marx shows how, in my opinion, a socialist society or a better society is presupposed by capitalism as its dialectical outcome and its necessary condition. In the earliest critical realist accounts the stratification of reality went hand in hand with the differentiation of reality, they are two parts of the same thing. **We are living in open systems which contain a multiplicity of structures and agents,** we are living in a sort of mish-mash world. This is precisely why scientists need experimental closures, why they need to absent themselves from the topsy turvy nature of all ordinary life and go into the laboratory and set up an artificially controlled experiment. The differentiation of reality is just as dialectically necessary a part of the thematics of critical realism as a stratification of reality, they go hand in hand. So, I think, in no way is critical realism vulnerable to post-structuralist critique, that it abolishes differences. I think the working class is tremendously heterogeneous, everyone is different. What we do in dialectical critical realism is that we have a notion of **dialectical universalisability** which is completely different from abstract universalisability. There is a universal component in it, but then there are always **particular mediations**, there is a geo-historic rhythmic to it, and each element in a situation is an idiosyncratic particular. Perhaps the same reality never occurs twice. Nietzsche formulated the doctrine of the eternal recurrence. He was very close to saying you can never get the same thing twice. Everything is always slightly different, and that is what is entailed in the concepts of dialectical universalisability and concrete singularity. Let me give you an example of this. This means that in so far as Marxism implies socialism, then we would understand what this means: we are in favour of equity not equality, we do not believe in uniformity, we do not believe in treating everyone the same because everyone is different, we treat everyone according to their differences. Where the differences are the same then they are treated the same. And that means, women, for example, can be treated differently from men according to norms of equity.

* * * *

Question.

Roy: Immigrants is another category which is excluded. They are excluded in lots of senses. They are excluded from the academic discourse, they are excluded from the electoral process, they are excluded from benefits, etc. Nothing is so appalling about western thought as its US-centric bias. When you talk about a global culture, it is the globalisation, it is the scientistic export of capitalism and 'western ideology' that goes with it. I believe that eastern thought, to take your example, has enormous resources for radicalising tradition and social change. I am working on it. I am working on an attempt at unifying eastern and western philosophy. I find that eastern philosophy is a very important critical resource.

* * * *

Question: Clarifying the golden nugget: How can positive contraries be transmitted into negative sub-contraries, and how can practice and theory transform reality.

Roy: What happens is that one has an inconsistency, one has an error. If this inconsistency is widely held, then it must be explained in terms of something missing, something absent from the categorial structure. All error is rooted in the absence of something or other, or be truistically something which would correct the error. In scientific and social totalities what is absent is often a level of depth, or a category of people in the social world or relations. For example, in vulgar versions of Marxism there is no dialectic of nature, of the inter-play between nature and humanity; nature is treated in a Promethean way, as a sheer other of humanity. There are no subtle connections, no symbiosis. One would attempt to reconstitute an ecologically sensitive Marxism by building in the symbiosis between humanity and its natural environment and show the way in which capitalism is destroying it. And once one has reconstituted that totality one could then use it and develop concepts of four-planar social being, in which I tried to show how we are set in a natural environment. Everything that we do in society is in a natural context. When we do that, then we can change our practice. We can change our practice in such a way that we behave in an ecologically sensitive way, or we can make arguments against capitalism on the way in which it is spoiling our natural environment. So we have build up a bigger totality, we have allowed it to inform our transformative action.

Patently there was something wrong with 'actually existing socialism'. When I said that Marx's analysis of the capitalist mode of production was fundamentally correct, I did not mean that Marxism was complete. Marxism is very far from complete. It contains huge lacunae, and it is our job, in so far as we identify with Marxism as a research and political programme, to identify its lacunae, to identify its tensions and weaknesses and to remedy them as Marx would have by recourse to a greater totality.

The **theory of surplus value** is an elaborate account to show how the whole pre-history of political economy up to his day could be situated within the context of Marx's own categories. So, it is by transcendence to a greater totality that we remove the tensions and contradictions in our thought, which allow more effective and coherent political action, and therefore, allow a greater possibility of transforming the world in a better way. This is not just a cognitive dialectic, because what sets off the feeling that something is inadequate in our theory is a human need like suffering, hunger, something like that. And that itself is an absence, a want, a desire, which we can not fulfil, which makes us enquire into the causes of the non-fulfilment of that want or desire, which leads us into the train of social scientific theory which sets us into this cognitive dialectic and then we fit it into political practice. But within the political ground similar learning processes should operate. Political associations and parties should learn from the mistakes, and in so far as they are Marxists, of actually existing socialism, actually existing Marxist parties.

I think one of the reasons for the popularity of the **politics of identity and difference** is the fact that actually existing socialism and most socialist parties are operated according to a command structure characteristic of instrumental, manipulative modes of reasoning and according to norms of abstract rather than dialectical universality. The masses would set over, or the people or the party members set over on the side, and then there was the elite of the executive, the politbureau, on the other side. The politbureau manipulated the members that carried out instructions. And this is **mimicking the mode of reasoning of capitalist society**. And this is why, and this is coming back to the point of the platinum plate, the politics of identity and difference is so popular amongst men of, broadly speaking, our generation. Because so many people have found the politics of actually existing socialism inadequate, they look for **an a-political way out to political problem**.

* * * *

Question: Something concerning subjective discourses and absence.

Roy: I think there is a growing acceptance of inter-subjectivity. The question is: do the theorists give these inter-subjectivities a right in contemporary social theory into subjectivity as often modelled on discourse? And this can be very dangerous because there are lots of things that the discourse paradigm leaves out. For example, we are having a conversation and we see a peasant digging the ground, and this was said to me by quite a famous philosopher: 'The first thing we should do is ask the peasant what he is doing, and the peasant would tell us he is digging the ground, and that is all we can say'. 'No', I said, 'we can ask him who is paying him, and why is he digging the ground, how does he keep his family by digging the ground, under whose instructions, on the basis of whose authority is he digging the ground, is it his autonomous reaction or not?'

* * * *

Question: Elaborate the concept of negation.

Roy: To negate is to absent and thereby transform. All praxis is transformative. Your question was transformative of the situation. It depends upon negation, it was an act, and all acts negate, they negate the status quo, they negate what is given. Negating what is given is transforming it, transforming it is absenting something which is already there and making present something which was not there. In a dialectic, it is quite common for a factor to be absented.

Let us take the **paradigm of science**. When scientists decide that that factor is not all that important after all, it is completely played down, and then, at a later stage of the development of science, one just forgets about some domain of phenomena. At a later stage in the development of science one finds something analogous to that phenomenon, and needs to be reincorporated in the totality. That is the model of the dialectic and the negation of the negation.

But it is too crude to think it is restoring. It is not a simple restoration, it is a restoration under change of descriptions. If you believe as I sought to believe in primitive communism I think actually poverty, scarcity, many things are a product of capitalism. I would like to believe in primitive communism, and I think if one can sort of believe in primitive communalism they you can see the whole history of master—slave society, money relationships building up to capitalism, the negation of the ideals, the bones of primitive communism, and then you can say some future society is the negation of that negation. But it will not be the restoration of primitive communism it will be a vastly differentiated, hopefully much richer society than we have ever known before.

Capitalism, and all class society, all master–slave society may be the negation of primitive communism, if and when communism becomes actually existing, then it will not be the restoration of primitive communism. It may be the restoration of some bones that were torn aside or completely occluded by capitalism. I would not place too much reliance in the formula of the negation of the negation. It is negativity, the continual process of negation that I see as all-important.

* * * *

Question: (Ricardo) Wittgenstein, spontaneous dialectics.

Roy: I think that the rational kernel of dialectic was a general theory of learning processes and the learning processes are operated in all rounds of social life.

We are saying they are parts of reality which transcend language. That surely is correct, but that is not a normal interpretation of linguistic philosophy, and is not the normal interpretation of **Wittgenstein**, who seems to be tied to the position that the limits of my world are the limits of my language, the identification of language and the world which I call the 'linguistic fallacy'. I think it is wrong to identify language and the world, or it is wrong to posit a one-to-one correlation between language and the world. The word existed before any languages, it exists outside, including the social world which exists outside language. We have experiences which we can not describe linguistically and we act as totalising transformative beings, materially embodied with some linguistically articulate understanding of what we are doing, but only a limited understanding. The dialectic is to enrich that limited understanding and to act in more totalising progressive ways towards the goal of universal human emancipation, which I believe to be implicit in the most primitive need or want. So I think we are basically agreeing or perhaps you can tell me where you disagree with what I said.

* * * *

Question: Further question from Ricardo.

Roy: I certainly believe in the priority of praxis but **philosophy, understanding, science, are also practices, discourses itself is a practice, everything is a practice in the totality of practices.** I do not think one can escape from concepts like totality by relying on the concept of practice itself. We are all willy-nilly acting, the question is whether we are acting correctly, whether we are acting to transform ourselves and society in a better or a worse way. Questions about the value of our action, its truth or adequacy, come in the very moment you pose the question of practice. The whole essence of critical thought is to subject yourself to the possibility that you may be acting incoherently or less than fully coherently, or less than fully adequately, or you may be failing to satisfy yours and others' needs.

* * * *

Question: What is the social world made of?

Roy: I would like to look at the social world in this way: there are four planes of social being which ordinate it (the social world). There are **material transactions with nature**, so the social world is constituted by nature; there are **inter-personal relations between agents**, that is the sort of thing that is going on now, discourse between us; underlying those there are **social structures which pre-exist us and form the conditions of possibility of our actions.** Such things as languages, modes of production, modes of political practice, those are social structures which provide the conditions, the means and materials for our transactions with nature and with each other. And then there is the **depth stratification of the personality**, of the psyche, of the individual, and in principle collective human subject.

There is also a dimension of **collective human agency** and institutions and practices; that can be reconstructed from the others, I think. So, these are the four planes. If we attempt to exclude nature from society, or attempt to reduce society to inter-personal relations, or we attempt to reconstitute society from our depth stratification (unconscious, all the other levels of our psyche, etc.), **if we leave out social structures, or if we only have social structures and we leave out nature or inter-personal relations, then we are in a situation of absence, dialectically erroneous absence.** What we are forced to do in reality is rely on an implicit totality to cover up mistakes until they became too glaring.

And then we will isolate the absence and remedy it by recourse to a greater totality, and that at the moment seems to me to be a good general schema for understanding society. I think the distinctions you made between first- and second-order inter-pretations is fine; I mean it posits the possibility of critique, but that distinction is anyway implicit in any speech action, any human interaction between us two now. I can do a critique of you without standing above our relationship, and certainly all communication embodies elements of first- and second-order level. If we did not differ about something, there would be no point in communicating. If we felt, acted and believed exactly in the same way there would be nothing to do. It is the differences, the second-order component, that makes communication so interesting, and indeed ultimately necessary. So, I do no like that conceptualisation, although I understand it at a logically and rela-tively primitive level, but I actually thing it is implicit in all speech action. It is the difference between monitoring our behaviour and being able to reflexively monitor the monitoring of our behaviour, the capacity of second-order step back from conscious-ness. Four planar social being I think is the minimum necessary to constitute an adequate totality. Then we have to put the whole thing in motion as process and the whole thing depends upon, and presupposes, social practices.

* * * *

Question: About social structure.

Roy: Our discourse about it is an interpretation. Agents themselves have their own interpretations. When I talk about reality, I am not assuming we have any privileged access to it. I am saying that any statement I would want to make, that any statement we make about reality is fallible. That statement is itself real and purports to be about reality. So **our mistakes are real.** I am not trying to deny that the social world is constituted in part by conceptualisation and interpretation. I am trying to give a very radical interpretation by saying that interpreted structures, what the tradition that I am attacking calls interpreted structures, must be seen as categories, some of which are false and are inherent to reality itself. You can have any interpretative schema you want, but if you go to a shop and try and buy a newspaper the only interpretative schema that counts is money. **That is the interpretative schema intrinsic to our society.** You can think of it as having a pleasant conversation with the newsagent, or you can be interested in the newsagent's daughter, or buying his premises. You can have a lot of meanings. The totalities we construct in social life are all differentiated, they are asymmetrical. **The dominant one would be the financial exchange**; you pass the money to him or he will not let you have the newspaper. That is the constraint, that is the dominant structure at work in that relationship, the structure of money. We are all actors, we are always actors. You can step out of the totality, exclude yourself from it and then describe it as an observer or participant; that is certainly true.

But if there are real relations between you and that totality, then you are going to make a categorial error, you are going to be false to the reality at work. For example, you can say: 'I am an academic, I am an observer, I am not concerned with such things as money or material structures'. But then what happens if your grant does not come through? **Sooner or later that categorial structure will catch up with you.** The world is increasingly englobed by very basic, very crude structures which have become disembedded from any possibility of voluntaristic conscious choice. So if we as philosophers or academics exclude ourselves from the totality, we can do that up to a point: when we leave our study we are back in the reality that we have denied, and that is doing a disservice to the norm of truth.

* * * *

Question.

Roy: The reality we are trying to explain pre-exists any agent's interpretations. The agent is interpreting the situation. S/he is interpreting the situation which pre-exists him or her, which constrains them, and which in large part limits or empowers their possibilities of action, and unless they understand that structure, they are going to act erroneously. If you talk about the conceptually dependent nature of social structures, that is correct. But I think there is a philosophical difference between us, which is that you are not accepting categorial realism. You do not accept that categories such as money, such as the categories of race and racism, such as the categories of class and class structure, such as the categories of master–slave society, **all these categories are intrinsic to reality as much as the categories of causality, space, time, substance, process, inter-relation.**

They are all part of reality. It is fine to have an interpretation which is distinct from those categories, or to have a very radical interpretation, but the question is: can you leave it out? Where is the unity of theory and practice? What you are failing to do, I think, **if you adopt a purely Kantian interpretative approach, is that you are failing to satisfy the reflexive criterion of philosophy,** which is the capacity to situate and to sustain your own content, your own conditions of possibility of being. You are sitting on a tree and you are sawing the branch off as you do so. This is clearly what most academics do when they do not concern themselves with material structures. They think: 'we are sitting in the library and we are not worried with human suffering or human oppression or such a brute thing as money. And then of course their careers and their actual activities are entirely driven by motives which are related to money—they are living a contradiction.

* * * *

Question: Merleau-Ponty and phenomenology.

Roy: You can tie Merleau-Ponty's remark to the Gibsonian ecological approach to perception, which is: when I come into a room and I see a chair, I do not see it as an exclusively material object. Rather I see it as something I can sit on, I see it as an affordance for sitting. We perceive the world in terms of the affordances it endows us for our human needs and wants. We go into the world, with certain pre-structured, categorially necessary presuppositions—in this case because of our biological constitution and our stage of geo-historical development, which makes us sit rather than squat. If we were in a different continent or a thousand years ago we probably would be squatting. Where I disagree with Merleau-Ponty, that is a geo-historical process, the different ways of perceiving things are geo-historical products.

* * * *

Question: In relation to the concept of the unity of theory and practice, and theory as guiding practice, in relation to what Ricardo said, this concept of spontaneous dialectics. At this moment in human history there is nothing more important than grasping the dialectics of nature, that nature is itself dialectical. But this should not be confused with the spontaneous dialectics which leaves our own concept at a primitive, immediate level. Surely, as we develop our own dialectical concepts, this is a process of ref-lection, we are penetrating deeper in the dialectical nature of nature. There is different strata, so it is true that this real nightmare that happened to materialist dialectics, was this terrible dialectical materialism which was this sterile schema that was developed in the Soviet Union. We should not allow that to prevent us from trying to re-establish that sort of man and nature, dialectical man reflecting dialectical nature.

Roy: I agree with that entirely. I believe nature without humanity contains almost all the categories of the dialectic. One of the things that it does not contain is conceptually dependent, categorial error, because that is a human construct, which I think is closely related to the establishment of master–slave relationships, class society, exploitative exchange, money and manipulative forms of reasoning. Apart from that, it contains almost all the categories of dialectic, including inter-related totality, etc. Take our ordinary concept of an event. An event is just a single happening. But in biology and physics we have to think of an event as consisting in a distribution over space or a succession over time. It is far too simplistic, our ordinary notion of an event, it is undialectical, it is undialectical for society and it is undialectical for nature, it is modelled on an atom, on a sort of atomic billiard ball, and the simple movement of the billiard ball or simple sort of material-object levels of reality which is so resonant with bourgeois modes of thought. All the categories, absence, negation, transformation (not transformative praxis, and not conceptually categorial error, and it is odd to say that reality itself is false although you can say reality itself is only implicitly full developed), apply to nature. And we have to understand our relationship with nature as being intrinsically dialectical.

* * * *

Questioner: Mind changes nature, human beings change nature . . .

Roy: And nature is going to revenge itself on humanity unless humanity treats nature with much greater respect.

Chapter Three

Critical Realism and Discourse Theory: Debate with Ernesto Laclau*

Ernesto

... It is difficult to provide . . . a direct, clear comparison between the theoretical approach of discourse theory and that of critical realism. Discourse theory is something which is embedded in 'scientific'—whatever that means—practice, which is the analysis of text: in the strict, narrow sense of the term it is a set of methodological rules for the analysis of text. Critical realism, on the other hand, is a whole ontology with some kind of epistemological consequences. So the first thing we have to do is see how we can establish a terrain on which a comparison of the two approaches is possible. Now discourse theory, as it has been developed here in Essex, not only by myself, but by a group

* *Alethia,* September 1998.
This is an edited version of a debate which was held at the University of Essex at the suggestion of students in the Department of Sociology. Each speaker was allowed half an hour with ten minutes to reply. As the transcript was somewhat defective, we have sometimes aimed to supply the gist rather than the literal record of what was said. The spoken has also sometimes been altered to conform more to the canons of the written word. A lengthy discussion which followed the debate has been omitted.

of people working with the same type of approach, involves definitely some ontological assertions and some epistemological assertions, so I'm going to do a bit of violence to our work in order to find a terrain on which a comparison is possible.

I would say that form this more general point of view there are four principles which are central to discourse theory. First, there is the assumption that there is a basic grammar within which possible objects are constituted and that this mediates any kind of contact with reality. This grammar, which is what we call discourse, is largely unconscious. Just as you speak your native language before you learn its grammar and the task of the grammarian is to bring out the immanent grammatical structure which constitutes that language, so the task of the discourse analyst is to explore the immanent grammars which underlie all kinds of meaningful intervention.

In the second place, by discourse we should not understand simply speech and writing, i.e., there is nothing specifically linguistic about it. The notion of language has been submitted to sustained critique over the last thirty years and as a result the specificity of an object which was called language in the strict sense has largely dissipated, and language on the other hand is a dimension which constitutes any possible experience. For instance, Wittgenstein's notion of a language game is not involved only in a linguistic dimension; it is a combination of linguistic elements and the action in which these elements are embedded, and the resulting totality of words and actions is what he called a language game. This is precisely what we call discourse. This enlargement of the notion of discourse is largely a result of the increasing formalisation of structural linguistics, a process whereby linguistic structures have become less and less dependent on the materiality, the 'substance', of speech and writing. And it is in this sense that discourse is a relational system which can be applied to any possible object.

In the third place, what we have insisted on is that the pluralisation of objects on which discursive practice operates means that we cannot remain at a purely constative level, for the performative dimension is inherent to any linguistic operation. So that action is something which is entirely inherent to discourse. The notion of discourse could, if you prefer, be replaced by that of practice. I myself prefer to speak of discourse for two reasons. First, by arriving at this point in which practice and discourse become almost synonymous, through the whole set of steps involving the linguistic derivation, we reveal some aspects of these practical discursive structures which would not be evident otherwise. More frivolously, practice is a very neutral term, i.e. it is unlikely to provoke the indignation of anybody, and concepts which do not provoke the engagement of people are necessarily boring. In order to get some kind of excitement and enjoyment, I prefer the term discourse.

Finally, discourse theory is opposed to various forms of ontology and epistemology, but the main philosophical approach it is opposed to is idealism. Now, while idealism is a conception which presents historically a variety of features, there are essentially two features which I regard as central. First, the reduction of the real thought. For example, if I am asserting in an old realist way that there is an equation between thought and the thing, what I am saying is that there is a basic identity between thought and thing, and this reduction of the material elements to something which is ultimately the universal form is exactly the essence of all idealism. Now, in so far as discourse analysis sustains the irreducibility of the real to discourse, it tries to break from this point of view with the idealist tradition. The second aspect is that if idealism means something, it means the unity of the mind, the unity of the subject; that is to say, the unity of apperception, of the 'I' which accompanies all my representations—this is something which belongs to the essence of idealism. Now, it is precisely the category of the subject which is put under threat by discourse theory, because there is a plurality of subject formation which cannot be reduced to any single unit.

If I present the argument in these terms, what are the points of convergence and divergence with critical realism? I think there are two basic points of convergence. The first is the critique of empiricism, that is to say the analysis according to which the problem of induction and the problem of what has been called transduction are irresolvable for it; the reduction of ontology to epistemology in the end begs the whole question. The second lies in what we call the transcendental term; that is to say, we are dealing with a transcendental realism, not with any kind of direct ontological realism. Here, however, is where my difficult with some of the positions of critical realism starts, because the way in which the transcendental is understood creates immediately some problems for me.

I would say that the main bone of contention between a discourse theorist and a critical realist, beyond all the agreement, is the distinction between the transitivity and intransitivity of objects. I have no quarrel with the notion of transitivity, if that would differentiate critical realism from any naïve theory about the direct apprehension of the object in thought; rather with the concept of intransitivity. Some problems that emerge for me are the following. Firstly, the intransitivity of objects in the work of Roy is alluded to rather than ultimately defined, or he even speaks of structure, about generative mechanism, casual powers, and so on. But obviously these are not synonymous, each of them has specific theoretical consequences, and the theoretical consequences have not been entirely worked out. So what about the transcendental term and its relation to the intransitivity of the object? In the first place, the non-transcendental solution is excluded by critical realism. That is to say, well OK, all my representations are variable approximations and so on and so forth, but there is something, which is the intransitivity of the object, which is there and which has a structure of its own which I can not determine at least a priori and in some basic dimensions. This would be a dogmatic approach, because why exclude from the transitive variation this object which is beyond the realm of transitivity? But the argument Roy's presenting obviously is not that it is not the dogmatic argument, it is an argument which passes through transcendentality. The question he is trying to ask is how the world has to be if science is going to be possible. That is to say, he takes from Kantian transcendentalism the more general form of a transcendental argument, although he does not follow Kant all the way though.

Now it is the factual character of science that for me is at stake, for Kant is clear that the factum of knowledge was not put into question and once the factum of knowledge was there, the problem was how to establish the conditions of possibility of that which existed, how synthetic a priori arguments are possible in physics and mathematics. (The factum of morality was also the starting point for the second *Critique*.) This presents for me a set of problems. In the first place, to what extent can science as a factum be there as a totality in which there is no plurality of scientific discourses, each of which have conditions of possibility which are very differentiated between themselves? To what extent can we work with this notion of science as a total unified code?

Secondly, the question which I don't think is asked here is whether science is possible in its own terms. What if we adopted, for instance, a pragmatist or a conventionalist view—which is not exactly my position—and said, 'Well, our discourse—the scientific discourses—is not something that is anchored in anything that is the object in itself.' For instance, Husserl was trying to put the conditions of possibility of scientific activity by inscribing it within the whole life world and the whole experience of the transcendental subject. In some sense the conditions of possibility of science are there from the very beginning. Now let us suppose that I ask, what are the conditions of possibility for astrology, which is also a factum? Why am I going to accept a discourse of physics instead of a discourse of astrology? Now I can immediately establish the conditions of possibility of astrology in a set of ontological considerations about the way in which the world has to be for astrology to be possible. But why this discourse is not accepted is not because it is incoherent in itself, it is simply because our experience is organised in a set of discursive sequences which are incompatible with the presuppositions of this ontology. In the same way, scientific discourses in the contemporary sense of the term are much more credible because they are able to hegemonise a field of experience which is much wider than the discourse of astrology, but these discourses are all the time changing. For instance, let us suppose for the sake of argument that I can falsify a scientific prediction on the basis of a factual observation. What this factual sequence is, is a set of other discourses in which facts are constituted. The point is that the plurality of these discourses is not unified, anchored in a coherent whole; there is no unity of science as conceived within logical positivism. Scientific discourses, as critical realism accepts, are changing all the time, and there is no way of anchoring the change in something that is beyond this world of discursive variation. This is not relativism, because the plurality of discourses constituting or organising my experience is a plurality which is simply the elaboration of my relation to the world, it is not a mental product, discourses are simply anchoring institutions organising a set of experiences, and in a sense meaning is the most material of the dimensions of reality. On the other hand, the world that is organised in this way is only one of the possible ones, the world of science is constituted on the basis of eliminating a variety of dimensions in the object. Now, this intransitivity of objects which is supposed to be behind all experience as the ground of all the regularities in experience is simply one more discourse which can not be conceded to be different in quality from the discourses which are seen as transitive. I would accept the hypotheses of critical realism, but I would integrate this notion of the intransitivity of the object as one more discursive element, so that the intransitivity of the object is in itself transitivity.

Let me say something about social theory. In the first place, I see critical realism, not as something that discourse theory would reject entirely, but as one of the possibilities for discursively constructing the real. However, these possibilities are, I think, much wider than what critical realism accepts as some sort of final ontology. For instance, if we pass to the social world and a problem like the limits of naturalism which has been central in the discussions of critical realism, it is not at all a problem that could have been posed in those terms in discourse theory. For naturalism is some form of discursive constitution of the object, which in this sense refers to a deeper possibility which is the discursive field constituting the basic grammar of society. In the same way, problems such as holism and individualism are problems which are going to be put in different ways by critical realism and by discourse theory. I share with critical realism the rejection of methodological individualism and the holistic approach to the social, but I would say that this social whole, this structural whole which constitutes society, is by definition incomplete, and this incompletion gives place to a set of practices by which the unity that society is unable to reach at the level of the structural is going to be reconstituted at the level of the imaginary. One of the basic assertions of discourse theory is that totality is not a ground but a horizon in the phenomenological sense. It is through this necessary incompletion of the social whole that I would approach the problem of agency and structure. It cannot be solved via the universalisation of either of these two categories, nor is it going to be solved via any kind of easy structuration which puts together things which are conceptually compatible. It is going to be solved only if we accept that the problem of incompatibility between agency and structure is not a problem of our theory but a problem inscribed in social reality itself.

Finally, I would like to say a few words about the question which for us a discourse theorists is essential, which is the question of negativity and antagonism. I do not see exactly with what conception of antagonism—something which is negative in itself and which cannot be retrieved by any form of positivity—a naturalistic conception of the social could work. However, I could see, for instance, Hegelian dialectics as one way of reducing the disruptive character of the negative to a certain principle of unity because the dialectical movement operates only in one way and any contingency is eliminated from this. So for us antagonism, for reasons I have presented elsewhere, is constitutive of the social, not as the result of empirical reason but for formal logical reasons. Social totality, being necessary, cannot however constitute itself. In this sense, the basic argument that I have presented is that antagonism is not something internal to society but is actually the moment in which social objectivity finds its ultimate limit. Now, I don't see that critical realism at this point has developed a notion of antagonism and negativity, but anyway it is something about which I would like to have the response of Roy, as to the many other issues that I covered.

Roy

Basically I had prepared a talk. Instead I am going to construct my remarks around Ernesto's. As far as I could see, Ernesto talked about three main topics, the first ontology, he brought up some nice distinctions, the second about the nature of social theory, and the third about negativity. And I think the third point is just—pardon me for saying so, Ernesto—wrong. I have written two very big books, *Dialectic* and *Plato Etc.*, which are concerned precisely to hammer away at what I think is the fundamental failing of western philosophy, which is to give only a positive account of being, a thesis I call ontological monovalence, and I assert the priority of negativity, the priority of absence over presence, and I define dialectic in terms of absence. . . . I think this is one of the strongest points of that development of critical realism over the last couple of years, dialectical critical realism. It does mark a break from the first phase of development, but I do not think we are vulnerable to your attacks on that ground.

Secondly, I quite agree with what you say about totalities, but it is one of the themes of critical realism that totalities must be open. We are entirely against any premature closure of social reality. Social totalities, all totalities, are open, and the myth of a closed totality, a closed system, is an empiricist idealist ideology. There is no such thing. And I like your remarks that totality is a horizon, not a ground, except that I also want grounds; so there are aspects of totality that can be totalities recursively embedded within other totalities, and one totality can function as a ground for another. But the fundamental thing that totalities are open is absolutely correct.

So on the question of totality, but not of absence and negativity, I am completely at one with where Ernesto wants to go. If he wants to talk about the negative, that's fine. I think the social world is structured around concepts of contradiction, absence, dialectic. I think Hegel did a tremendous disservice to the dialectic in his actual practice. He is ontologically monovalent. This was one of Marx's great insights and also of course of Left Hegelianism, that you can not do that sort of conjuring trick on reality, that world. There are four terms of the critical realist dialectic—you remember the Hegelian dialectic has the terms of identity, negativity and totality. In the critical realist dialectic we have the concepts of non-identity (I am going to take you up on what you said about transitivity and intransitivity)—non-identity between beings and things, between causal laws and constant conjunctions of events, between structures and events, between the real and the actual, and the actual and the empirical, between the positive and the negative. This is a constant refrain, a critical refrain in critical realism. The second moment of negativity we have already discussed. This is the crucial one, in terms of the ontological power of absence over presence, because this is due to the nature of the negative. The third moment is totality, which we have seen is open. The fourth moment, which is completely lacking in Hegelian dialectic, or at the end is lacking, is transformative practice. Transformative practice will ensure that history never comes to an end. Even if we succeed in blowing up the planet, there will be some kind of processes going on at the end.

So much for the two points, that I don't think should be in dispute between us, about totality and negativity. I think there are matters of substance in relation to ontology. Now what is ontology? Ontology is the theory of being. Now a whole tradition in western philosophy has tried to reduce being to knowledge, to epistemology, and I think from Ernesto's remarks he is against this tradition. So he actually does want an ontology. Now what I think is absolutely crucial is that this tradition—the basic form of western philosophy—was anthropocentric. To get away from this anthropocentricity is one of my motivations is actually trying to thematise the character of extra-discursive reality. I am making things very simple before we get on to transcendental arguments, but we believe in the possibility and actuality of a world without human beings, and therefore without discourse. What critical realism says is that we can actually say something about the general character of that world, we can say that it must be structured, differentiated, open, governed by laws which are transfactual, constituted by its own kind of contradictions and antagonisms, and without reason, intelligibility or discursive practice. How can we say all this? By transcendental arguments. Ernesto says there is an extra-discursive reality, we agree about that. Critical realism says that extra-discursive reality has a certain shape, and that it is very important to get its shape right. If you get it wrong, this is going to be implicitly secreted into your theory of knowledge. An example of this can be given from Habermas. Habermas does not believe in ontology at all, and he does not believe in positivism in respect of the human sciences.

Yet in his account of instrumental reason he assumes that the natural world is structured by constant conjunctions of events, and that causal laws can be reduced to empirical regularities, but that explanation in natural science proceeds by deductive subsumption. And all these things are false, not just for science, but actually ontologically false for the character of the world.

Ernesto is going to say to me, 'Well, what you are doing in your transcendental argument must be based on certain premises, what are your premises?' This is where the critical points become very important. I took as my initial premises experimental activity because there was a whole ideology of science—the empiricist ideology—which says that experimentation is the most important thing in science and that the one reason why we can not do social science is because we can not do experiments. It is a fact that the natural sciences, some natural sciences, can conduct experiments and they do attribute value to what they discover in experiments. So it is a reasonable move polemically and critically to argue against empiricism that they have got their analysis of what the world must be like for experiments to be possible wrong. Do I need to go through the analysis? It is basically that, in an experiment natural science the scientist sets up an artificially closed system; her artificial activity is necessary to gain an invariant conjunction, an empirical regularity—outside these closed systems we do not get such regularities. The significance of this activity is that what happens inside the experiment gives the scientist epistemic access to what happens outside it and what would happen outside it if the experiment had not been done. Let me give you an example. The law of gravity is tending to pull us down from the sixth floor of this building to the ground floor. This law is operating irrespective of the fact that countervailing forces are preventing it being manifest. It is part of a correct scientific description of the situation. So we have a certain shape to the world, a certain shape for ontology is presupposed by experimental physics and chemistry. Is this position and presupposition, that we are intervening in nature and that nature has its own structures and transfactual character so unfamiliar to us? If, for example, we make a cup of tea and put some sugar in the tea, we expect it to dissolve; if it doesn't dissolve, we assume there must be something in that tea which is preventing the sugar from dissolving, or the sugar must have some impurity. So it is not in fact all that arbitrary. I would argue that you can move from experimentation in physics and chemistry through to ordinary practices and see that they also presuppose the same general character of the world.

I would make certain claims that the world is structured, that it is governed by transfactual laws, that is by tendencies, that there are a multiplicity of mechanisms and structures at work, that the world is constituted by open systems, some of which are internally related to others, that discourse is a case of an efficacious mechanism which operates on the world and is embedded in the world, and the world impacts on discourse—this is perhaps another point that we would want to discuss more finely later. But I would say that the initial premises of transcendental realism from experimental activity were really to generate a critique of empiricism on its strongest grounds, and I think that critique is invincible and provides an adequate account of the experimental natural sciences. You could just stop there and say, 'Well, now we know what physicists and chemists assume about the world, we can make a more interesting contrast with the conditions of social science or of geology or biology, where they can't do experiments.' That is interesting enough in itself, but what I am suggesting is that when you argue from a transcendental premise you are arguing from something you have to believe. Undoubtedly, all transcendental arguments are going to be relativised to a premise, and I agree with Ernesto that in principle there are an infinite number of premises, there are an infinite number of practices. Experimentation of the classical sort is impossible in the domains of the very minute (quantum mechanics) and of the very large. So we could argue from some other aspect of scientific activity. So it is all going to be relativised to some form of activity, but then your practice in the world is going to implicitly assume a certain ontology. Let us take the case of Hume. Hume says we have no better grounds for going out of the second floor door than the second floor window. Isn't that absurd? In our practice we do—we must—make some sort of commitment. We may make it on the belief, that Newton's theory of gravity is right, or we may make it on some other more recondite belief but that is how we actually do act.

That is the first line of defence. If you don't want to use transcendental arguments to establish the general shape of the world from experimental and applied scientific activity as then possible in the experimental natural sciences, then you have to do so from some other, equally sound premise to act at all, to engage in any discursive practice. My second argument is that the shape of ontology that the experimental natural sciences presupposes is entirely continuous with what we can establish by transcendental arguments from very simple, mundane activities in the other sciences, in the arts, in everyday life.

What, then, of transcendental realism's assertion of the existence of an extra-discursive reality, given that we have discourses? Of course, in discussing the general shape of the world, the general kind of ontology, the character of ontology, the content of ontology, I am polemicising against Kant as much as anyone else. Your remember Kant said that we constitute a phenomenal world, but there is of course a real noumenal world behind that. I think in a way there is a tendency within Ernesto to want to say that we constitute a phenomenal world in our discourses, but of course we are not denying that outside those discourses there is something to which they can ultimately be referred. I am saying the character of this world can be known, it can be known by transcendental argument, relativised always to the conditions of possibility of some social practice. So we can not have philosophy unless we also have discursive practices, but philosophy can tell us what the world would be like even if we did not have discursive practices. But what can philosophy tell us about a world in which we do have discursive practices?

This is where we come up against a dualism which is very familiar to philosophy, a whole set of dualisms: between mind and body, reasons and causes, the intelligible and the purely natural. I get a feeling—and I may be wrong—that part of the thrust of discourse analysis is falling in line with this dualism. What would discourse analysis be like if I was wrong? We would have to say that discourses, discursive practices, are in continual causal interaction with the material world. That ideas are causally efficacious on the world, practices are causally efficacious on the world, and that the world itself is causally efficacious on practices. We can see the effect that global warming is having on our social practices, we can see the effect of years of neglect of the London transport system on social practices in London. Nature has a recoil, and I would argue that it is impossible to get at reasons irrespective of their material efficacy. Let me take someone—Bill, will you hold up your hand? What has happened here is that I have given Bill a reason for doing something, I did it in virtue of my material effect on the world in issuing a sequence of sounds, Bill understood me hermeneutically and held up his hand; and that effected a change in the material world. I think that unless you allow that reasons are causes and that mind and body to interact—that society and discursive practices are embedded in nature and the biosphere—we end up with a philosophical dualism that is totally unacceptable. I am not saying Ernesto does this, but that I feel it is a tendency in his work and perhaps we will reach a point of agreement before the evening is out.

So instead of giving a long spiel about critical realism and discourse analysis, I have really just responded to Ernesto's points. I would just like to re-emphasise, first, that we need to know something about the general character of the world, we need to have a philosophical ontology, and the character of that ontology is crucially important for special practice as well as social theory. Secondly, where exactly do Ernesto and discourse analysis stand in relation to the causal interactions between discursive practices or reasons and extra-discursive realities? I accept of course that all extra-discursive realities are constituted within discursive practice, from the point of view of their intelligibility. But that is not to say that they are constituted in discursive practice from the point of view of their causal impact. We can assume that global warming went on long before we had the concept of it, and this is true. We come to the concept of most diseases long after they have their causal impact. So where does he stand on the causal interaction between discursive practices and things which are not at the moment discursively cognised or things which are clearly extra-discursive or things which are part of a material world or things over which we have no material control like the cosmos? It is on these two points that we have honed down a nice difference.

Ernesto

We need a philosophical ontology, I absolutely agree. The point is, What is this philosophical ontology? For me, it is exactly everything which is constituted within discourse. . . . It is the level of constitution of any objectivity. In the case of natural science, which has precise conditions of possibility, these go back to a more basic ontology, which is what I call discourse (scientists would say scientific practice), and that it is able to constitute its object on the basis of regularities depends on sedimented social practices and a variety of discourses, and the constitution of its objects has discursive conditions of possibility which comes before.

Regarding your second point, I do not accept such a distinction between the discursive and the extra-discursive. You ask what is the effect of discourse on the external world, well, for me the external world is also discursively constituted, not in the sense that it is constituted by the mind of men, but in the sense that any kind of practice is embedded in the elaboration of the linguistic world. This involves at the same time interaction between subject and object, for if I am going there and I open the door, on the one hand I want to open the door, on the other this forces me to a material act, which is to open the door. The performance of that act is what I call discourse; it is not that discourse produces some kind of material effect, but that the material act of producing it is what discourse is. That is why, at the beginning, I insisted that the performative dimension is inherent in the discursive operation—it is not something that is added to it—and that is why I said that finally discourse and practice are a single category.

Obviously all practice, scientific or not, is based on some assumptions about the world. These assumptions can be perfectly contradictory. For example, in legal practice, we assume that punishment requires a free legal agent, that it was discussed with the agent who is responsible in committing some act or not. On the other hand, in scientific discourse we believe in universal determinism. These two responses operate with assumptions about human beings which are totally at variance with each other, and there is no guarantee that there is some kind of unity that is going to put all these practices together. That is why I think any kind of practice, whether scientific or not, has to pass through the treadmill of making itself credible in front of a variety of other practices. I can easily construct a perfectly coherent discourse which has assumptions about the world—an implicit ontology and so on— but this discourse is not going to be accepted because it is coherent in its own terms, it is not going to be accepted because it clashes with many other discursive sequences which organise our world. So in this sense any kind of scientific practice, I would say, would have to be hegemonic, that is to say, it has to be proved in front of a tribunal which is constituted by a variety of other practices. My objection from this point of view to the notion of the intransitivity of the object is not that I do not believe that it is important for organising our practices, but the point is that, if you say about the intransitivity and transitivity of an object a set of things, these things are said on the basis of assumptions which are themselves challengeable, and in this sense, the very distinction between intransitivity and transitivity is itself transitive.

Roy

I think this is very interesting. I would like to make a series of dis-tinctions between philosophical ontology and scientific ontology, and between ontology and being. Now the subject matter of onto-logy has to be broadly conceived to include absence as well as presence, totality, internal relationality, reasons, causes, whatever you like. Everything has being, and some things have being or exist quite independently of their constitution in scientific or philo-sophical discourse, and there is a distinction between these two. Once you accept that, it opens up the possibility of saying how the general character of the world is; you can use what you estab-lish on the basis of a transcendental argument which is credible for you. Astrology obviously is not credible for you. Concerning your example of universal determinism and free will, I think the two are actually compatible, but I have argued that elsewhere.

What is the argument for ontology? The most basic argument is referential detachment. To refer to something, to say anything about the world, I must detach myself from that to which I refer. This is a function of all agency, all desire. If I desire water, I must detach the water from the desiring subject, this is the referent of my act of desire. Are you saying that no referents exist independently of their discursive constitution? If you are, I can not agree with you. The world fifteen million years ago or the planet earth fifteen million years ago existed independently of its discursive constitution.

Ernesto

No quarrel.

Roy

No quarrel, OK. This is a point where you may quarrel. Did global warming exist prior to its discursive constitution? Did cancer exist before it was identified and discovered as a particular form of disease?

Ernesto

I am not saying that global warming did not exist independently of the discourse which called it global warming, because that would be absurd. What I am saying is that global warming is a way of classifying something which is there with. . . .

Roy

You admit that it is existentially intransitive with respect to discourse, but you then want to take it back to the level of the signifier or signified and say that this object only exists in my discursive constructions. In other words, you are contradiction yourself to say, 'Here, that thing has a reference independently of human beings', but at the same time you do not have a rigorous enough concept of reference, you are pulling the referent back to the level of the transitive, to its constitution in discourse.

Ernesto

My quarrel with you is not that.

Roy

Now, I would want to extend the category of reference to include causal laws, the general structure of causality, to include what I call transfactual efficacy.

Ernesto

There I would not agree.

Roy

All right, so you just want to enclose things. I would extend the category of reference so it would include open totality, I would extend it to include absences, I would extend it to include that aspiration to freedom which I think is implicit in our most element desires. So I want to make a huge claim for the intransitive dimension. I want to say that everything that I say about it is of course constituted in my discourse now, but that is at the level of the signifier and signified; at the level of the referent it either is or is not the case, or perhaps possibly is the case. We can give any epistemic value to that, but ontologically, either the earth had a certain shape fifteen million years ago, which is in some way captured in my discourse, or it didn't, or it didn't exist.

I think what is absolutely crucial, and what a lot of post-structuralist theory does not do, is to articulate the concept of what I call the semiotic triangle (not a concept unique to myself), that is to say, clearly distinguish the word, the signifier or the sentence, and its meaning or the signified, on the one hand, from the referent, on the other. And whether the referent exists or not is an interesting question, and it is not determined by the constitution in the transitive dimension of science of the signifier or signified.

Chapter Four

Critical Realism and Ethnomethodology: Debate with Rom Harre

The Ontology of Social Life*

ROY

Andrew Collier, in his book, *Critical Realism: An Intro-duction to Roy Bhaskar's Philosophy*, describes my first en-counter with Rom Harre as intellectual love at first sight. I do not know whether I would go so far as that but there was an affinity and I was very grateful to have Rom as my supervisor. We were working on parallel lines. From the start I think we more or less saw eye to eye on the philosophy of natural sciences. His *Causal Powers* came out at the same time as my *A Realist Theory of Science*. *Causal Powers* consisted in a critique at the idea of the sufficiency of Humean and Popper–Hempelian criteria for laws, adequate explanation, etc., and *A Realist Theory of Science's* inno-vation was a critique of their necessity. I was saying that the Humeanism was not only just insufficient, but rather that it was actually false. I think my early upbringing as an economist helped me to come to the characterisation of the world as being an open

---

* Part I, SOAS, London, 7 November 1997.

system and thus supplementing the more formal critique of Rom. So we basically agreed about natural science but we have agreed to disagree in a friendly and mutually rewarding way for the last twenty or thirty years about the ontology of social life. That is why we are here together today because we have often been in such contexts and I at least have found our engagements fruitful.

I should perhaps start on a very positive note by noting some of the sort of permanent contributions of Rom's work in the philosophy of social science apart from its realism which I take as being read. I do not want to go through all his books but the most important in the area of the philosophy of the human sciences is the *Explanation of Social Behaviour*. This came out in 1972 when behaviourism and all forms of positivism were completely rampant and he had the striking notion that we should treat for scientific purposes people as if they were people, not some sort of dolled up machines. People were powerful particulars, the philosophy of social science we were both adumbrating stressed the role of causal powers, and Rom focused this by agreeing that people are centres of causal powers. This is a very powerful notion. Where we might disagree on this, and we do disagree on this, is that I say that people are not the only encumbents of causal powers in the world and that people's reasons are causes and norms, reasons, etc., and can all satisfy an adequate scientific criteria of causality. Social structures are like the natural environment, in so far as they can generate, that is constrain or enable, effects. The critique of the empiricist criteria for describing reality was a critique of the limited view that what was real was what we could see, touch, feel, taste or smell—I think I have gone through all the five senses. Where the new, what I call trans-cendental, realism went beyond that was saying we could ascribe reality to things like magnetic or gravitational field, even if we could not actually perceive them as long as we could identify their effects. So if we saw someone fall to the ground from the top of a building we quite naturally and properly ascribe this to the force of gravity. I want to argue that this notion of people as centres of causal powers is true, very true, but people are not the only centres of causal powers in the world and also I want to make reasons, norms and such like causal properties in the fullest possible sense.

The second striking feature of this book was what Rom (his co-author was Paul Secord, so I should mention Paul as well) and Paul called the open souls doctrine. This is basically that people, and this was quite foreign to the sort of behaviourism of the time, have a pretty good idea of why they are doing what they are doing most of the time they are doing it. This is almost a definition of intentional action. This capacity that we have not just to act but to monitor what we are acting, to know the reasons for our acting, and to know why we are doing what we were doing, was a great and underutilised resource for social science. And for me this is in fact the beginning of social science. The first step in any adequate methodology is to identify what it is that the agents think they are doing. Here again, perhaps I will go further than Rom by arguing that we do not stop there, that is the starting point, we can retroduce causal explanations grounded in natural environments, social structure, ideologies, such powerful particulars of the social world, to explain perhaps why it is they think what they think they are doing and perhaps even show that what they think they are doing is not actually the reason why they are doing it. In other words, what they think they are doing is wrong. Nevertheless, such a critique presupposes the move that Rom and Paul made. This move of course had been prefigured by the hermeneutics of Gadamer and Heidegger before that and is a familiar theme of critical theory and all theories which take a hermeneutical moment. But for me hermeneutics was contingently critical, it was a starting point, not the end result of social science, and so I characterised my position, critical naturalism, as being equivalent to a contingently critical hermeneutics.

A third aspect that I would like to praise Rom for (and I come to praise and not to bury Rom) came out in his next book relevant to the philosophy of the social sciences, *Social Being*, where he introduced the very powerful categorial couple between the practical and the expressive orders. This was a time when Marxism was pretty rampant and there were some rather reductionist forms of Marxism around at the time, not in keeping I might say with Marx's spirit or true intentions. Here the notion of the expressive order was very valuable, an important corrective to the crude materialism that was circulating at the time. His next book in

philosophy of social science, *Personal Being*, in 1983 was an absolutely brilliant tour de force and for me this is probably one of his
finest books, and I think he is rewriting it now under a different
title—the *Singular Self*. The thing that I want to stress here is that
if there was a tendency in his works of the 60s and 70s to veer
towards individualism, then this was corrected in *Personal Being*.
He became or espoused Vygotskyism, the individual was constructed from social dyads, tryads, polyads, the individual was a
construction from a wider society. This is really complimenting
at a different level of analysis Wittgenstein's private language argument and in a way I feel in that particular book Rom may have
gone too far. Because the cover of *Personal Being* showed about
six or seven absolutely identical faces, the assumption was really
that society is so, as it were 'determining', that it was very difficult to have any singularity. Perhaps in his new book he is going
to show us how it will be possible to be a social singular, but that
was a problem for me in that book.

About this time he brought to the fore the notion of the
conversation as being the primary social reality. This is taking us
on to our main topic today. Rom has come out with a number of
dualisms or dichotomies, the exact status of which I think we
have to press him to clarify. In *Social Being* it was a practical and
expressive order, it is not clear whether these were mutually exclu-
sive or supposed to account for the whole of society, but anyway
there was this striking dualism between the practical order and
the expressive order. A little bit later he, and particularly in the
excellent festschrift to Rom Harre which I happened to edit called
Harre and His Critics,[1] he said basically as far as we know the
only two social realities are individual physiology and the collective conversation. This was 1989. Let us think about this individual physiology and the collective conversation. Obviously one
has got to ask whether that can possibly exhaust the social world
but then what exactly are the mechanisms by which the collective
conversation has real effects on the material world. For example,
the conversational discursive act in virtue of which Clinton ann-
ounced that he was resetting the Kyoto targets for reduction of

---

[1] Blackwell, Oxford, 1990.

greenhouse gases drastically by a horrendous figure, in fact for thirteen years. This is a discursive act which had an immediate real effect, ideologically, and presumably if it is carried out will have a real effect on the human environment. That is an effect of conversational or discursive acts on the environment. But it seems patently obvious to me that if I ask Alan, what is the time, 2.20, this actually resulted in a material exchange between Alan and myself, in other words it had a material effect. If I shouted 'fire' in a sufficiently animated voice, you would all get up and leave. Of course you may get up and leave for other reasons as well. But anyway this is the sort of question that I would like to pose to Rom: what precisely are the links, accepting this duality between the collective conversation of which the individual is a special case, a special, socially constructed case. By this time Rom was calling himself a social constructionist, and the physiology or the physical order.

A little bit later about the time we did a joint production with lots of other art people last autumn in something that has been published as a special issue of the *Journal for the Theory of Social Behaviour*, June–September 1997. On the ontological status of ideas, Rom said basically there were two realities. As I remember him saying at the time, there were molecules and there were people and that was it. This is prima facie rather surprising in view of Rom's very complex ontology of the natural world. His very neat demonstration of the stratification of reality in nature. Why can we not have a stratified social world, why can there not be emergent powers? Even if people are in some sense primary, a point which might be disputed, there certainly can be emergent powers in the social world from people, and I will go on to be more specific about that. However, to bring the story up to date, at the moment Rom's basic duality in the published version of this special issue is basically between molecules and their structured interactions, and people and their skilled performances. In other words the emphasis has turned to the act or the event.

I think that there are four things wrong with this general approach. There is a dualism there and it is unmistakable. First of all I think it is unnecessarily restrictive, that is my first objection to it. And it is inconsistent with the general thrust of his critique in philosophy of natural science of empiricism. I re-emphasise here particularly the fact that we both share a causal criterion of ascribing reality; and this opens the field to emergent properties of the social world, to consideration of the reality of all the modes of interaction between human beings, social products, nature etc. It seems to me to be inconsistent with Rom's project for the natural world. I can understand it being part of a critique of behaviourism in psychology or social psychology but I do not think he needs it. The second thing is that I think it is restrictive, that he actually omits certain elements of the social totality. For example, I have given one already, unless speech is real and causally efficacious, no science is possible. I will come to my own or critical realism's systematic reconstruction of the nature of social reality in a little bit but suffice it to say that it includes material transactions with nature, social structures, and the stratification of the personality plus their secondary and tertiary elaborations as well as personal inter-relations between people. And the personal inter-relations between people are not for a critical realist restricted to discursive or para-discursive acts. Thus, for example, the employment contract or the capital labour relationship which is hardly glossed as a discursive act, although it entails and presupposes discursive acts. So what I am going to do as I list these four moments of what I think is wrong with his approach is relate them eventually to the categorial structure of dialectical critical realism. The first point is that it is unnecessary and inconsistent with realism. So the second critique, the second point is the omissive critique and this relates to the second moment of dialectical critical realism which hinges on concepts of negativity and absence.

The third thing wrong with it is that it is auto-subversive, it cannot be coherently sustained. Rom himself is making a massive causal intervention in the social world, he is materially affecting everyone's way of thinking, and unless his discursive acts had causal reality and were in some sense an emergent feature of that social world, it would be very difficult to make sense of his own project. In this way I think we have two results. We have a failure of totality, because all these dualisms result in a split between the social world, a split between the material or the causal ground and then the rational or the intentional, ideational realm, we have a split which if you focus on one pole of a split results in the formation of an implicit totality. We have quasi-causes or quasi-reasons where the other half of the totality is reflected or they are then combined and an implicit totality is formed and we have what in dialectic I call a TINA compromise form. So we have basically alienated implicit totality and I think that at the end of the day Rom is forced in virtue of his very acute realist perception of the social world to admit that under disguise, categories such as social structure and nature are sui generis part of the causal nexus of the social world. So in other words we have an implicit critical realism.

The fourth thing that happens corresponds to the fourth moment of dialectical critical realism. I think that at the end of the day Rom cannot sustain his own discursive practice because he, like I, was having an effect on Alan or you, hopefully having an effect on you: he has had an immense effect on other people so it fails to sustain the criterion of reflexivity. Close to these last two points a failure to sustain the criteria of totality, rational totality and reflexivity is I think a failure to sustain the tremendous moral impetus that is behind and sustains Rom's work. I feel that he is basically a humanist and he wants all the right things but without becoming a full-fledged critical realist he will not be able to get them. What I want to do to be slightly more systematic is to go through the nature, what I think Rom's position on what I will call the four moments of dialectical critical realism is and I will do that by defining the moment, then saying what Rom's position on that moment at a meta-theoretical or meta-physical level is; then I will go into the critical realist position very briefly and it's critique of Rom's substantive position.

I am not going to justify in detail here what I have tried to explain elsewhere, and that is I think that the system I developed as dialectical critical realism turns on four spheres of categories: the first turning on ontology and the critique of the reduction of being to our knowledge of being, that is the epistemic fallacy, the critique of actualism and so on, that is fairly well known. That I call the first moment. The second, the dialectical moment, turns on an attempt to revindicate negativity, notions of transformation, change, space, time, tense and absence. The third turns on totality, interconnection, interactivity, and is becoming familiar to us in the ecological turn in recent social thought. The fourth turns on reflexivity which is the ultimate criterion in philosophy, that is the capacity of a system of thought to sustain its own intelligibility, its own mode of production, its own content and context.

Taking the first moment, the actual realist moment, here we come dead up against Rom's dualism. In his critique of my notion of social structure he says, 'as far as we can determine this is the exact and only basis for Bhaskar's conviction that realism is transcendental'. What is this? 'Bhaskar concludes that the power of causation transcends any moment of its occurrence or detection either in closed or in open systems'. I think that is pretty powerful really and if you have a realism which says that whether things are real are not determined by whether they are detected, detectable or any epistemological characteristic at all then that realism is the only sort of realism I would defend and I do not take that as being an objection. But of course we are concerned in science with knowable realities and I would hold that certainly social structures, the natural environment, our own past formation do constrain our social life. The social structure of money radically constrains where I can live, what I can do in my spare time, whether I can go on holiday or not; the social structure of money is absolutely ubiquitous, it is a living reality that we encounter in every transaction almost literally. Traditions, grammars which are allowed as social realities by Rom obviously determine the discursive possibilities of our speech acts. But so do lots of other things. So I really think that if we are going to allow grammars and language and people in the social world, accepting that people are causal agents with causal powers who have real effects then Rom has no reason not to accept social structures, the natural environment, material transactions with nature, things like the capital–labour relationship, global warming as all constituents and proper objects of social scientific investigation.

I say proper objects of social scientific investigation guardedly because Rom says in his latest piece that actually there is no difference between sociology and psychology and I think this is a part of the problem about our positions. Because Rom came in through a very powerful critique of psychology, social psychology, whereas I came in through a critique, literally came back into philosophy, came into academic philosophy from being a student through a critique of standard economics and with an interest in social and political theory. But certainly I do not believe that we can reduce the social to the psychological or vice versa. I think that Rom's actual definition of what we would both call a form of dispositional realism which allows that what is real is real as a bundle of dispositions, independently of whether those dispositions are exercised and independently of whether, if they are exercised they are realised in any particular outcome and independently of whether, if they are realised and exercised in a particular outcome, they are perceived by human beings. This is in fact all you need to sustain all the entities in the social world that I want and Rom apparently does not.

The other interesting feature of realism which bears on his remarks to the effect that realism in the social world has got to be really quite limited, like a constraint imposed on our imagination by grammars, his understanding of the implications of what I call categorial realism. This is saying something more than that social reality is conceptualised. For a start, in the natural world, for a consistent transcendental realism, and this is the only consistent form of realism there is, we have to say that the categories, whether we have got them right or not, exist independently of our philosophical investigations. We do not bring into being space, time and causality. Such features are, and we can get them right or wrong irrespective of our categorisation. Now the situation is slightly different in the social world, in that the social world is similarly categorised. But in virtue of the concept-dependent nature of social reality, it may be falsely categorised and this brings out the role of the notions of ideology and the critique of consciousness and the idea of the critique of the person's own accounts.

I have been pinning my critique of Rom on this dualism, questioning whether dualism is exhausted of reality and how he can explain, or fail to explain, the links between the poles of the dualism. But critical realism is also very impressed with the dualisms of orthodox social science. Let me list a few of the dualisms which it attempts to transcend. The dualism between naturalistic positivism and anti-naturalistic hermeneutics. This was the first dualism, the dualism which was transcended, I hope, in critical naturalism. Notice, however, that to transcend a dualism between two poles is not to give the two poles equal status, because it seems to me patently obvious in reading the works of hermeneuticists and critical theorists that the positivist pole is dominant because the hermeneuticists have not critiqued positivistic ontology, and this is generally true of post-structuralists and post-modernists. They critique the epistemology of positivism but not the ontology. Anyway, the first dualism was the asymmetrical dualism between positivism or naturalism as it was understood and hermeneutics, or anti-naturalism in a critical naturalist account.

Then there was the familiar dualism between structure and agency. This is a very well worn but interesting dualism. Of course what we are (or at least I am) against is reification and voluntarism. The interesting thing is this, if you elaborate an account, as I attempted in my transformational model of social activity, to show how the social world was reproduced or transformed by our agency, but not created by it, this does not mean to say that the two poles are, as it were, on the same level again. Because if the social world is constituted by reified agencies, money, capital, perhaps the nation state, perhaps the nuclear family, all of which are reified entities, then they have to enter into the description of the social world. There is a certain sense in which by accepting categorial realism we are accepting that master–slave relationships, instrumental reasoning, alienation, reification, intellectual sins are out there in the world as real practical sins and it is our job as social scientists to help the transformation of social reality itself, so that we will have a social reality which is free of the category mistakes which are intrinsic to oppressive societies such as we have known for most of our history. That is just a brief aside on reification and voluntarism. I might say on reification and voluntarism that I think it is obvious that Rom is more voluntaristic than me. I think that what Rom thinks is that when we go to sleep the social structure shuts down and when we wake up in the morning, whatever it is that is the social structure is reconstituted. I think that is also pretty close to what Tony Giddens believes, and I think that is false.

Then there is a dichotomy which critical naturalism tries to transcend between individualism and collectivism. Both are pretty abysmal. Take the collective, the idea of the nation on the march as a unit of social analysis. It seems utterly repulsive, and then the notion of the nuclear, homuncular individual. This is equally repulsive. What is the self after all? What sort of self is this? Both must be thoroughly rejected. I argue for a relational conception of the subject matter of the social sciences, in terms of which we understand this as being constituted by the enduring but transformable relations between people and the roles that they occupied.

Another dualism that I attempted to transcend was the mind—body dualism. I argued for an emergent powers materialism, that is situating them in the same totality, putting them in the same grammar. Mind is an emergent power of matter, it reacts on matter and matter effects, conditions mind. Mind itself can be regarded as ingredient in matter, as an emergent possibility of matter. Really this is a dichotomy which should be thrown out of the window. Similarly reasons and causes. Once we accept that causality is a very generic category, which is that it has nothing mechanical at all about it which applies to magnetic and gravitational fields, there is no reason not to allow that reasons may be causes, and in fact there is good reason to argue that we can only sustain a coherent sociology or a coherent ethics if we can make the distinction between an agent's real reason for acting and his imagined, supposed, conjectured or rationalised reason for acting. The final dichotomy that critical naturalism attempts to transcend is the fact-value dichotomy, and I argue that we can move from facts to values by a route which is well known to you.

What critical naturalism tries to do is to show how social science becomes possible in virtue of the nature of the social reality. What we have tried to do is define the characteristics of the social world that might make it knowable to us and they are the activity, concepts, space, time, social relational, dependence of the social world, together with the critical limit that I have referred to earlier. I think that the form of argument in the social sciences is exactly the same as the form of argument in the natural sciences. It is retroductive in virtue of the concept-dependent nature of social reality. It has a hermeneutical moment which may make it transcendental and in virtue of the fact that our belief systems may be categorial false it may be dialectical. But dialectical and transcendental arguments are proper sub-sets of retroductive arguments and that is the method common to science. And I think that method is one of which dialectic forms the most general learning process.

Just to consider a very vexed topic, turning to the second moment of critical realism, the chief moment of the second edge of critical realism turns on the concept of absence. Rom argues that absence is basically unnecessary and that everything we can say about absence we can say by using the concept of the possible. We are both modal realists in the sense that we both believe that the possible is ontologically, logically, epistemologically prior to the actual. There is no difference between us. But I dispute that absence is the same as the possible. My concept of absence is of determinate absence as well as nothingness and this is a very rare concept. Almost always when philosophers from Parmenides on have discussed negativity, they have discussed nothingness, which is, as Rom says, an infinite category, a pretty useless one. Thus the only negative notion Hegel discusses as such is nothingness and, coming after being he proceeds immediately into their synthesis in becoming. Thus negativity is effectively eliminated from Hegel's dialectic by that move.

My paradigm of absence is a very simple one, it is determinate absence. It is patently obvious that we are sitting in a room in which rain is absent, this is an important fact about it. Fire is absent as well. Time is also running out for me, it is becoming absent, which is very pertinent. That is the first thing; I am concerned with determinate absence which is exactly on a par with determinate presence, except I would argue that it is ontologically prior. Secondly, absence is not the same concept as the possible because we can of course have absent possibilities, and possible absences, recursively embedded in one another. The concepts are completely different. Although the concept of the absent includes the non-actual possible, the concept of absence is far broader than that of the non-actual (although we both agree on the sense that the non-actual is absent); here is the residue of a prejudice, which I have called the doctrine of ontological monovalence, which leads to the emasculation of the negative, taken from Parmenides and Kant and further endorsed, if not enshrined, by Hegel. I cannot conceive of a coherent discursive act which is not constituted by spaces, absences in some way. The importance for the ontology of social life is precisely this, that the paradigm of social activity, on a transformational model of social activity, depends on absenting. *Agency just is absenting*. It is transformation, it is negating what is given and what moves to the fore in critical realism is the notion of activity as work. This is a very Aristotelian concept and there is some irony in the fact that Rom called his last meta-theoretical statement on it 'Aristotelian'. I could also argue here about the presence of the past, about emergence, about tense and lots of other things. But I have more than stretched the tolerance of the chair. I am sure we can come to these topics later. I would just like you all to remember all the nice things I said about Rom in the beginning.

ROM

Well if you have a star pupil what can you expect! I have got a lot of small things to say which may add up to something altogether. I begin by reminding Roy of the cover of my *Personal Being* book. It is the famous painting of the Chumley twins in the Tate. If you look at it from a distance you might think they are identical, if you go up close you will find every single detail is different. They have obviously been dressed by their mum or their nurse or whatever to be distinct. That was the point of the book. Stand back a bit from human beings and you might think they are all the same, get up close and you will see there are a huge variety of minute differences and these differences make all the difference. Roy pointed out that I have lately made a lot of use of the notions of Vygotsky and I would just like to remind you briefly about the general conceptual structure of a Vygotskyan point of view which I think is not only applicable to child development but to all sorts of matters in which people are with one another for one reason or another. I could draw a nice Cartesian pair of axes between the public and the private on the one hand and the collective and the individual on the other. So we have an axis from public to private and we have an axis from collective to individual and the Vygotskyan idea is that a human being is born somewhere into the public collective quadrant and has properties which draw on and bring out the activities of the people interacting in that quadrant, primarily conversationally, which gradually becomes privatised by the individual, which Vygotsky calls appropriation and then eventually become individualised. So there is a subjective realm of course, and there is a non-subject realm, I would not like to call it objective, but what is in here? Well, in my view it is the public conversation, and it is that conversation which transforms nascent human beings into people. That idea I think is something we have to bear in mind in the whole of our social investigations, that people are never free of a societal matrix which is transforming them in one way or another. And it is doing it by the sort of process that Vygotsky talked about—in this basic schema there is a constant circulation between what is going on in the conversation which becomes privatised and individualised and eventually may return to the public world via the other two quadrants. We produce in the public world individual acts which may succeed, a joke people may laugh at, innovation may be accepted or they may simply be ignored, enter into if accepted, taken up into the conversation.

Now to the question of causality and I want to sketch out in a bit more detail what it is I think are the basic set of notions that we need to understand what people are getting at, what physicists are getting at when we talk about them informally, we talk about things being brought about, being made and so on. The idea that Madden and I had started to develop, an idea which was taken from the physicists of the seventeenth and eighteenth centuries incidentally, was the idea that causality must be thought of always in terms of entities and not in terms of events. So that part of what led Hume astray was to think that the ontology of the world was an ontology of events. In fact if you read the first chapter of both of Hume's books that is the very first move, it is a world of events. It is either impressions or ideas depending on how far inside the individual person we are going. He is sceptical about powers, about substances, he is not interested in entities. Now we argued that if you look closely at the physical sciences you will see that, whenever notions like causality are employed, formally or informally, it is entities that are in question. What is the powerful particular that is doing something or other in these circumstances. This is a very tricky notion because I did notice that Roy, uncharacteristically, slipped in that he thought that the gravitational field was what was pulling the object towards the centre of the earth. Not in physics it isn't, it is the earth that is pulling. The earth creates around it a gravitational field which we can describe in terms of dispositions. That is, if released at such and such a point an object will fall with such and such acceleration and the generic notion in physics is that of a charge, a charge and its field. The field and the dispositions, the charge is the power, it goes for magnetic poles, it goes for electrons, it goes for the whole story. So we talk about gravitational charge and that is essentially a massy body with a certain mass which is its gravitational charge. So we think of charges and their fields, active entities and their dispositions, which are distributed in space.

Now the move we want to take in the social world is very closely parallel. If we ask what are the entities that are involved, the entities are people. They correspond to charge, they are the powerful particulars, and of course they have all sorts of skills and dispositions which in the human case are distributed over time. It is a kind of temporal field where the skills and dispositions of people are deployed. The physical world, the interactions between the powerful particulars via the fields creates a world and I argue that the interactions between people via their skills and dispositions creates a social world. Now what are the primary skills and dispositions to do? Well there is a vast, huge variety of such things. But the ones that I think we should focus on which are so characteristic of the human social world are those which have to do with discursive acts. I am not saying for one minute that discursive acts are exhaustive of the secondary productions of the social world, they are properties of human interactions, yes, but not the only properties, there are all sorts of other properties. But discursive acts are incredibly important. I want to remind Roy of something about money. I do not know whether you have seen any money recently but here is a bit of it, and look it is all written all over, and it is just a chunk of paper with writing on it. Incidentally it is written by the right person, yes, my goodness, it is a chap called Kantfield who is the chief cashier, and you have to look and see if his name is on the stub because if anybody offers you something written by Bhaskar, I would not take it. What is Roy's problem? It is another piece of writing because the right things are not written in his bank account, so when he takes another interesting discursive entity like this and pushes it through a machine, this is a piece of writing too, and it comes to his bank account and the right number of 0's written on it are missing, then he cannot buy the latest hi-fi or computer that he wishes to. So bear in mind Roy that money is of all things the most discursive object of all. It says, I promise to pay on demand, it used to say a pounds worth of silver, but I do not know what they promise to pay now, Euros I guess, but we will see.

This is a terribly important idea, the distinction between the powerful entities and the dispositions that they have which determines the field of possibility. And then the actions or activities or performances brought about by those things. Like falling bodies, like speech acts and so on. So the general idea then is a very close parallel between physics and the social sciences. When you come to look a little bit more closely though, it is the hierarchical structure that has a quite different interpretation in my view. Both Roy and I acknowledge that the physical world and the social world have a hierarchical structure, that is for sure. The question is what is its ontology, what does it consist of. Well the physical world consists of structures of entities and we track down causality through those. So I offer you a molecule and it has got certain causal powers. So are these its causal powers? Well no, not really, because it is a combination of various atoms which have certain charges. Are those its causal powers? No, we have to go into sub-atomic particles and perhaps even to quarks and perhaps more things which are yet to emerge from obscurity. So in the physical world we are tracking a hierarchical structure of entities. At each level there will be certain sorts of dispositions of those entities which interact to produce the world, analysed at that level.

Now when we come to look at the hierarchical structure of the social world, the question we want to ask ourselves is what are the entities. And in my view the entities are, there is only one level of entities, namely people. Why is there a hierarchy? Because there are hierarchical structures of acts. If you want to understand the hierarchical structure of the social world you have to see it as a hierarchy of acts. The acts produced by individual people are used to perform higher order acts, which themselves coalesce in yet higher order acts and the hierarchy is a structure of acts. This is one of the things that Seccord and I argued for long ago, and the more work that has been done along these lines the more satisfactory this point seems to be. Let us take a very simple example. That in the course of a recent notorious trial in Boston all sorts of acts were performed by individual people, which so to say added up to higher order acts, and now there is a further range of acts at that level being contemplated which will themselves add up to yet higher order acts and so on. So in our view the hierarchy of the social world is as real as you like but it is a hierarchy of acts rather than a hierarchy of entities. Other social entities are properties of the discourse, the discursive productions of people working together to do things. That means that when we are looking for agency we have to make a sharp distinction, and we need to do this about our ontology between agency and activity. We can see that all sorts of things seem to have some kind of activity about them, to bring things about, the question for the ontologist is, what is the agent in for, what is the original, as they used to say in the seventeenth century, of that activity. In the physical sciences we know where it is, it is in the charges not in the fields, in the social world by parity of reasoning, I want to say it is in the people not in their acts. Of course acts are active, they bring things about, but only because they are the acts of the agents in the situation, the people. Then you put a bit more spin on that.

Roy is inclined to say that reasons are causes. Well, I do not think we should use causal language at all. I think it is highly misleading. Let us talk about agents and work with that notion. What are reasons. Well, if you ask yourself what is the offering of a reason doing in social activity, what is doing some work or other, on who's behalf is it doing the work, on the person who is using it. Just as you might come across someone who is hammering. Thus there is a cylindrical piece of iron with a point on the end and they are going like this; you say what is going on here? And you say well this hammer is pushing in this nail, but wait a minute, it would not do this if this person was not doing it, what is he hammering for? Well, it is some project that somebody has in mind. They are hammering the thing in to stop the ladder slipping. So we have to ask ourselves for everything that anybody does, what is the project in which they are involved. The moment you ask that question you begin to find room for another metaphor. That is the tool–task metaphor. And I think that all these things that Roy mentions, natural objects, reasons, bits of paper etc., these could all be thought of as tools for the accomplishment of certain tasks. And that leads us to the idea of instructions.

One of the ways in which we make use of the natural world, the physical world is via instructions. We tell someone to do something and they, understanding our instructions or the discursive act, move something about. Mr Clinton says cut the emissions. It is the United States of America, so immediately the senate and the supreme court stop his instruction from having any efficacy. So we know very well that emissions will not be cut. But that is not because he did not issue the instruction. It is because various other contrary discursive acts were put in which frustrated it. I tell you to do something, you say go jump in the lake. I have still given you the instruction even though of course I have not thought about what I wanted you to do, except maybe I wanted after all to be encouraged to swim. Wittgenstein made that point. One of the best ways to get someone to jump is to say, look, look there is someone who needs rescuing and they all jump in. The task–tool metaphor is I think of the very greatest importance in tying people to the world. The world both of material things and of the discursive acts that people had before. Just think about that a little bit. An exercise you could contemplate. You might wander around Westminster and imagine that some strange thing has happened, that some gust has emerged that has obliterated the writing on all the documents, there are no documents in the world, just blank sheets of vellum. All the writing has gone. No road signs anymore, no 70 mph signs or anything like that. We would find it very very hard to imagine sustaining our world. Roy says lend me 10 quid and I pull out a blank sheet of paper. Imagine all that has happened, Roy's bank account is just blank. He puts his credit card in and up on the screen comes nothing. Imagine that the tower of Babel has indeed happened and we do not understand one another. Have you ever tried to order a cup of tea in Budapest? You will have the same sort of experience, or Estonia where they speak Finnish, a language only they can understand. It is a very strange experience when nothing you say makes any difference and nothing that is said to you strikes any chord. Well, in the view of people like myself the social world has evaporated. There is no such world because there is no possibility of a performance of acts which can add up to hierarchical higher order acts. The whole thing has disappeared. Goodness knows what sort of world we would be in, because chimpanzees do not live in that kind of world, chimpanzees live in an already quite conventionalised world. So when you carry out that sort of thought experiment you can begin to get some sense of just how crucial the discursive activity is.

Now Garfinkel has got a nice little ironic phrase for words like class, nation, etc. He calls it glorious words, and of course this is meant to be ironical. Huge words, I would like to call them, vast words which pick up some hierarchical structure of discursive acts and give them a name and so make us think of them as entities. Now I think Roy really believes that only entities can be causally efficacious, but he is far too promiscuous about what he thinks are entities. This is what I was arguing, that Roy is too ready to accept things that we would be sceptical about as having the characteristic of entities and thus being able to be powerful particulars. Social structure, yes of course there is social structure, but it is a property of a series of human acts. It is not an entity. If we are true to the causal theory that Roy and I both want to agree on, then social structure could not possibly have a standing as a source of activity, it is not an entity at all, let alone an efficacious entity. So of course we can still talk about, use these glorious huge words, but let us ask ourselves very carefully with a great deal of scepticism, let us ask ourselves just exactly what it is that would be claimed if someone was saying this is an entity. It is quite a different matter to see it as a property. And properties of course had to be properties of entities. Properties of what? So ask the 'what question' in a fairly sceptical tone of voice.

There are quite a number of other things that I want to pick up. First of all, the question of immanence and transcendence, that is again a point, a bone of contention between Roy and myself. I think that the transcendence, immanence notion can be made sense of in a very modest kind of way, on a very small scale. And one of the things that Seccord and I were trying to do in our book was to make a distinction between transcendence and immanence with respect to the social psychology of everyday life. And in particular with respect to the notion of a rule. It seemed a good idea, and I am still to some extent attracted by it to think of the orderliness of life, its normativity as something having to do with rules. Now we had to be extremely careful and we were, I regret to say, rather sloppy even though our hearts were in the right place with that notion. Let me just spell it out a little bit more carefully. There is a sharp distinction between the role of the notion of a rule when we are talking about something trans-cendent to the action. So for example, when someone is taking part in an unfamiliar ceremony and they have a rule book, they consult the rule and use it and do what the rule says. Or ulti-mately what the writer of the rule says, not the rule that is doing it per se, but what the writer of the rule says. And then compare that sort of case with something where we all know very well how to do what it is we are doing and someone tries to write a rule book for it. For example, speaking your native tongue or riding a bicycle and things of that sort. But how do we write the rule book. Well, that is definitely not transcendent to the action. So how does it come about that someone can speak their mother tongue in a normative and orderly fashion, not because they are following a rule. Now Wittgenstein distinguishes between acting in accor-dance with a rule, where the rules are immanent in prac-tice and have to be extracted by a social psychologist or gram-marian or someone, and then written out, and where we treat the rules as a set of instructions, as transcendent to the practice. I am quite happy with the notion of transcendence and immanence at that level, but if we go any further to look for something transcendent to the action, I am sceptical of making sense of that notion. We might have a large-scale sociological treatise, as in Karl Marx or Tony Giddens, that might serve in some way as a representation of society transcendent to the action. It might or it might not. And we know the catastrophic effect of treating *Das Kapital* as a set of instructions for setting up a new society. Not a very good idea, however brilliant it might be as an analysis of mid-Victorian ways of doing things. So the transcendent immanent distinction is very important. I believe that most of the glorious things, in Garfinkel's words, are transmitted immanently but not transcendentally. There is nothing in that sense transcendent to the action except of course the action itself. And we should not mistake higher order acts for something transcendent to the action. So when a little person is born into a human conversation, the individual is transcended momentarily by the conversation of its elders, and then it very quickly comes to partake in that conversation.

The next thing I want to say is a little bit about the complications that arise if we take this view. And we are trying to make sense of the idea that there are only molecules and persons as entities in the world. There is a lot of complicated stuff about that which I shall not go into. But if we try to do that then we are inclined to say well, causality in the physical sense applies to collections of molecules, and if we take the task–tool metaphor we might say that the human body and its brain has a collection of molecules functioning as a tool. And we might be interested in its mechanism. How exactly does the brain work, well that will tell you something about how I might use it to remember something or to perform a calculation or something of that sort. But I could equally take out my diary or calculator and do it vicariously or somewhere else. It looks as if we would neatly partition then the account of things in the material world using notions like causal mechanism based upon the idea of atoms or quarks as powerful particulars and we are looking at a different kind of account of orderliness in the social world, but in terms of immanent and transcendent rules, and by and large as I was arguing, the vast majority of these rules are immanent. That leads to a kind of problem for understanding what social psychologists are doing. And how they could have fallen into the extraordinary idea that you could do experiments in social psychology. How did it even seem possible that you could trigger a causal mechanism to bring about social actions?

I think the reason for it is because there is a third category of human action which is tremendously important in everyday life—namely, the category of habit. We have on the one hand intentional actions in which we can talk about projects and plans and so on. On the other hand we have the operation of body as a mechanism, a tool and then there is a habit. A huge amount of our life runs by, on habit. Habits look very much like mechanisms. I think that part of the reason for the old style social psychology was the confusion of habitual action which looks automatic, simulates automatic action with causal action, strictly where there is a strictly identifiable causal mechanism. From what I have just been saying, the resistance to that assimilation, returning one to the discursive point of view, is that what looks like habitual actions are to be assimilated to just the character of normative activity; only the rules are immanent. That is, we are not in any sense at all doing rule following. My old friend John Searle recently came up with a wonderful diatribe against people who think there are unconscious rules which people are unconsciously following. Immanent rules are simply a metaphor for all sorts of ways of people doing things and then the psychologist or sociologist comes in later and writes down the norms as rules. There are no unconscious rules, habits are just habits.

I want to finish up with a little bit about a new idea that I and some of my friends have been working on recently. We started with a study on peace in Iran. We started with a study of the Ayatollah and the problem we were concerned about was a problem that goes deep into sociology and very much into the territory that Roy has made his own, namely the territory of transformation. It is a very striking thing, is it not, that after the end of the French monarchy in the French revolution, two turns of the wheel, or really one and a half, and we have Napoleon crowning himself emperor. That is the difference between Napoleon and Louis XIV, not much. We have Jo Stalin setting up what amounted to a Tsarist regime, the Odpoo becomes the KGB, what is the difference, not much. The Ayatollahs have set themselves up with their regime, weirdly like the regime of the Shah, corruption is perhaps even more flagrant in Iran now than it was in the Shah's day. How has that come about? Is it not weird that despite the fact that large-scale changes are made in the macrostructure of society, all sorts of different ways of organising matters on a large scale, how does it come about that, after a couple of turns of the wheel it looks as though nothing has happened at all? What is the bearer of that particular kind of conservatism. I started this years ago on my own with some researchers to understand how it comes about that the world of hedox generation after generation in a particular community, let us say southern England, keeps on being just the same. How does that come about? I thought and I still think it probably right to some extent that the world, the autonomous childhood world in which all sorts of social practices are passed down from children to children, continues on, there is even evidence that some of it is the same as it was in Norman French days because they still use Norman French terminology. A kind of groundswell of practices which maintains all sorts of crucial things about the larger social world. Well these are simply matters like how you greet each other. Or how do people sit at a table. These are the unnoticed bearers of the structure. Because they are what determines the way the discursive world operates. So in our view it is even more microscopic than we thought before. It is these tiny things that carry what Garfinkel calls the glory responses. So this is the way you greet people, this is the way you organise your family life, this is the way you walk down the street, then that sort of thing will carry through in subtle ways to influence the whole of the discourse. And if we are right the social world is a discursive creation. It is going to influence the whole of the discursive world and hence all of that hierarchical structure of acts that, unless we are very careful, we may be tempted to reify into what I take to be a serious violation of Okham's razor, a reification beyond the realm of duality, namely making these things which are really hierarchical acts generated in the discourse, making them into things which seem to have causal efficacy. As far as I believe only people are the sources of activity in the world and there is nothing else.

ROY

I think that the ground is becoming clearer, the ground for the differences is becoming clearer between Rom and myself. There are basically two sorts of reductions which I think Rom may be guilty of. That is the reduction of the social ontology to people on the one hand and the reduction of social ontology to conversations on the other. I am not quite sure, but these certainly are not the same. Let me just assert something. Firstly, there is no reason to suppose that activities cannot have a structure. Certainly people are born into a world which is pre-structured for them by language, economic traditions and so forth. I think Rom may agree with all this, allowing that people or conversations or both are the bearers of structures. Now we are getting closer because he is not actually denying that social structures exist, he is saying that people or conversations are the bearers of social structure. Now I want to say an agent's activity is a necessary condition for the reproduction of a social structure. But it is not the same thing as it. There is something more to the social structure than that necessary condition. That is in relation to the people dichotomy. In other words, an agent's activity is necessary but not sufficient for claims about social structure. Secondly, I want to say that social reality is concept-dependent but it is not exhausted by concepts. Again, concepts are a necessary but not a sufficient condition for the existence of social structure and other social items. I will not complicate matters by asking how exactly nature fits into this because I think these are very clear questions which we can put to Rom now, if he is prepared to accept this formulation that structures exist and are born in virtue of things like activities which may be possible or actual. Then we could finesse the whole issue by saying that they are people-dependent, but not people-exhaustive.

Money has lots of functions. The promissory note idea is a very weak function of money. It is noticeable how quickly Rom put the ten pound note back into his wallet, suggesting that it has other functions than being a nice piece of writing promised by his bank manager, by the manager of the bank of England or what used to be the bank of England. But I think we are coming very close to it. Accordingly, to critical realism social activity is yes, people-dependent. Social structures are people-dependent but they are not exhausted by people. In exactly the same way, social structures are concept-dependent but they are not exhausted by their conceptuality. Now are we in agreement Rom?

ROM

I think there is still something absolutely fundamental, lots of things that need straightening out. First of all I do not think, and I do not think I have ever said that any agent could bring anything much about. John Shotter and I have been arguing for two decades that the only possible way an agent can enter into his or her agency is in joint action. There is no such thing as individual action. Even people soliloquising or even people daydreaming, in so to say within a conversational framework, even if the interlocutor is notional. I simply do not believe in the possibility of that individual agent creating a social act. It has got to be groups of agents in one way or another. That is one point. Secondly, I do not think for a minute that concepts are the substance of sociology. It seems to me that it is activities and in so far as activities are given meaning by the people who are performing them, either directly or vicariously or by virtue of the positioning of the problem by somebody else, then of course they do display for those who want to see it that way, concepts. So for example someone who says something disagreeable to someone, it displays a concept, namely something like rudeness or something of that sort. But that is work done by them discursively via the commentators upon the action. So I certainly do not want to go for the idea of an individual as capable of performing social acts all on his or her own. Now the key difference between Roy and I has to do with this notion of structure. That is where it is at I think.

Because I think that Roy still thinks, despite the eloquence of my last half hours' dissertation, that structures are somehow or other there as well as people and that they have an interpretative status. I said who am I to deny the existence of social structures, but as what? Property or entity. And that is where it is all at. So my argument against Roy's version of critical realism was that he assimilated structures to entities and that causal power theory was based upon the idea that causal efficacy is reserved to entities. Now entities can do things, can bring things about and what they bring about jointly are discursive structures of various sorts. Of course they are structured, where are these grammars, not up there, not language, not *saussure's langue* but *parole*, and grammars are only there in the discourse. They do not exist outside it. They are a term of art used by grammarians to describe what they write down in their books, something that we might employ when we are trying to learn a foreign language. So I really am at odds with Roy over structure. As far as I am concerned structure is a property of properties, it is a second order property not an entity. I have got the same war going in psychology, but because psychologists are just as promiscuous, you find them talking about beliefs. Beliefs, what on earth are they? Maybe they talk about memories, but hang on a minute, what is a memory, what is it as an entity. I can understand remembering, I can understand people talking about the past, but what would a memory be, what would an opinion be. I can hear people telling you what they think, but what would an opinion be. And worse, when you get that travesty of folk psychology by the Churchlands into people's heads they put beliefs and desires as if these were entities floating around. They even sometimes call them mental states or mental entities. Beware, there ain't no such thing. There are people thinking, talking, jumping up and down, and what they do, have certain attributes, properties of properties, properties of performances. So it is the same war everywhere. It is this war against reification. I thought my pal here was one of my allies in the war against reification and if you are then what are these structures doing here?

ROY

What I would like to say to Rom is that his dichotomy between a thing and an event seems to me to be far too crude, even in the natural world. We have to redefine our notion of an event in contemporary physics and Rom is very aware of this. An event is not a single instance, it can be a distribution of space or time, it can be highly enduring. What exactly is a thing? It is not at all clear. A system of relationships? There seems to me nothing wrong in calling an economic system like capitalism or like the banking system or like the system that the IMF presides over now as being an entity. It certainly has all the properties of being a bearer of causal powers which constrain and enable us. If that crash that started off in East Asia had gone on we would all have felt the pinch. Luckily for us it did not go on. But if the banking system in this country were to collapse, this would have momentous causal implications for all of us and it seems to me patently obvious that language, economic systems, social systems, the structures of cities enable and constrain. Moreover, let us think of structures as being systems of relationships. Let us move away from this crude thing event ontology. Let us think of relationships. Let us think of different paradigms of things. Consider what language enables and constrains. What was the feminist critique of language? It was that it constrained certain possibilities of women, that language which was called sexist actually had a determining influence on the options available to them. In the same way the possession or non-possession of a ten pound note makes all the difference in the world if you want to get a taxi cab home or you want to buy a nice book (like one of Rom's or mine) in the shop.

ROM

Language does not constrain women, linguistic practices constrain women; that is what constrains people, it is practices. Now what are practices, they are activities. We have to be very careful at drawing on the analogy with the physical sciences, because if you do take that analogy seriously, the crucial thing about causally efficacious entities in the physical sciences is that they have criteria of identity. They are enduring, and that is a very important characteristic; the only thing in the physical world that has that characteristic is not practices but people, because people perform practices.

ROY

We have got it in a nutshell now, because at any moment of time the possibilities open to people are constrained by something which I am calling structure. Now that structure is reproduced or transformed by peoples' practices, that structure does not exist independently of the prior practices of people at an earlier moment of time.

ROM

Why do you need to put in that term?

ROY

Because we are constrained by the presence of the past.

ROM

How, exactly how?

ROY

I believe that we are living in an abundant world. It may be a very romantic notion but I believe that scarcity could be eliminated over night. And I believe that the nature of human needs is finite and that we need have no economic crisis and that we could have a rational social order. Now the constraints on our doing that lie in the nature of the global system in which we live, which we reproduce or transform, and which we must transform—that is change, now.

ROM

No, Roy, it is the nature of the global discourse in which we partake.

ROY

And the one is very closely related to the other.

ROM

There is not any other.

ROY

This is very interesting you see because in a way there is another way in which Rom and I are moving closer now because I have been stressing categorial realism and I have been stressing that money is not just a thing, a concept, it is actually a category which is constitutive of the nature of social reality itself. Rom is saying a global capitalist economy is a matter of discourse. I am saying it is certainly a category. So we are not so far apart. But it is also a reality. It has all the causal powers of any other category. When we look at society in this way we can see that both crude materialism and crude idealism are completely unacceptable. Because categories are constitutive of reality, they are also the sort of things that philosophers and political theorists and economic theorists talk about, but they are the bearers of causal powers and I think it is totally absurd to say that there are not causal constraints on the future of Bangladesh.

Chapter Five

Critical Realism and Ethics: Introducing Transcendental Dialectical Critical Realism*

Realism about transcendence

I would like to relate three of Doug's points in particular to what I am going to say, which isn't a sort of resumé of *From East to West,* but rather an introductory background to it. The three points I would particularly like to take up are first, the question of realism about religious experience, which I would broach under the broader category of realism about *transcendence.* Secondly, I think talk about god is eased in a dialectical critical realist context by being seen as talk about an—or the—*ultimatum.* Thirdly, I want to focus on that dialectic of *co-presence* which

---

* *Alethia,* April 2000.

After Doug Porpora's presentation a question was raised, in effect, whether religious sociology, as distinct from the sociology of religion, has a proper place within critical realist discourse. The corrigibility of experience is a central realist tenet, and indispensable to explanatory critique of, say, fascist experience. How can religious experience be corrigible given that there can be no agreement within the scientific community concerning its object (or whether, indeed, it has a real object)? After some discussion, Margaret Archer (in the Chair), suggested that Roy should be allowed to provide the 'hinge' on this issue, because the discussion was cutting off epistemology from ontology, which is not what Doug does in his book, and what Roy wanted to do was swing the focus away from the experiential to the ontological groundings Doug invokes.

is the dialectic of autonomous and heteronomous—or real and irreal—determinations. I will argue that transcendence as such is a phenomenon which has been much misunderstood and is essential to science, and in particular scientific discovery.

So I am not going to argue about specifically theological or religious transcendence as such, but I would like to say a few words about the dispute into which Doug got embroiled. There are two interesting takes I would like to suggest on the démarche Doug seemed to get landed in. The first is that, within the continuum of being, is there really such a huge difference between realism about god and realism about any other being—for instance a galaxy which is beyond the expanse of our current most powerful microscopes? Secondly, suppose that god was in fact the self—that god was the missing self or at least was to be included in it, i.e. that god was part of the missing self—then there might be an interesting new angle on Doug's question.

However, what I primarily want to defend in this talk is realism about transcendence. One form of transcendence is the sort of transcendence typically found—or claimed to be found—in acts of religious worship: meditation, prayer, communion or whatever. So that is one of the things I would like to pick up from Doug's talk. The second thing is really, more specifically, his realism about god and I would like to subsume this under the question of realism about ultimata. In *Dialectic* and other works I distinguished various levels of being, and it is clear from what Doug is saying (and I am bouncing my ideas off Doug's now to make for dialectical continuity) that for him and for many Americans god is an ultimatum. So I am going to be talking about realism about transcendence and realism about ultimata. Ultimata have particular qualities and one of their qualities that is relevant to our discussion is that they are in some way *ingredient* in lower orders of being, so that if god did exist and if god was an ultimatum one would expect god, as a basic property of the universe, a basic constituent or categorial structure, to be for instance in this room—and indeed in some sense in each part or aspect of it (without however saturating the room, so that we should still have to say that there were other things besides god present in the room).

Irrealist surface, realist deep structure

A third interesting idea relating to Doug's book is the peculiar paradox we find in American society between the ontological necessity for Americans to be selves and their absence of a sense of self. For what we have here is the co-existence of a presence, namely reasons, or their belief that there are reasons for everything they do, and an absence, namely their being unable to cite or justify the belief that there are reasons (or that these—such-and-such—are the reasons). It is the same or a parallel contrast between the existence of the self and a lack of a sense of that existence of the self. This is a perfect example of the dialectics of copresence, and this takes me to the theme of my talk. There is what strikes me as being a huge paradox about realism. Most philosophy and most societies are profoundly irrealist in character. Now I claim realism to be true, and we critical realists believe realism to be true; so we have a juxtaposition between an irrealist categorial structure (and I mean this as part of what I call the platinum plate in Hegelian dialectic, viz. the way in which one can use a philosophy as a diagnostic clue to the character of our society—and I think it is true to say that our societies are in character profoundly irrealist) and our belief that realism is fundamentally true.

Now this pattern or figure of an irrealist surface and a realist deep structure is paralleled by similar motifs which vibrate, recur and resonate throughout western and indeed eastern thought. For example there is the assumption that Marx and Rousseau had that man is essentially free—that at a deep level, he/she/we are *even now* essentially free—but everywhere in chains. Then that essential freedom which we possess is occluded and overlain by structures of what Marx called ideology and what the Vedic tradition in India regards as *maya* or illusion. So the structure of these two forms of thought in respect of freedom and in respect of realism are very similar. We have the idea of an irrealist categorial structure masking and overlaying and acting as a surface filter to a profound deeper realist structure which is waiting (and wanting) to be free of this irrealist superstructure. And the idea of autonomous human beings in some basic sense aspiring to be free, that is to be shed of, or rather to shed themselves of the heteronomous structures that impede and prevent the liberation of humanity. This seems to be a fundamental theme, which I touched on in my talk in Örebro, *the* fundamental theme and presupposition of western radical thought—it is amazing how prevalent it is in radical critical and libertarian thought and philosophical writing.

Now besides these paradoxes of irrealism and freedom there are other similar paradoxes. We could say that the universe is necessarily one and whole and seems to be bound together by holistic forces. In the ethical domain one would look to instances of love as a great binding force. And yet the world as we know it is also overlain and occluded by structures which are highly divisive, alienating, split. In the ethical domain the overriding emotion remains one of fear. Our world is dominated by fear, not love. Then again, this is a world, one could claim—I would certainly claim—of enormous abundance, yet it is also a world of extraordinary poverty. This is a world without (non-dialectical) rationale. For we can have good reason to believe that we can cut oppression and suffering to a minimum; yet it is at the same time a world characterised by massive oppression and suffering.

Dialectic of co-presence

So what seems to be happening is that we have a view of human beings as essentially free—the structure of the world as essentially realist and essentially harmonious, or one in which something like cosmic love could manifest itself—being *occluded* and *overlain* by heteronomous or irrealist categorial structures or determinations. In arguing for categorial realism. I have argued that categories are real so there is nothing wrong in talking about categorial structures as features of the universe: they are in fact the most basic features of the universe.

There are two mechanisms operating here: perceptual occlusion and causal determination—the fact is that the funda-mental essential freedom or autonomy of human beings is both hidden *and* overlain by structures of oppression, master–slave relationships, reification, duality, alienation, split and the mystified world of ideology in which we all live most of our lives. Thus we have both a perceptual mechanism and a causal mechanism. These are difficult to disentangle except conceptually. For are not all beliefs experientially (and to that extent perceptually) informed, or to the extent that they are to be efficacious, e.g. as manifest in the form of wants, do they not include or depend on a perceptual component? At the same time all causal determinations in the human world are informed by cognitive and thus perceptual claims. So the perceptual (or more generally cognitive) and the causal, or the cognitive and causal, metaphors I have used—the surface structures of society occluding and overlaying the deep structures—fit together very neatly.

And this is the basic structure of a dialectic of co-presence, which is very central to dialectical critical realism and critical realism, crucial to the thought of Marxism and the western radical tradition generally, but which is equally to be found in the eastern Vedic tradition where the world of ordinary, surface everyday life is characterised as a world of duality, alienation, split. The central idea here is that man is essentially godlike, subsisting and acting in a world of relativity and duality. A difference springs up only as a product of illusion. And it is the essential nature of man to come to see through this illusion and to realise their self-consciousness as free and/or godlike. We need not go into the details of this basic structure of thought, but it has the characteristics of a dialectic of co-presence and it is equally central to critical realism and western radical, and much eastern, broadly libertarian thought.

Liberation and disemergence

What is the process of liberation then? This must be understood within the context of the development of a dispositional and a categorial realism in which we have the central idea of the multi-tiered stratification of being. Now if the autonomous or the realist level, the potential level, is already in some sense actualised, but overlain and occluded by the heteronomous or irrealist level, then to become fully free, an aspiration which would be reflected in a realist categorial structure of the society, what we have to do is to shed, let go, get rid of the heteronomous levels or orders of determinations, the alienations, constraints and reifications that dominate our contemporary society. And I would argue along the lines of Andrew, but in a different way, that such a society would be based on an ethic of love, unconditional love rather than fear.

Is such a dialectic of liberation anything more than a pipe dream? I think so; for what a pipe dream is the supposition that this world of heteronomy, of irrealism, can carry on indefinitely, because the stratification of being is such that there are one-way relations of dependency between more basic and more superficial strata. Thus the existence of master–slave relationships is entirely dependent on the creativity of slaves. And when we realise that, we realise that if slaves cease to be creative, master–slave relationships would be no more. But, conversely, the creativity of slaves, or the creativity of free human beings, can persist without the existence of master–slave relationships. So it is not that we have to hope that an autonomous or realist society will magically manage to spring into existence. It already is in existence. It is the heteronomous and irrealist world which is entirely dependent on it. This is itself a liberating thought, though thoughts are only truly liberating when geared into action. But it does mean that the world of duality, split, alienation, illusion, ideology, fetishism, money, reification can only survive for so long.

As to what can happen, there are only three possible solutions in terms of logic. One is that the realist, the autonomous, the free, the loving could be entirely suppressed. I am arguing that this is impossible because heteronomy, irrealism, etc. are all parasitic on the truth, on freedom, on love; vice is parasitic on virtue, so that is not a live option. Second, the vicious world could destroy the virtuous world physically and our planet could be destroyed. In that way the vicious world would not sustain itself any further, but the virtuous world would cease to be complete, would not exist, in isolation by itself, as a whole, untainted by heteronomy; and arguments could be adduced to show that this incompletion would have to be remedied (namely by a new round of a dialectic of embodiment). The third is that we pursue a dialectic of liberation and disemergence, of shedding. This is the only feasible solution for humanity, the only way we can go.

I would argue we do this through dialectics of action and inaction, and the chief dialectic of action is the dialectic of desire to and for freedom, which I set out in *Dialectic: The Pulse of Freedom*. There are other dialectics of action, some of which I articulated there, and others of which I develop in *From East to West*, but I have not explored dialectics of inaction, except in my recent work, to the same extent. Basically, if you want proof of realism, or autonomy, of your own freedom and sense of self, what you have to do is *access* it; so you need a dialectic of access, and this ties up with the point Doug was making about religious experience, which is a specific form of a dialectic of inaction. Then you need to *shed* those heteronomous, irrealist, alienated levels and layers of determination. Thirdly, you need to fully *embody* or embed the autonomous real, in all the existing strata and levels of society, so you need something like a dialectic of embodiment. And finally you need a dialectic of *witnessing* or self-consciousness because this has to be subject to rational control and critical scrutiny and done to the level at which humanity's full potential and powers, including powers for further development, flourish, as an embodied, emotional and a rational species.

Transcendental experiences

Now I said I would say a little bit, picking up from Doug, about how transcendence and ultimata fit into this.

First transcendence. If we go back to Hegelian dialectic, I have argued that the four central features of Hegelian dialectic are its *rational kernel*, its *mystical shell*, its *golden nugget* and its *platinum plate*. The rational kernel consists essentially in a dialectical learning process which involves transcendence to a greater totality, depending upon the resolution of oppositions, conflicts, contradictions, aporia, and the restoration of lacunae and other incompletenesses, by resort to a greater totality; and of course the greater totality we are concerned with in this human world is the totality of the human race in our natural environment (in what I have called four-planar human being). The mystical shell is ontological monovalence, or the absence of absence. The golden nugget is the dialectics of co-presence, and the platinum plate is the diagnostic value of philosophy. What the mystical shell, the absence of absence, does, is to occlude the central moment in the rational kernel. This is precisely the very moment of transcendence in which we reach for a new, greater, synthesising, transcending concept. It is that moment of human creativity which comes *ex nihilo,* out of the blue, which can not be sustained by reference to inductive or deductive norms; that moment of transcendence which inspires the scientist and the artist and which people find or claim to find in religious worship that we have to start investigating and taking seriously as well as critically. Every human act, every genuine transformative human act, comes *ex nihilo* from the absence on to a more or less well prepared immanent ground, prepared by prior rounds of transformative work, and consists in the operation of a transcendent cause on that immanent ground. This starts to put religious experience in the same sort of category as transcendental experiences in general, from moments of scientific and artistic inspiration to moments of a more quotidian nature but essential to all human transformative praxis.

Now where does the ultimatum idea come in? Higher order or more basic categories are epistemologically transcendent, but ontologically immanent, and in particular, ingredient in lower order or more superficial categories.

And so one would typically expect something like a new idea which was coming from 'out of the blue' or from an undiscovered stratum of reality or dimension of being, to be coming from a stratum which was both *epistemologically transcendent* and *ontologically immanent.* Now it is important to note that god or the ultimatum, whatever it is, has to be ontologically ingredient in all the lower order strata to some degree and in some respect or other. So this would justify the view, if we were going to talk about god, of the ontological immanence of god in man. This may be thought to raise the questions: does god create man or does man create god, or is man in fact god, or is the true essence of god man rather than the true essence of man god, is that what god is? However, if there is an ultimatum, whatever the value of such speculations, this idea of ontological ingredience must not encourage any sort of anthropocentricity. Because if there is an ultimatum it will far outweigh humanity. So we should not become too conceited by the idea that man's essence may be god-like. Because man's essence, if it is godlike, will itself be part of a totality which is far greater in width and depth than man himself, so this idea gives no cause for a resort to anthropocentricity. God, as an ultimatum, is ingredient in, but neither exhaustive of nor saturated by, man and man's world; that is to say, god id partially manifest in it, and, as part of him, as it.

I hope these few remarks have justified, a little bit, the legitimacy within a critical realist discourse of making the points Doug was making. I have put them in the contexts of a more general realism about transcendence and realism about ultimata, because I want to get away from existing disputes we have about religious experience. There are very many forms of religious experience. Ontological realism about god is consistent with epistemological relativism about our modes of experiencing him and judgmental rationalism about religious beliefs and experiences—not all of which are legitimate and some of which are no doubt heinous. I am trying to get a debate going by putting Doug's talk of religious experience and the talk of others with religious experience within the category of transcendental experiences, so that they can then have a place in the scrutiny and the discourse of critical realism. And if we can think of god, breaking free from customary connotations, as the ultimate categorial structure of the universe—which is what I think people who talk about god do in fact think of god as—in fact, then we can get a different perspective on the philosophy of religion: one which makes god immanent in man but gives no grounds for anthropocentric conceit. For, to repeat, god neither exhausts nor is exhausted by man or his world.

Powers of liberation and survival

However, it does give us grounds and support for arguments in favour of liberation. Because, if we have within ourselves, whether we believe it is god or not, all the powers of the ultimate constitution of the universe, dispositionally real and indeed actualised in ourselves, though occluded and overlain by structures of heteronomy, alienation and irrealism, then there is nothing we cannot achieve. The main thing I think we want to achieve is freedom, and to achieve this all we have to do is to shed the illusions and the ingrained structures which hold us in thrall. But if we can come to the realisation that at the deepest level we are autonomous, that if we are slaves or otherwise creative, we are nevertheless free, a freedom upon which all oppression ultimately depends; if we can realise that we are such beings as a dialectical critical realist and perhaps a transcendental dialectical critical realist describes, then we do have grounds for the belief that ours is the struggle for the survival of humanity. For humanity can not survive unless we become free. Conversely, if we become one with our ultimatum or godlike essence then we have all the powers of the universe at our disposal, and there is a chance that, if we learn as much from Marx and perhaps the Vedics as we do from contemporary sociology, we may yet win through to a world in which we can live in a stance of unconditional love for ourselves and each other and for every other being (or for that matter nonbeing) in our environment.

So these were just a few ideas picked up from Doug's talk, but which I go into in a systematic way in *From East to West*.

Margaret

You say that the ultimate human desideratum is freedom. I would question whether freedom is the ultimate desideratum on the grounds that freedom is either a freedom *from* or a freedom *to*, which implies that it is incomplete in itself. You said it would lead to our acting in unconditional love. I would be very tempted to put those two the opposite way round: yes we need to be free to live in an unconditional love but the ultimatum, the ultimate state to which the whole of humanity is groaning and struggling is that creative expression of ultimate fraternity.

Roy

What I meant is, what we need *now* is freedom. The ultimatum is not freedom. The desideratum is freedom, the ultimatum is unconditional love. It is interesting that in your very words, when making this point with which we both agree, you talked about creatively expressing unconditional love, so creativity is essential to human being. I do not think that, either for human beings or for a generalised psychology of them, action is such a great problem. I believe that we have got to think through all the categorial domains of dialectical critical realism and that this transcendental deepening or radicalisation of dialectical critical realism (which I am calling transcendental dialectical critical realism) will lead us to see that really the best action, and indeed most action, is basic, that is, it is pretty spontaneous; it is not calculating instrumental action. Moreover, most action is not narrowly self-motivated, although thinking action may often be so self-motivated. Indeed I would say that we are faced with an option in ethics of two ethical stances; one based on spontaneous unconditional love and the other based on instrumental conditional reasoning, and I think particularly that unconditionality in love and in reasoning go hand in hand and that our society suffers from a surfeit of conditionality and instrumentality superimposed upon basic action, whereas good action is spontaneous and pretty natural. It is the sort of action, if one had to use an analogy, of the sun or a flower. The sun does not try and shine, it just shines; a flower does not try and grow, it just grows. And human beings left to themselves are lovely, they will find out how to use language, they will love each other, we can organise a society without reified structures (including ultimately I believe money), just give us a chance.

Question

I have a problem with the word/concept freedom. Kant defined it almost as one phase—you would not want to define freedom as freedom from causal determination, for example. Part of the causal structure of the world is other people with complex wants, desires and beliefs.

Roy

What you say is absolutely true: humanity is essentially one, but each human being is essentially unique, concretely singularised and each is different. I can not see a huge social problem there, we still have to negotiate, we will still have problems caused by the complexity of whatever wants we have, but we may find our wants moving in an unexpected and more simple and easily satisfiable way, there is no reason why not. Take the structural wants in our existing society: you have to cars, what do you want next—three, then four, this is absurdity, there is a finite number of cars that any family or any person needs. And so, it is not necessarily true that greater freedom will result in an indefinite perpetuation of wants or social conflict; it could result in greater simplicity, greater harmony, greater love of the elements, greater enjoyment of each other's company.

Margaret

There is another side to this which is very compatible indeed with your stress upon creativity, because just the celebration of the unconditionality of love without introducing the wisdom, the prudentiality, the consideration of the good of the other being, or what Andrew calls in his St Augustine section the loving in due order, is not actually going to resolve any of those problems. But the optimistic thing it seems to me is that just as all these distortions happen on our freedom because of the society in which we live, nevertheless we can see endless exemplifications of the creativity of unconditional love exercised in wisdom and judgment in the ordinary ways in which, for example, a mother interacts with her child, which is not to say yes to everyone, but it is to exercise a discretion and leading out, and encouragement which is all of those things, or what you mean by the necessary creative moment in the exercise of love.

Roy

Yes, and I mean that I think that such a society will be characterised centrally by difference and change, it will not be stagnant.

Question

You said that 'categorial structures are . . . the most basic features of the universe'. Was this a slip, an endorsement of some sort of grand idealism, or what?

Roy

Transcendental and critical realism has always insisted on categorial realism. Now, what are the categories? They are things like substance, causality, arguably space, time; in the social world, things like housing, education, money and so on. Now for the critical realist, causality is not a schema imposed upon the world as it is for a Kantian; causality exists in the world. It is not just that Ohm's law or causal laws exist in the world, but that causality and lawfulness and causal lawfulness are real features of the world: so categories are really in the world. Now, if god is an ultimatum or a most basic structure then he/she/it would be something like a categorial structure of a very high order, and this was appreciated by Hegel and Spinoza. However, by talking about ultimata I have tried to defuse it from a lot of theological issues and aporiai; nevertheless it remains of paramount importance to stress that categorial realism is an essential part of critical realism.

Question

So you did not mean conceptual structures?

Roy

No, I mean a category like causality could exist in a world without concepts at all. The conceptualisation of it is in what I call the transitive dimension. It is true that when you have human beings you have both categories and conceptualisations of them but you get wrong conceptualisations of categories, as the Humean theory of causality is the wrong conceptualisation of the category of causality.

Question

Why do we talk about causal structures and also about a category of causal structures, I am not sure about this idea.

Roy

The concept of a category is a basic philosophical concept. It is a concept, but it has a reference, it has a referent in the world. There will still be a difference between talking about the reality of causality as distinct from the subjective or objective idealist notions and talking about the reality of a particular nominated causal law. To say that substance is real or that time, space, causality, holism, totalities or the self are real, these are all ultimately categorial claims because they are claims of a very basic significance, and what they denote is that the object of the term, which is called the category, is real. Categorial realism makes it clear that you can be wrong in your basic characterisation of the world. Therefore when you talk about irrealist and realist categorial structures it is important to distinguish between your conceptual categorisation of the world, which is in the transitive dimension, and the real categorisation of the world, or the categorisation of the world as it is in itself, which is in the intransitive dimension. Categorial realism is a deep part of ontological realism, which is initiated as the reference of our epistemological attempts to classify the world categorially and sub-categorially.

Question

Is god categorially real?

Roy

If god were real, he would be categorially real.

Question

Is the ultimatum real?

Roy

For the purpose of this talk, the ultimate ultimatum is real.

Question

And if it is god, he is responsible for everything, for all the bad things as well?

Roy

Absolutely: the condition of possibility, that is why I talked about this one-way relationship of dependency.

Question

The Church's subjects say that god is responsible for everything.

Roy

It is not quite as simple as that, because this ultimatum provides the conditions of possibility, but does not determine what happens at lower-order levels. This is the true basis of free will. God, if you like, provides the enabling conditions, man determines, selects, picks out from them, from the totality of possibilities which god affords.

Question

God is unconditional love. This is two people loving each other unselfishly?

Roy

Perhaps one wants to generalise that even further and talk about the whole room loving itself, and all other people in all other rooms, and ultimately the whole universe, unconditionally.

Question

In your book, *Dialectic: The Pulse of Freedom*, the pulse of freedom is something contained within the historical, the social; it is always there, and always reminds you that it is there. The ethical impulses are quite tightly controlled within that book. What you seem to be doing now is severing the relationship between the historical and the ethical. The idea that 'man is born free but everywhere is in chains' sets up quite an antinomy between freedom and determination, autonomy and heteronomy, and that seems to be open to the criticism that you are simplifying a relationship between the ethical and historical, political and social in a way that gives one a sense of almost: with one bound we are free.

Roy

All these institutions, all these structures are largely historical and social; that moment is there and that is the life blood of it all. What is lacking perhaps in *Dialectic* is a clear idea of the actuality of autonomy, the essentiality of creativity, the immediacy of that transcending moment which is the inspiration and driving force of every human act. To say *we are* essentially free, that *we are* free in actuality, although this is occluded and overlain by the structures in which we live, is a profoundly liberating thought, and it will inspire that impulse, that pulse which I described in my book

Dialectic. The pulse doesn't just come when the slaves revolt, the slaves are in revolt because they realise they are essentially free. It is this realisation that must be built explicitly into the structure of critical realist thought, before it was there only implicitly. Critical realists think they have got the truth, or something close to it, about the categorical structures of society, but everywhere we see the dominance of irrealism, as for instance in postmodernist or positivist thought. Perhaps it is important to assert the reality and actuality of those real and auto-nomous structures as *there*, even though they are so invisible to us. Perhaps in this moment of time we need to grasp them, realise we are free and we can do it: humanity can survive; the world is fundamentally realist and human beings are essentially free. But they still have to realise this freedom, they are not only essentially free, they have to become *only* free: they are essentially free but in actuality oppressed, so that they are both free and unfree, or less paradoxically only partially free (because their freedom is overlain by oppression). This is putting the dialectic within a context which looks antinomic initially, but isn't really because the dialectic, involving the co-presence of freedom and unfreedom, is stratified and moving the whole time. In a way, it is just making clear that the basis of the drive to freedom rests on the actuality of our essential freedom.

Question

Despite your qualification that universal love was only the ulti-matum, I have noticed that several times in your books you talk about universal love as the immediate necessity, as if it is what we all need to be driving to. Now, it strikes me that this was Feuerbach's philosophy. Feuerbach was a humanist who wanted to liberate people's potential, but as Marx pointed out he could not do that because he was not able to identify the right ques-tions was unable to draw the class divide correctly, and was not able to analyse the structures of capitalist society. I am not accus-ing you of being a Feuerbachian, but I think that you should de-emphasise the idea of unconditional love in your work. Relatedly, in your four-fold dialectic of liberation you gave the final, fourth dimen-sion as being a philosophical reflection on what had been achieved, but it seems to me that the philosophical reflection needs to go in before. This is something I don't understand about your treatment of Hegel, you seem to treat him as almost like a bourgeois sociologist rather than somebody who through philosophical elaboration managed to re-establish the dialectic in modern philosophy which was the ground for Marx to be able to then write his books.

Roy

First, there is a sense in which Marx was also a humanist, although he was quite correct in his critique of Feuerbach that he left out the necessary social and historical dialectical mediations. So I am not a Feuerbachian. In respect of Hegel, I think that maybe in *Dialectic* I was too tough to him and didn't give sufficient merit to him. The rational kernel of the Hegelian dialectic was a profound rediscovery and I accept my (perhaps) underplaying of it in *Dialectic* as a self-criticism. But it is still the case that in the mystical shell there is ontological monovalence—the absenting of the concept of absence—and with the concept of absence goes transcendence and the capacity to move to a greater totality, which is the rational kernel of the dialectic. So he does eventually undermine himself. I don't think that there is much difference between myself and the questioner.

Question

You say that the slave has a right to say no, but your concept of freedom seems buried in the ontological depths; in the context of the world, in the context of political action, it does not engage in any level of practicality.

Roy

I think that what you are saying is that it is a very deep freedom, but Marx realised that it was characteristic of capitalist society that we had free labour—the worker had a choice (of a kind) whether to be a wage slave or not—and that differentiated it from, and was a progressive advance on, former modes of production. It is at that level of generality that I am talking about freedom. Unless you accept it, you can not get very far in a liberatory or emancipatory direction. Once you accept it, you still have all the spade work to do. What I am trying to do is to restructure or reorient the parameters of our thought on these basic issues, not to say that we should not be thinking about the local elections, or day to day bread and butter issues. . . . Unless you start from unconditional love you will not get the right answer.

Question

How can we start from unconditional love? There are many problems about the whole concept that need to be unpacked. How for example can I love the tribe of fleas that infect my body and carry the plague, how can I love them unconditionally?

Roy

Firstly, you have to accept some sort of hierarchy of being. You talk about a moral dilemma for you, so we have to do this in discussion and presumably there will be rational ways of resolving it. Secondly, you have to consider in talking about unconditional love for a person what it is that you love about that person. I would say that what you should unconditionally love about a person is their intrinsic self, essential nature that would be what would have been called, in the olden days, their higher, noblest or best self, not all their vices and irritating habits, let alone the fleas that dwell in their pores.

Question

But we have to love all these things surely?

Roy

No, other things being equal, if it did not get in the way of humans or other beings we should love fleas.

Question

But it is part of a flea's essential nature to bite me. But you tell me that I should love them.

Margaret

No, he is talking about a hierarchy of being, just as Andrew's book was about this.

Question

Andrew was saying we should love all being.

Margaret

. . . In due order.

Roy

There are two things: first there is a hierarchy of being, and secondly there is the question of what is it about those beings that you love; and you love their essential, best or highest qualities, and certainly biting you is not a very high quality of a flea. If you could have a population of fleas, isolated from human beings, there would be no reason not to love them because they have their own existence as a species.

Question

This is getting away from the point. Purpose, analysis, politics, practice. It is just not helpful to keep talking about unconditional love.

Roy

This is a starting point. We must still recognise different levels of discourse and philosophical discourse. In particular at the level of generality at which we are talking now, philosophy is providing a tool kit for the set of tools that you actually use in social analysis, it is underlabouring for underlabouring. It is at a very high level of generality and refinement, but it is necessary to get our concepts clear. Unless we get our categories clear, we will not be able to do all those nitty gritty things that some members of the audience want us to turn our attention to. That is the heart of social work and social change and social analysis. And that is what we talk about most of the time, but we have philosophical workshops and seminars like this to enable us to do our social analysis and social transformation in a more clear headed and hopefully more inspired way.

Question

You said that we are actually free, not merely potentially free, but then you say that we are actually oppressed.

Roy

Yes we are essentially, actually but only partially free, not completely. We are both free and oppressed: that is the dialectics of co-presence. The dialectic of liberation is a dialectic of disemergence, which turns fundamentally on shedding that part of ourselves which is heteronomous or unfree.

Interlude

Critical Realism, Transcendence and God*

*R*oy circulated the twelve propositions below, shortly after the discussion from which Chapter five is drawn, for an informal discussion with critical realists which he contextualises at the beginning of the discussion.

Twelve Propositions on Transcendence, Critical Realism and God

1. <u>Ontological realism</u> about God [in the intransitive dimension] is consistent with <u>epistemic</u> (more generally experiential) <u>relativism</u> [in the transitive dimension] (including pluralism, fallibilism and diversity) and <u>judgmental rationalism</u> [in the intrinsic aspect]; and in particular with the view that god

   (a) manifests himself; and/or
   (b) is accessible (e.g. as a transcendent entity in moments of transcendence) in a variety of different ways.

---

* Debate with Critical Realists, London, December 1999.

[In particular note that ontological realism about god is consistent with the view that there may be one, many or no gods; and if there is at least one god that there is perhaps something more fundamental than (cf Taoism) or co-equal to (cf Dualism, Manichaeism) it].

2. The <u>experiential</u> (or epistemic) <u>transcendence</u> of god is consistent with his <u>ontological immanence</u>, immanence within being, as indeed constellationally overreaching it as the ultimate (dispositional but constitutive) <u>ingredient</u> categorial structure of the world and the alethic truth of the rest of it. But god is neither

(a) saturated by; nor
(b) exhaustive of the rest of being (including man).

3. As ontologically <u>ingredient</u> [though arguably perhaps only in moments of transcendence] but not <u>saturated</u> by man, god is both

(a) ontologically immanent; and
(b) ontologically transcendent—defining an immanence/transcendence spectrum discernible in particular religious traditions and practices.

[God can be neither completely transcendent nor completely immanent. For god must be at least partially immanent if experience of him is to be possible and at least partly transcendent as wider and deeper than man/and/or if non-experience of (at least part of) him is to be possible].

4. As ontologically <u>ingredient</u> but not <u>exhaustive</u> of man (or four-planar social being), god provides only the conditions of possibility of man's activity. God affords or enables, but man selects and determines. The existence of god is thus consistent with error, evil, illusion and 'structural sin'. In particular the presence of god may be occluded and overlain by levels of objectified illusion, alienation and other modalities of structural 'ill-being'.

5. God is at once <u>real</u>, as an alethic ground of (inter alia) pure dispositionality; <u>actualised</u>, as both transcendent being and immanent (ingredient) constitutive structure; and experienced and <u>experienciable</u>, in different ways, by man, most notably in moments of transcendence.

6. God <u>creates</u> (cf as *a* or *the* ultimatum), <u>contains</u>, unifies and bounds [as a fount of unconditional (unifying) love], <u>categorially defines</u> (as existentially constitutive structure) and (as existentially constitutive structure) and <u>grounds</u> (as alethic truth) the rest of the universe, including man.

7. The <u>grounds</u> for god's existence are experiential and practical. And god may be more or less experienced and realised by man.

8. The <u>telos</u> or role of human being is to maximise the presence of god in man, society and the rest of being.

9. God is a <u>transcendent</u> being, although also ingredient [cf as ultimate categorial structure and alethic ground of all grounds] in and experienced by man. What is transcendent lies beyond or between experience, but may be in principle (as in the dialectic of discovery in science) accessed in experience. It may be unbounded or bounded and god may be experienced in either an abstract or a concrete, e.g. personalised, form. And the experience of god may be non-dual (e.g. one of identity or engulfment) or dual (e.g. one of adoration, accompaniment or witnessing).

10. <u>Transcendence</u>, like transcendent, is a relative term. But within the transcendence of a position, situation, problem or dilemma (e.g. in a dialectical learning process) there is a moment of transcendence, characteristic of creation *ex nihilo* in science, artistic inspiration and transformative practices generally. Such moments of transcendence may take the form of awe and/or engulfment in aesthetic and/or religious solitude (e.g. the silence of a Quaker meeting) or in the bustle of activity. It may be dual or non-dual. When the experience is one of god it is typically called spiritual or religious. The qualities of god may be apprehended, as effects, and described as such after transcendence experiences, even if they are in themselves beyond apprehension or in those experiences (perhaps necessarily) beyond description [since they may be ones of subject–object identification].

11. Man is alienated from god, the cosmos and his intrinsic nature. Dealienation depends essentially upon dialectics or practices expressing or informed by—that is, of—<u>unconditional love</u>. Such love expands, heals and unifies (whereas fear contracts, divides and splits). And dealienation then becomes a process of

love for, and therefore union with, the source of all union with the universe—its fundamental binding ground, god or pure unconditional love. Unconditional love is fundamentally for god and the presence of god in the world (in being) is fundamentally that of unconditional love, as the unifying, totalising, liberating force of the universe.

12. As god is its highest order condition of possibility, the ultimatum in the stratification of being and the fount of all possibilities, a permanently or enduringly 'fallen world' characterised by conceptual, real and self-alienation and the alienation of man from God and the rest of the cosmos is not a sustainable one.

* * *

I will have to contextualise this slightly first. Doug (Porpora), Andrew (Collier), Maggie (Archer) and myself are intending jointly to write a book on "Transcendence: Critical Realism and God".[1] We have spent two weekends, both at Brahmes Hall,[2] discussing issues of transcendence, and we found a high degree of convergence, but not identity. It is an independent initiative which is developed from within critical realism but reaches outside it. The first part of the book would be a manifesto which would be written jointly by the four of us. These are twelve propositions which are central to the manifesto which I have formulated. They are my formulations, so I alone take responsibility for these propositions; though I even disagree with one of them! It is not supposed to implicate the CCR or critical realism in any way, it just is twelve propositions on transcendental realism, critical realism and god. As you read through it you will see where the

---

[1] Roy has since withdrawn from this project, which will be published by the other three, with his good wishes, by Routledge, London (forthcoming). According to Roy the main difference between him and his three colleagues lies in Roy's emphasis on ingredience (which is thematised in the discussion), which makes his position at once more compatible with a purely secular interpretation and also to an immanentist understanding on the presence of the divine within being.

[2] In East Anglia, where Roy was living at the time.

critical realism comes in and I think the best thing to do, before we have a general discussion on it, is to ask me questions or make comments on the propositions.

I suppose, to break it down, the first proposition asserts a very general theorem of critical realism, that ontological realism goes alongside epistemological or experiential relativism and judgmental rationalism, and to apply that theorem to god. Now in the square brackets I imply that ontological realism about god is consistent with no god (as well as one or, many gods); so that would make atheism an ontologically realist position. Now in one sense that is right. But in another sense, and this is the only bit of the propositions I disagree with, it is sort of missing the point. Because the whole thrust of this is to be ontologically realist about god in the sense in which, in *Dialectic: The Pulse of Freedom*, I am an ontological realist about structure, contradiction and process.

So what I would like to say is that there are positions about god which collapse it into an epistemological or a purely judgmentalist position (so committing the epistemic fallacy) or which reduce it to its role in society (and I am thinking about constructionists, fictionalists etc.), which are not consistent with ontological realism generally. Against this the ontological realism about god that I am defending here is actually saying that there is, as is clear from the thrust of the next six or seven propositions, in fact something like god which does <u>manifest</u> and is to human beings, and is <u>ingredient</u> in them in specific ways. So that would take us on then to the sort of grounds for such a proposition and the simplest ground lies in experience and the particular kinds of experience that people do have who engage in specific forms of practices, which need not be religious.

These experiences are what I call transcendence experiences and the two crucial propositions here really to get the whole argument going are 9 and 10; and so you might want to take me up in the first instance about this because this should be pretty common ground for all of us.

I think the notion of the transcendent is actually presupposed by transcendental realism and the notion of transcendence is presupposed by dialectical critical realism. So if we can agree on those propositions then we can move through to other ones, say the notion of an ultimatum, which is a category that I used in *Dialectic* and again used after Doug's talk as a general definition of god, which in some way abstracts from his religious (using the word here in a gendered way obviously only for heuristic reasons), from his specific, spiritual, religious qualities. So my suggested way of dealing with this would be to look first at transcendence and the transcendent.

Andrew Collier

I am wondering why, when Roy spoke about god or, he said god or something like a god and that seems to me to be a big possible difference, and one question I would have would be, what would be the difference between substituting the word humankind with a capital H, wherever god is put in this paper. The second point I would raise is there cannot be any such thing as creation *ex nihilo* in science, artistic inspiration or transformative praxis.

Roy

I would like to take you up on both those points. I think you cannot substitute humankind for god just simply because of the non-anthropocentricity which has always been characteristic of transcendental and critical realism. Man is very obviously in the universe and if I am defining god, as I do in my book *From East to West*, basically as being the ultimate categorial structure of the world, which is ingredient but not exhaustive of man, and which is ingredient but not saturated by man, so at this most basic categorial structure of the world must also encompass in some manner and in some form things besides man. It must be wider and deeper than man, so that is why we cannot simply substitute humankind for god, because god, whatever he is, whatever the ultimatum or the absolute or whatever you want to call it is, is going to be the widest and deepest category in the world.

Alan Norrie

I would come back on that and say that by humankind I would not mean man. Humankind as a species being is of course both a social and a natural animal.

Margaret Archer

I still think your emphasis is anthropocentric. One thing we can concede to Alan is that god like any other category or concept is something we can still only know under our own particular descriptions.

Roy

The whole force of transcendental realism is to assert that one can make propositions about the world as it exists independently of human beings and I am applying that same logic to argue that the world is structured, dynamic, is totalising and I want to say ultimately is holistically unified by an ultimatum category which is something like god. Now Maggie's point is in a way an obvious one but it is worth stressing, whatever god is and whatever a structure is, whatever a person is, whatever object of experience it is always known under a particular description in a particular way and that is where the epistemic relativism comes in. So I do not think we disagree on that, or we should not disagree. Now on the question of transcendence you are absolutely right. If we turn to proposition 10 there are two basic inflections of transcendence, one is a relative on which we talk about the transcendence of a situation and you yourself in your brilliant commentary and reading of *Dialectic* have seen that emergence is the general positive bi-polar dual of absence and transcendence is what happens when emergence takes place, and I think that the first part of the next sentence makes it clear that this is a very general characteristic of all dialectical learning processes.

We talk about the transcendence of a position, a situation, problem dilemma, relationship whatever. It need not be a dilemmatic one, it can just be when you move to a new higher vantage point even without a tension.

But the point is that this is absolutely crucial and this is where creation comes in—that the point is that at the moment of creation, the point of emergence itself cannot be induced or deduced from the pre-existing situation. It is the irruption of something qualitatively new, something that was not there before and this is what I called creation *ex nihilo*. But it is of course always, from a transcendent cause on to an immanent ground, it.

Creativity only strikes fertile ground. It is never simply algorithmic. It is always a sort of miracle, a marvellous miracle which is intrinsic to human nature. Moreover, in so far as praxis is genuinely transformative, it always embodies an aspect of creation *ex nihilo* and this defines the novelty, the irreducibility and irreversibility in the development and evolution of the human species. I think it is a remarkable feature about the world that emergence occurs, that it is irreversible and tensed, that new things do happen and this is just what the old deductivists and inductivists logic could never account for science.

All creativity and creation is *de novo*, and all creativity *de novo* contains a moment of creativity *ex nihilo*, from the epistemically unmanifest. But the epistemically unmanifest is not necessarily ontologically non-immanent. (In fact it is difficult to see what is meant by the ontologically non-immanent.) If it is ontologically immanent then it could come from within and/or without, the first tends towards platonic anamnesis, the second to a self-revelation of an alethic truth of another being to or in an experience which is prepared for or attuned to it. The first points in the direction of an immanent ingredient ground (in which possibly all other truths may be enfolded). The second points to its ground in something like the cosmic force of love. On the second we have the accessibility of an alethic truth outside us, in virtue of something like the cosmic force of love, at the level of what I have called the ultimatum, an ultimatum, which in virtue of being one universe is going to enfold us all and make access from one region or experience or part of it to another in principle possible, as the ultimatum would contain the ground of all alethic truths; this ultimatum is always going to be greater than any particular ingredient within it.

Now, to revert to transcendence, in that sense, that moment of transcendence within the transcendence that is absolute transcendence, it is creation from nowhere on to an immanent ground, and that has correlates in the sort of inspiration that artists find when they suddenly make a breakthrough or the inspiration you might find when you are going for a walk in nature. I personally, if you want to know my own personal experience of god or what I would call god, they come as much from nature or music as they do from anything which is a specifically religious practice and these are experiences of transcendence. Now in this particular context where they are experiences of something other than oneself they typically break down subject–object identity, they are typically experiences in which one finds oneself in a non-dual state in which one is engulfed, in which one is inspired, in which they are experiences of awe, or identity (but not necessarily), they can also be dual experiences where you experience some being or entity or thought which gives a specific quality to one's experience. Which here I say non-legislatively allow it to be self-defined as spiritual or religious which is an experience which the person who has it calls one of god or the ultimate or the absolute. So there is really a three-way progression, there is transcendence in the relative sense which is very unproblematic, there is transcendence in the absolute sense which is the moment of creation *ex nihilo*, then there is transcendence in the specifically spiritual sense which may be either dual or non-dual where what the person who is experiencing believes subsequent to that experience, or in that experience he is experiencing is an experience of god himself.

What we are dealing with here is clearly a dialectic, involving the co-presence of duality and non-duality. Now duality sows the seeds of dualism and dualism inevitably generates a contradiction, conflict and split. Reasserting the role of non-duality, more generally the role of the transcendent, which I here identify with the ultimate ingredient in man, allows us to capture a sense in which the reaffirmation of that realm of non-duality can set the agenda for a dialectic of disemergence, which would liberate the elements of heteronomy at present overlaying that essential ingredient element; and roll back the realm of duality, generating dualism and oppositional split, so better enabling us to fight the war between war and peace, heteronomy and autonomy, duality and non-duality. This is a different war, a different struggle to the wars and struggles within the realm of war, heteronomy and duality. It is a war on and against the ground of the dichotomies and oppositional splits which occupy most of our thoughts and attention today. Recognising the realm of non-duality is the first step for liberating it and allows us to shift the balance of forces in the co-presence of duality and non-duality, and so empower the dialectics of disemergence or shedding both within us and outside us, in the rest of creation.

Now, to go back to the experience of god, the condition of possibility of this is that god is ingredient in man, that is my own thesis. That to be able to have this subject–object identification with god or the divine, we must ourselves be in some manner or part, divine, or godlike. I argue this in more secular terms at the meeting on critical realism and ethics when I said that we are essentially free but our freedom is occluded and overlain by layers of illusion, alienation, dualism, split, reification, commodification. This form, this dialectics of co-presence, the dialectics of autonomous and heteronomous determinations in man, is characteristic of the structure of both western and eastern, both libertarian and mystical thought.

Andrew

So is there anything special in saying that god is ingredient in man, are you prioritising man in that?

Roy

I myself would say, absolutely, each species has to be concretely singularised, and the ancient Greeks had a dispute about whether each species should not have a different god because each species sort of formed god in its own image. I would say that at the basic structure of the universe god would be ingredient in everything. One could even say that god is ingredient in evil, though only in the sense that the energy and power of the most ultimate level in the universe would need to be utilised or abused in some way in order to sustain itself within that universe.

To say that god is ingredient in man (and to suppose that this ingredient is a particular person's alethic truth or essential nature) is to say one or both of two things:

1. That there is actually a bit of god in man; and/or
2. That there is actually the potentiality within that person or being, the potentiality to access, in virtue of the ingredience of god in man, all the alethic truths of all other things which are bound by the same ultimate which sustains the whole

universe and manifests in particular forms in particular beings as their own deepest, most essential, nature or their specific alethias.

To go back to the question of the particular form of god, and the form that we find easiest to worship, would be a form in which it were embodied in, a personabilistic or human lifelike way. Thus if you were a Christian you would say you worshipped god in the form of Jesus or if you are Hindu in the form of Krishna, a Buddhist possibly in the form of god. You can certainly combine an impersonal conception of an absolute god, such as the Hindu Brahman and a relative or personalistic conception of a particular deity or form of manifestation of the absolute. And this is also the way in which a fundamental monotheism, at the absolute level, is susceptible to a variety of different religious declensions and within any one religion interpretations or practices of communion or worship. In other words one can accept that there is a single god which manifests itself in a variety of different ways to peoples of different religions. But I am not a theologian. I am an ontologist and this is relatively new territory for me. I have only been interested in these issues seriously for the last couple of years.

Andrew

I suppose your response there would knock me back to my first question which is why not talk about humankind, if you are going to say that it is ingredient in man, that there is some special nexus there then you are as anthropocentric as I was.

Roy

Not at all, I mean this is the way we know him. I may have grounds for believing there are lots of other universes besides the universe I apprehend but the only universe I can describe is the universe I apprehend. I can certainly posit the possibility of universes other than the one I know, and I may know that there are universes (or at least many things) that I can never know because of the limits of my own sensibility. Put it like this, for me god is the basic structure of the world, that basic structure of the world is also ingredient in man, but in a concretely singularised way: that is in man as a particular species, and then within each human being, as concretely singularised members of that species. So for me, and this may or may not be a far out theological position, each person would have a unique godliness about them. God would both be ingredient in them and may at the same time manifest himself to them in a uniquely singular way. This ingredient may or may not be what Christians have referred to as their souls.

Andrew

It strikes me that you just added the word godly to what *Dialectic: Pulse of Freedom* says anyway.

Roy

If it is justified then it is certainly an important addition; or it may be that godly might be there implicitly or godly might be implicitly in it, but if so it is there without any conscious intent, because certainly god was very far from my conscious thoughts when I wrote that book. However I would say that there is a dialectic, a process at work in intellectual development, in which you will inevitably discover a tacit presupposition of your own work which you had left out. In this case the tacit presupposition lay in the realm of the ultimata. But I think this is the only way of making sense and resolving the antinomies that I went through at that meeting on critical realism and ethics. The antinomy of western libertarianism including communism and Marxism, believing that man is essentially free and that freedom can be fully realised and yet is everywhere in chains, for instance in societies amock with reification and commodification. The paradox of the fact is that we believe realism to be true and yet the surface categorial structure of our society is irrealist. The dialectics of co-presence makes understanding this possible, and I think it can be very liberating. People do often use god as an excuse, as a substitute for action. But if you realised that god in a way only works through you or that god and freedom are two different ways of saying the same thing, or that god and freedom or creativity are only different ways of saying essentially the same thing, slightly different nuances on a basic level of reality, then I think this thought is quite empowering and puts a great onus on the agent.

Margaret

I accept the transcendent moment in science, but how is this a development of critical realism which until now, as I understood it, has based its claims on rationally?

Roy

What I do in my forthcoming book[3] is to try and show how dialectical critical realism, through its different moments, successively uncovers deeper and more elemental presuppositions in the stratification of being, thus not only dispositional but categorial realism, not only transcendence but also transcendent totality, at a level which is ultimate, which together amounts to a rough approximation of what some traditional theologies would have called god, but also has an experiential aspect, in what people apprehend, as spiritual experience as the experience of the divine. So I am only making out a plausible case; it is not like an ontological argument, it is not a proof of god's existence, it is just saying that this is consonant with critical realism, critical realism can make sense of a lot of theology, a lot of religious or spiritual practice, while in its judgmental rationalist aspect critiquing practices from many points of view; and from many points of view I should say religions are the worst enemy of true spirituality. I can make sense of it and it actually expands our conceptual repertoire if we begin to talk about ultimates; and then translating it into slightly more human terms, we talk about categories like love. We have all been very critical of instrumental reasoning and reification; but we have not talked about, have not theorised, so how do we suppose we understand the practice of their opposites. Do we really know what kind of society we want; and what would be the binding forces of that society if they are not to be money.

---

[3] *From East to West*, Routledge, London and New York, 2000.

Mervyn Hartwig

. . . I can see that one can easily get to ultimata and call that god, I do not mind, but what logical steps do you take to get to love. And I would prefer to leave out the unconditional to be frank. Why don't you just call it love?

Roy

The point of calling it unconditional is because most love in our society is conditional and therefore it is not love. Most love is a kind of instrumental reasoning or exchange in terms of which you are working out what you can get for what you give, which is something which is best expressed in the market and not called love.

Mervyn

But how do you relate the ultimata to love?

Roy

There are a set of arguments which relate the ultimata as the fundamental category of the universe to being the binding totalising power, which holds things together, and to the properties of love as expanding, healing and unifying, bringing entities and things together. It might be argued that love is a misnomer if not applied to the human world. However I want to go further than that. In fact I think with suitable graduations you can go from it to the ultimate categorial structure of the universe, the binding holistic power of the universe to love as what I called the cement of the universe (in a deliberate ironical reflection on Hume), to love as a unifying force and a liberating force for human beings. Of course if you only want to use a concept like love to refer to present human forms of love then you are going to find it very difficult to apply it to non-human beings let alone to pure examples of great spiritual love, not to mention the universe as a whole. But part of the dialectical process of thought is stretching our concepts so as to capture realities which we have barely comprehended let alone begun to live.

Maggie

We are going to need some new kind of binding force for socialist post-monetarist utopias, if what is going to hold us together is not going to be the principles of the market.

Mervyn

Is it because we need a concept for what the universe consists of ultimately, that we can relate to that you call it love?

Roy

The argument, if you start with the ultimate categorial structure of the universe, that is the structure that keeps the universe together, that is the binding force, that is the totalising force, this is the sort of thing that we mean by love, as a power of uniting, healing, and dealienating.

Question

How do you arbitrate between some crazy group of sects and a well authenticated religion?

Roy

This is where judgmental rationalism comes in. You have to be very careful about going from ontological and experiential propositions to judging particular claims about a particular tradition. I would have to know about the particular sect in question. I do not know much about many of them. But I know quite a lot about capitalists, Quakers, Buddhists, Muslims, Hindus and I know that they all have authentic claims to authentic experience. I also know that many of them engage in practices which can be criticised in terms of the traditions, doctrines and experiences and original intentions of the traditions which they inhabit. Fundamentalism and all kinds of religious chauvinism and communalism are completely contrary to the basic premises of almost all religions. On the other hand within almost all religions you will find a great overlap and sometimes quite surprising ones. For example Sufism and Kabalah and Gnostic Christianity and Yoga and Vedanta and of course many Buddhist and Taoist practices all show great affinity, they practice similar forms of meditation, and they offer similar characterisations of the ultimate and the way to the ultimate as well as interpretations of the journey of life; they are amazingly convergent. But then of course there are many other traditions which are very different again. Exactly the same in science.

Tony Lawson

I am happier than Mervyn with the things we have been talking about but I am a bit lost when you say god is the widest and deepest structure of the universe. Is that a definition or the development of an argument or what?

Roy

It is the development of an argument, which is why I have a certain objection because the way the rest of the propositions go make it clear that whatever god is, god is the ultimate, the ultimate categorial structure of the world, and I think this is really our position, at least that is my position. There is a sort of meta-ontological realism. I am just saying in my opinion god is, and that whatever god is, god is the ultimate. I am saying now that it is not possible for there to be a more basic category, contrary to what is said in the parentheses in proposition1. I do not actually believe that propositions 2 to 12 are consistent with the idea that there is a higher category than god. So for me it is pretty definitional that god is the ultimatum. But I do understand that there are religious and spiritual traditions which assert the contrary, though, say in the case of Taoism, I am not even sure that the greatest thing or the greatest ultimate, which is absence or emptiness out of which both heaven and earth emerge, is not also god.

One motivation for referring to the ultimatum as love is because the absolute or ultimate would also have to have all the properties, including the holistic, binding, liberating power which in the human world we call love. Which we insisted must be and is only unconditional.

Question

So how does that differ from life force?

Roy

It is not different. It is the holistic, totalising, evolving, unifying, expanding. . .

Could I just take us to proposition 4. It is ontologically ingredient but not exhaustive of man. A higher-order structure provides the conditions of possibility of a lower-order structure; it does not determine activity at that level. That is vital. Physics defines the conditions of possibility of biological human phenomena, human phenomena define the conditions of possibility of social phenomena. God provides the conditions of possibility and man selects them. And so man and man alone is responsible for evil and in his social aspect for what we call structural sin. That is structural ill being. Now this is really a neat way of resolving or coming close to adequately conceptualising the problem of evil by putting it in the context of a dialectical critical realist concept of the stratification of being. Because god's goodness is untainted by man's evil, if I can put it that way. Now the thing is of course that it is most important to insist that god is both beyond and yet contains though does not cause evil.

If you just take the stratification of being, a higher-order structure will be immanent in, ingredient in but will typically transcend or exceed or overreach a lower-order structure. The model of the relationship between god and man is exactly the same as that. I myself would think it very unlikely that the ultimatum did not manifest itself in a plurality of different ways and forms but that is my personal view.

Mervyn

Did you really not think about god before? This is astonishing to me, everyone knew it was going to lead to god. I am merely asking out of journalistic responsibility.

Roy

The honest truth is that I had transcendent experiences in my youth, I became agnostic, atheist in my late teens. I have never been unsympathetic to any forms of experience, I have always been open minded and tolerant, but I had no interest in spiritual or religious phenomena, no particular interest in arguments about god. Up to and including the time that I wrote *Dialectic* and *Plato Etc.*

Mervyn

Did it not occur to you that you might be opening that box?

Roy

No, I can honestly say that it did not occur to me. I was so immersed in the immanent critique, the actual process of critique that the next step did not occur to me. That often happens to scientists, or philosophers or writers; they are so involved in their work that they cannot see the next step whereas someone from the outside can. I had a period of physical illness in the sense that I had a couple of months in which I had a succession of colds and I could not finish another book, which was to be called *philosophical ideologies* which was about ten pages away from being finished. I took a holiday and started thinking about these things, Christmas of 1994. That is the honest truth. Since then I have been trying to integrate practical experiences with philosophical developments in a new direction which is as yet very far from being complete.

Tony

Can you tell me a bit about how you defend proposition 8?

Roy

In so far as we want to say that we have a purpose in life then it must be to realise our true essence. Now the highest order structure within man must be god, if god is ingredient in man. Because by definition he is the ultimatum and our heteronomy and evil, illusion and all the ills that befall humanity come from other emergent levels of structure, which heteronomously block our freedom and so by maximising the presence of god, our godliness in ourselves, in society and the rest of nature, we fulfil our true intrinsic nature. That is human flourishing. The ethic that brings this out very nicely for me is actually the Bhagavad Gita which makes the very simple point that man is basically like the sun or a flower; and when you think about it, the sun does not try to shine it just shines, so that what we ought to do in our life is to fulfil our true intrinsic nature, our innermost essence. Now for all the reasons I have given, our innermost essence is free, is godlike, is actually a fount of unconditional love and of tremendous untapped possibilities. Put on a social scale it is the free development of each as the condition of the free development of all. And that I see is quite frankly our role in life, that is why we are here, that is the purpose of human existence. And if you try and denude human beings from teleology then I think we are going to end up with a mechanism again. Now some people might have said well, dialectic does not have any use for teleology, but then your external outsider would have said well, it is bound to lead to it sooner or later, and of course there was an implicit teleology in it and this is just bringing it out.

You have got to follow the truth wherever it takes you. If I had gone for popularity I would never have published *A Realist Theory of Science*.

Tony

Strategy does not matter, truth matters.

Roy

I just want to say that I believe the time for this turn is right, it may not turn out that way when my book is read, when all the books are read, when our joint book is read, it may not seem so outrageous, just as it is not so outrageous to you or to Sean or to Tony, even though we have not come to the same conclusions. It may seem outrageous to some critical realists now. But then you have to ask were they good critical realists, were they actually accepting arguments on the basis of truth or merely because of gut feeling or popularity or something like that.

Tony

What human practices get you to the idea that our telos is to maximise the presence of god.

Roy

Well there are arguments from the ultimata, arguments from the binding power of the universe, its holistic totalising properties, arguments about the necessity of understanding human beings as evolving, about the co-presence of the autonomous and heteronomous and practices, about practices of love, spiritual inspiration, religious worship, scientific discovery etc.

The thing is that what I think we are all trying to avoid doing is to say: look, there is a simple argument for the existence of god and this is not like an ontological argument, we cannot prove the existence of god in that way. There might be a day we can work out waterproof dialectical and transcendental arguments for the existence of god. But we are not going down that road, at least we are not going down that road for the moment, at the same time we do not want to validate all forms of claimed religious experience, we are talking about the possibilities, the possibilities of apprehending what Margaret has called the intimation of divinity, or what I have called transcendence experiences. For someone who has not had these experiences the notion of god will be a purely intellectual one and it will be that much poorer. For someone who has had these experiences it will be a rich experiential concept as well. To someone who only has those experiences, it will just be an empirical concept without the theoretical richness that it can have. So here again we need reasons and experience, we need the union of the two, just as in science. So you cannot do it by ontological arguments or theoretical considerations alone and you cannot do it by reference to spiritual practices or religious experiences alone; this turn is about the meshing of the two together and seeing how they cohere.

Chapter Six

Critical Realism, Co-presence and Making a Difference*

The first thing I want to say is that critical realism is not a fixed, rigid system of thought, it is not dogma, it is not a set of doctrines. I would like to begin by quoting something that Marx said which is quite well known about the dialectic. But if you substitute critical realism then I think that may also be appropriate. Marx said, 'in its mystified form the dialectic became the fashion in Germany because it seemed to transfigure and glorify what exists. In its rational form it is a scandal and abomination to the bourgeoisie and their docrinaire spokesman because it includes in its understanding of what exists a simultaneous recognition of its negative, its inevitable destruction, because it regards every developed form as being in a fluid state, in motion and therefore grasps its transient aspect as well and because it does not let itself be impressed by anything, being in its very essence critical and revolutionary.'

I think what we have got to do before we can see how and why critical realism makes a difference is to understand that critical realism acts like a stone thrown into a pond, producing ripples.

---

* Introductory Plenary and discussions at CCR/IACR Conference at Lancaster, UK, 18 August 2000.

Ripples that may gather momentum depending upon the circumstances and other agencies. It is a dynamic, multidimensional, expanding research programme in which each moment or aspect is only developmentally consistent with the next or succeeding one. Indeed it may be that from a certain perspective the next moment is the alethic truth of the previous moment; but critical realism is in spread-eagling motion and what part of that dynamic movement you, or any particular individual or collectivity or community or discipline or organisation, is affected by will be entirely dependent on your own particular circumstances, the state, discipline of your art or practice and what you as individuals find authentic and useful and above all true. It is not a dogma, it is not a fixed or closed system of thought; it is a process in continual motion, aiming to convert ripples into waves.

Let us take a few illustrations from the development of critical realism. I will relate this mainly to my part in it, though mine is only one aspect of the whole movement of critical realism. Then in *A Realist Theory Of Science,* for instance, the transitive dimension was sharply differentiated from the intransitive dimension, so ontology was separated from epistemology. That was very important because it was absolutely essential to situate ontology as an important and necessary subject for philosophical discourse. So then of course we have to ask what is epistemology, what is the subject matter of epistemology, systems of thought. But of course systems of thought are themselves part of being. Therefore epistemology has to be included within ontology, and so this very sharp distinction, this very useful distinction between transitive and intransitive dimensions, breaks down. In the same way— I did not realise that my own session was going to be immediately followed by a wholesale attack on my latest book! For the seemingly innocuous concept of the ultimatum that I introduced in the *Dialectic: The Pulse Of Freedom* became in *From East to West* the concept of the absolute which is customarily referred to as god. To be a critical realist you must have a sense of what I think is essential to all intellectual creativity, a being continually on the move. If you stand in the same place then you are basically reifying yourself, your thought and your activity. Moreover you are freezing the world and we as critical realists do not want to do this individually or as a movement. So the first thing I want to say is that critical realism is not a dogma, is not fixed nor a closed system of thought nor is it identifiable with any one text by any one author. The driving impulse behind critical realism, however, if there is a unified theme, is it does seem to me to be the drive to freedom. And in fact if you think about it freedom is opposed to every form of reification, every form of fixity, every form of rigidity. To be free is to be open and to be able to be continually on the move, to be in the moment, not to be structured, but not to be unstructured either; and it depends on being deep, on going very deep, as I will indicate later on.

What I am saying is that we are all essentially and basically, individually, completely and totally free. Absolutely free. But we are also oppressed and the basic dynamic behind the research activity of critical realism has been a kind of dialectic in which we progressively get rid of, shed, overcome layers of structures and systems of thought and ways of acting which overlay and occlude and are parasitic upon our freedom. This is by no means unique to critical realism. This is a very characteristic motif of radical libertarian thought. It is essential for the work of both Rousseau and Marx but also to the work of Chomsky and many other libertarians from different schools. The basic presupposition that I want to stress is that we have ourselves, at some level, actually got all it takes, are free and getting it right; but we have also got an awful lot else as well, in virtue of which most of our activity and our life is compromised. That is not just an individual thing, it is a collective thing, what we have got to do is get rid of those bits, those components of the compromise, which are not essential to us. How does this relate to the question of how critical realism or any other philosophical idea can make a difference. Why does it matter?

Well, I think critical realism is in the enormously unique position of being able to say why it itself matters. What critical realists say is that thought, reasons, intentionality are and must be causally efficacious—that is, make a difference to the world. That presupposes the emergence of reasons from physical, material causes and that presupposes that intentionality is causally efficacious, makes a difference to the pattern of material events that would otherwise not occur. That is a very profound and differentiating feature about critical realism, something which in virtue of its conception of emergence can sustain (but which many materialists would deny), the claim that thought makes a difference. For agency presupposes intentionality and intentionality presupposes, even when it is spontaneous, thought or belief or ideation of some kind. Moreover, not only is it the case that thought causally affects the world, but it is the case that if we have false thoughts or thoughts that are not true in the world then we are going to make errors and we are going to fall into illusion of one kind or another. Illusions are or can be (though untrue) causally efficacious, make a difference in the world—this is what I have tried to capture in the concept of the 'demi-real'. This immediately makes truth a very fundamental norm. Let us think for a moment about how critical realism in its development can, in virtue of providing truer conceptions of the nature of the world, come to better inform human practice and better inform our understanding of the world and better enable us to lead the lives that I think we are capable of.

I will briefly recapitulate what will no doubt be very familiar to a lot of you, what I think are the five main moments in the development of critical realism. The first was transcendental realism and that essentially situated ontology and it showed the necessity for ontology. Basically what we argued was that every philosophy of science, every epistemology, every system of thought presupposed an account of a world, and that was a very radical thought because people like Wittgenstein had said that there is no need to talk about what the network describes, just talk about language, just talk about the way we talk about the world. That of course was an extremely paradoxical thing to say because that talk about the world was itself in the world, so how do you talk about the world unless that talk about the world had a referent, namely the talk? So actually ontology is inevitable and inexorable. What transcendental realism did was it said not only is ontology inevitable and inexorable, but a particular ontology is inevitable and inexorable. The world is structured, differentiated and chang-ing. The pre-existing epistemologies of the 60s and 70s, just as the non-critical realist ontologies today, presuppose an account of the world as being flat, undifferentiated and unchanging. If the world is in fact structured and differentiated and changing this brings about a fantastically liberating change in our conceptions of the world. Because of structure there is a lever, because of differentiation we appreciate why we do not always see it and because of change we realise that we can use it. And use it we must.

The second major moment of critical realism was called critical naturalism. This consisted in the attempt to take the insights of transcendental realism over to deal with the specificity of the human sciences. And basically what was happening about the time of the 70s and is still happening today was that the social sciences were split by dichotomies between positivism and hermeneutics, between structure and agency, between individualism and collectivism, between reasons and causes, between mind and body, and between fact and value. In each case the critical realist moment was to say the dichotomies and oppositions were completely false, and that in fact there was a third sublating, transcending position which could situate both the truth and the falsity of the poles of the dichotomy, for instance in doing justice both to the generality of science and the specificity of the social sciences. That led on to the third moment in which explanatory critique came to the fore. Once we accept, as we must with critical naturalism, by the way on the second level that thought makes a difference, we accept the intentional causality of reasons, then of course it is immediately clear how critical realism can sustain itself and why truth is so important. For the explanatory critical moment said that not only is truth important if you want to avoid error, but that factual truth, truth about matters of fact are in fact presupposed by and can be shown to imply evaluative or factual judgments, so it broke the great bridge between science and morality that western philosophy had been lumbered with at least since, and probably well before, the days of Hume and Kant.

The fourth element in the development of critical realism, and again I must stress this is just my own interpretation of it, was the dialectical moment. This turns on what Alan Norrie has nicknamed the MELD formula. This was in fact a dynamic structure which turned on four moments. The first was what I called

1M, which is the first moment of ontology, of structure and most importantly of alethic truth. This said that if you go into a multidimensional analysis of truth, we can see that ultimately there must be a conception, a level of truth which goes beyond the feeling of trust me, act on it, which goes beyond the feeling of this, is an adequate representation of reality, which goes beyond the feeling of this, expresses the way the world is but goes deeper to the level of saying, this is the reason why the world is the way it is and when we get to that level then we get to the alethic truth of a matter of fact. And that is what characteristically happens in science when a scientist will find the reason for some superficial phenomena in a deeper one. According to the arguments I have lately been adducing *the alethic truth of irrealism is in fact realism*. Similarly the alethic truth of reification, of hypostasised and alienated structures depends on, that is to say the condition of possibility of that, is the essential creativity of human beings. The alethic truth, condition of possibility of heteronomy, of unfreedom is our essential freedom, an autonomy which is masked, occluded, overlain and suppressed, that is actually reduced by the more superficial structures which dominate it, socially and in our everyday practice. So the concept of alethic truth is a very important one. And it takes the whole idea that thought matters, a necessary condition for intentional agency whether in objectified, materialised or purely ideational form, undisputably the dominant force in human history, a degree further to say that getting our conception of the alethic truth of things right really matters and affects our practice essentially.

The second moment of dialectical critical realism was the most important one, at least for me, and this turned on absence. The whole of western philosophy had been dominated by a purely positive conception of being. But just think, for instance, how important the pause is between words, how important space, the gap, the hiatus is in any form. What was above all absent from western philosophy was absence. In *Dialectic: The Pulse Of Freedom*, I argued that the dialectic turned on absence, specifically determinate absence, and gave a recursive definition of it as being the absenting of absences (as constraints) on absenting absences (as ills). In this second development, what I called second edge, the key notion was of course dialectic itself. In a way I think in that particular book I did not do sufficient justice really to the rational kernel of Hegel. The mystical shell was ontological monovalence, the installation of a purely positivist account of being so that his dialectical idealism was in fact also, as Marx noticed, a tacit positivism. But the rational kernel is very important and very strong. It is a dialectical learning process, a developmental process in which apparent, positive contraries are turned, transmuted into special cases of a general or higher sublating position so they appear as negative sub-contraries. And this is the mechanism of scientific progress, the mechanism of every act of creation, this is the stepping, letting the fly out of the fly bottle that Wittgenstein famously talked about; this is what happens whenever we make a conceptual leap, whenever we feel that we have touched a new level or we have grasped a new truth, or we are to a greater degree free. This was the essence of the rational kernel. Now the actual mechanism of the moment of transition in this rational kernel involved what I have called the dialectics of *co-presence*, which turned on the way in which two apparently contrary things can simultaneously co-exist. I will come back to this in a moment. The fourth element in the dialectic was what I called the platinum plate and this was the way in which looking at a system of thought, especially (but not only) a causally efficacious and/or dominant system of thought, that was secreted by a society gave us a clue as to the character of that society. I would say that there is an extraordinary paradox here that realists have to face and that is this: If realism is true, if it is really true, why is it that irrealism is so dominant? Well irrealism is so dominant because it reflects the irrealist, reified, heteronomous, oppressive structures of the societies in which we exist. Realism can only be conceived to be true if it reflects a deeper, more basic level which most of us have not fully developed or have so overlaid with structures that are irrealist in character that we find it difficult either to see why most people are irrealist, reified or unfree or to believe that realism, freedom, spontaneity, creativity, love, can actually be alethically true.

Now most of us would accept. Whatever level or moment of realism we feel to be most important, whatever aspect is most sufficient for us, if realism is really true, then we will have the *co-presence of an irrealist superstructure and a realist infrastructure.* Now that is essentially the model of freedom that I tried to articulate in *From East to West,* this is that although we are all essentially unique, we are all essentially free and the only reason we cannot express this freedom is because that freedom is overlaid, dominated and occluded by structures which are nevertheless completely parasitical upon it. Just as Humean ontology would not work in practice if it did not presuppose critical realist ontology, the network of master–slave relationships could not continue without the creativity and dynamism of the slaves. Similarly no social form could survive which was not sustained at some level by relationships of solidarity and love. What we have got to do, and all we have got to do is to *shed* everything individually and socially that we are essentially not and realise everything that we essentially are. This is a project which can be seen to be continuous, a dialectic of disemergence, with my earlier definitions of emancipation as the elimination of unwanted and unnecessary determinations. Getting now to what we essentially are requires of course a conjugated process which I will simplify here. It requires some mode of access to your freedom and to our social freedom, whether it is in individual or collective form. In fact it is not difficult to get this access, because we utilise it all the time, it is our freedom, our creative ingenuity, our loving here which sustains the whole social edifice and our psychic make up. Realising this access, we become aware of the co-presence within our own being of opposed, autonomous and heteronomous determinations or elements. As it is the autonomous ones which define our essen-tial nature, we will be spontaneously set on a dialectic of liberation. A dialectic of liberation, a project of dis-emerging that which enslaves us. The requisite, the desideratum is the shedding itself: this is the moment of revolution, the moment of liberation, the moment of emancipation, the moment of our enlightened man. This then requires simultaneously the full embodiment, the complete realisation of that freedom in one's own being and in our social being. And finally it requires, at each moment, a conti-nual process of witnessing, of being aware of what is going on in and around one, of awareness without judgment; just being aware, that is witnessing itself; will spontaneously lead to the necessary action, flowing from our innermost nature, the ground of our being, at the moment heteronomously compromised. So all we have to do to be free is to get rid of everything that we are not.

****

How then does critical realism make a difference; and how is this connected to the theme of the co-presence of good and evil, truth and falsity, of freedom and oppression and all the other opposites we have talked about? Critical realism, in virtue of the causal efficacy of ideas, can make a crucial difference, especially once we accept categorial realism, to the way we think, feel and live our lives in that ongoing struggle, in which a world of non-duality, of transcendence and freedom is dominated and occluded by what it sustains. Critical realism can help to eliminate the perceptual occlusion and cognitive delusion which hides the alethic truth of human beings from themselves: namely the qualities of freedom, creativity, love and intelligence, which sustain, in their expression, in the activities of everyday life, all the structures of oppression which are currently hurtling the planet into crisis and into the very real possibility of an early demise. When we realise, contrary to the claims of vulgar (including I have to say Marxist) materia-lism, the enormous causal efficacy of ideas we can see how the philosophy of critical realism can come to empower the dialectic of disemergence or shedding, of emancipation necessary to save the human race and the other species with which we co-exist on this planet. In this struggle, there is one enormous factor on our side, namely that there is a relationship of unilateral dependency of those structures of evil and oppression on that foundational layer of good and freedom which I have identified here as the essential nature or alethic truth of man.

Question

I would like to ask Roy Bhaskar whether he sees the moments of critical realism as necessary or contingent, in the sense that they are compatible with other possibilities.

Roy

I would say both. Certainly I think each moment presupposes the next; and I would say that the alethic truth at any one level is the moment that succeeds it, so there is a definite logical order, at least in the way I have tried to develop and present it. However there are also always going to be many possible lines of development. It is a necessary truth that if there is one way to resolve a problem there is in principle and infinite number of ways to resolve that problem. And people in this room have been developing critical realism simultaneously and alongside me in all sorts of different ways. For instance Alan Norrie and Nick Hostettler have been pursuing the dialectical path, while people such as Andrew Collier and Margaret Archer have been working on questions of ultimata and god. But I do believe that all these steps are dialecti-cally related, that is my own belief, one can have sequential development and simultaneous spread. If you want to use one aspect of my work or of critical realism generally that is absolutely fine and if you want to reject a particular thesis or think that a line of research is not fruitful that is fine too. Anything else would be totally inconsistent with my belief in concretely singularised, uniquely individual freedom. Moreover no one's beliefs system should be static, and my view at any one moment of time will not be the same as another; nor in one context as in a different one. All this is consistent, organically, dialectically consistent with transcendental dialectical critical realism.

Question

Do you think that there is a correct or essential interpretation of your work, or is it consistent with multiple interpretations?

Roy

I think it is a completely false theory of meaning to suppose a single unique meaning to any concept, in any sentence or any text. Meaning is so multilayered, so multidimensional that an author is even not aware of all the meanings that he or she is utilising in trying to put across some point. The interesting thing if you think about critical realist works and critical realism is that we can accept entirely different interpretations of the same basic thesis or argument. Two of the best introductions to my work in particular are books by Andrew Collier and William Outhwaite. They both happen to be friends of mine and very substantial intellects; but they are completely different interpretations and both are completely authentic. Some people have said which has got me right? And that is a question I refuse to answer. They both got me right.

Of course there are certain propositions which I would deny could be deduced from a text; but there is much more in a text than any one author ever intends or knows. So I think what you are implying about multiple meanings is very true. Everything we say has meaning which is holistic, part of a pattern which draws on the past, several lines of development which looks out to the future, which has many levels of depth and has infinite potentiality. All those are, if you like, moments of critical realism. Thus infinite potentiality is a dispositional realist concept. So if we had a true critical realist account of meaning then any monistic account of my meaning, or the meaning of a single word or single sentence, any single meaning interpretation would be completely false. In fact I do not see how a language could be learnt or understood or what point there would be in communication unless we all came from different experiences and so put a different slant or spin on the words and sentences we used and the texts to which we referred, including that text which is the world.

Question

How did it come about that we acquired the baggage which needs to be absented at the moment arrive?
Was there an original state free of what you call heteronomy?

Roy

I would not entirely rule out conceptions of primitive communism. However I do not think at the moment that we can empirically validate them. Whether there was a point, a moment or span in space and time when we were completely, utterly free, is a very interesting question. However I think the development of our society is now the truly important thing—for oppression is accumulatively building up and ills multiply rapidly one upon the other. Now we are in a very precarious state in which we are actually undermining and destroying the ecology of our planet so it is quite likely and possible that unless we radically transform our social structures and our own individual collective ways of acting that planet earth will not exist as a viable habitat in the next fifty years.

Question

What does the word 'alethia' mean, where did you get that from?

Roy

Alethia really just means real. It is a Greek term for reality and truth. So it is our truth as reality. For me it is a conception of truth which is not an epistemic conception but an ontological one, specifying the deep or ultimate ground of something more superficial apprehended in our consciousness as an epistemically validated truth. It can be translated in Greek as being real or truth, but if it is translated as being truth then it has to be understood as reality as well, and if it is translated as reality it has to be understood as being true, so it is not the false, reified, superficial structures that I am talking about, but the underlying essential grounds. Our true nature, our true self would be our alethic truth. So there are different orders of truth and different orders of reality. We can say some realities are more real than others.

Question

In *From East to West* you highlight an important point about basic action, which is I think indispensable.

Roy

What you are talking about is what in *From East to West* I called spontaneous right-action and when you think about it most of us, when we are having a conversation or discussion or eating a meal, catching a bus or driving a car, we are not thinking about it, we are just doing it. This is a spontaneous unthought basic action; if you like, non-dual action, that is action not mixed with anything else. So acting in a way which is not mediated consciously by thought is both indispensable and often just right. Thus when you are in a critical situation, you will spontaneously do something which manifests the unconditional love you have within yourself, like rescuing a baby, saving someone else, perhaps saving them humiliation, it does not matter, it will be an expression of unconditional love. If you *think about it* you probably will not do it.

* * * *

Nick Hostettler

I am really much happier with the road you were taking in your dialectical work, than the way you are going now. For instance, when you say things like space time and causality are real entities that would seem to me to be [reifying] them, taking causality for example as an entity existing independently of us. But causality is not an entity, it is a category.

Roy

It seems to me that unless you accept categorial realism you are going to have to go down one of two equally disastrous roads. If you do not allow any level of rich, deep, philosophical description of the world to refer to the world then philosophy can have no purchase on the world. If you do not allow space, time, causality, law to have a referent in the world, then you are going to have to attenuate the totality of levels in being to a single stratum or point which you assume to be the only correct or real level, which would not then allow you to talk about both electronic structure and tables or both tables and the curvature of space. Or else, what you are going to end up doing, which is in effect almost what you did at one point, is to say that being is ineffable, that we cannot name or describe it in any way. I think that is what is going to happen. What I argue in *From East to West* is that there is a fundamental subjectivism about our categories in western philosophical thought, which you find in Kant, you find in Popper, which does not allow us to distinguish real categories in the world (described in an abstract or high level way by philosophical discourse) from their mis-description in social practice and the ideologies, including philosophical ideologies which reflect that practice. The world contains not just Ohm's law, Boyle's law and countless other laws, but lawfulness as such, along with space time, causality, process, totality; but also falsity and contradiction and error and evil, and so also of course thought, creativity, love and war—war as such, not just particular wars. Are we going to say that there are no processes in the world and that process is not a fundamental category in the world or that holistic causality or relationality does not exist, or that totalities do not exist as such independently of what account we give of them? Because if we say that then we are coming very close to saying something like capitalism does not exist for after all if you read Marx's *Kapital*, particularly volume one, which is an account of the capitalist categorial structure of society, this is very much an account of the relationship between wage labour, capital, money, all of which are undeniably categories for me. They are categories, and, as categories they are causally efficacious and crucial to the systems of the reified and commodified world in which we live, quite independently of our descriptions of them, and whether we get them right or wrong. You made a reference to Skinner. Skinner does not seem to me to have a concept of agency, but that does not stop agents acting, we have to say that agency is a real cate-gory in the world. The whole structure of the material world, as you call it—and I am going to come back to the 'material world' as described in *Dialectic*, is a categorial structure, the whole system which Alan calls MELD is nothing but a structure of categories.

The claim in *Dialectic: The Pulse Of Freedom* is that it makes an attempt at getting certain very crucial aspects of our reality right. It is a fallible attempt, an attempt which itself would be part of a process in motion. I actually think there are aspects of dialectic I left out, including an undertheorised concept of the transcendent. I actually think you are making too much of the difference between *ex nihilo* and *de novo*. I do not deny that the creative inspiration always breaks onto ground which is immanently very well prepared, but the inspiration comes out of the blue, in the space between thoughts, in a way which cannot be induced or deduced by a mathematical or mechanical algorithm.

In short categorial structures are real, our accounts of them are fallible, corrigible, correct or incorrect. Now our account of categorial structures are themselves part of reality, and a capitalist account of capitalism is a very important, reified part of capitalism. That is what I want to say about reality. That is all I want to say about categorial realism.

What then about materialism? (the other main objection raised by Alan Norrie and Nick Hostettler; and also by Mervyn Hartwig). What exactly do we mean by this? Everything that happens in the human world happens via, and as a result of, or is mediated by, human intentionality which is an expression of thought in the world. And I think it is a great weakness of the Marxist and the so-called materialist tradition to underplay the causal efficacy of ideas, I really do.

I think the thesis of the rise in the organic composition of capital is completely true, but it takes the form of a rise in the organic composition of ideas, and also I would add in the organic composition of nature. I think you cannot understand technology, machinery, or any of the processes that Marx began to analyse in the labour process and what would normally be understood as being material structures of society without taking into account the role of human intentionality. They are embodiments, externalisations of human intentionality and creative human intentionality is the driving process and underpins monstrous and reified systems like capitalism, just as it does beautiful music or poetry or science at its best. There is too much lack of thought in the blanket invocation of materialism. We do not really understand materialism, it is a woefully underanalysed concept. We do not understand what it is to be a materialist.

Now when Mervyn talks about the biological nature or the animality of being, yes of course we are animals, we are physically embodied, we live in four-planar social space, I never for a moment in *From East to West* attempt to deny that. All I attempt to do is to deepen the account of one aspect of that four-planar social being which is the stratification of the personality because I think that was very underdeveloped in the dialectic and I think it may be that I am trying to defend the possibility of freedom but this is not, I would have thought, a reactionary position as Mervyn was trying to imply, but something on which any liberation and indeed any thought at all depends.

I agree with Nick that I am trying to defend the possibility of freedom, even a little bit more freedom would be a great thing. Between Mervyn and Nick there seems to be an antinomy, because while you say I am getting too concerned about freedom, Mervyn says I am going all reactionary because in some way I am supporting a commodified logic. I really do not agree with that at all and I must say that I agree neither with a lot of new age nor with a lot of new left. So perhaps Mervyn's was an unhappy choice of description of what I was trying to do in the book.

I am not trying to defend an aspiration which certainly, as Mervyn said, Jesus and Buddha, but so too in a way did Marx and Rousseau, which depends on the possibility that we have an essential or true nature, so that when we have got rid of structural sin and all the oppressed, emergent social structures (including their internalised form within us), and when we have fully embodied and realised our true being, the result will be the sort of society which Jesus, Buddha, Rousseau and Marx all believed was possible. And I would like to hope and believe that is possible. Now if it is impossible I would like to know why. Just because it has not happened so far, does not mean it is not possible.

For instance I think that there are very good grounds for saying that everything we do in the social world depends upon and presupposes human creativity. Every transformative act is in a way a creative act, it contains a moment of novelty that is a *de novo* element within it. Someone who went on doing the same thing over and over again repetitively would be mimicking the kind of reified, hypostasised systems of thought and being which capitalism introduced or, if not introduced, cemented. We forget that it is the creativity of the worker, doing the same thing perhaps over and over again, but always under different and unique conditions, always liable to need to use his own creative ingenuity to keep the production line going that, in the last instance, sustains capitalism.

If every IACR or CCR conference were the same it would be terrible. What is distinctive about human life is our capacity to make something new, something that was never there before. Now transcendental realism from its very inception said that one of the things wrong with positivism, and that equally its idealist counterparts could not sustain, was novelty, emergence, originality, and together in some way you both seem to be saying these things do not exist. I am saying that they do and they actually sustain, and are the true underpinning of capitalism and all those other reified systems. If we could just be creative, loving and exist in social and natural harmony, then we would have shot of those reified structures and that is what I believe Marx and Rousseau, and in their own way Jesus and Buddha, believed, and that is what I believe, and that is also what I think you believe Nick!

On to ultimata and their relationship to god. When I introduced the concept of an ultimatum in *Dialectic* I was thinking of two things. One is the limits of our knowledge which I call epistemic ultimata in *From East to West*, and the other is the limits to a particular sphere of freedom whether we know it or not.

God comes in through a linking of the concept of the ultimatum with the notion of ingredience, with the notion of the way in which a very deep level or structure of being, as for example in science at the most basic physical level you can get to, say the level of quarks or sub-quarks or whatever it is, that level would be ingredient in higher order and emergent levels.

If there is an ultimate, an absolute structure of being then that being would be god. What properties would that being have? That being would have to be a binding being, and that binding could be translated into human metaphorical terms, by *love*.

Love is the binding force of the human world. Let us put it like this: there is a certain sense in which all of us know god and there is a certain sense in which none of us do. Any talk about god is bound to be slightly metaphorical. I do believe that we contain within ourselves infinite potentiality, infinite creativity, infinite power and I do not think it is just our species either. I think there is an element of the unbounded in us. And I do not think that element of the unbounded is unconstrained, rather I think it is very heavily constrained by our physicality. We can put it like this: we are potentially infinite, within the bounds of our physicality.

The model of the stratification of being always suggests that anything that happens at any one level, whatever level you are looking at, is going to be determined by things at that level, things at higher order levels and things at more basic levels. Our conversation is determined not just by the flow of our exchanges, but by the constraints of philosophical discourse, and the constraints of the physical structure of this building. It is determined by the texts we have read, by our inspirations in nature, by a host of very many, including many intangible things. We must get away from the notion of a flat, one level view of reality.

Chapter Seven

Part I: Reality Check*

Part I: Reality Check

Part I: Reality Check

H e has developed a whole new school of thought. There is a centre at a major UK university dedicated to the study of this movement. And his works are widely read across many disciplines. So why is it that the name Roy Bhaskar finds its way so infrequently to the syllabuses of philosophy programmes?

In the strictly demarcated world of academia, Bhaskar tends to be lumped with the social theorists, not the philosophers. So just, as John Searle puts it, philosophers inherit a 'dumb list' of standard problems to solve, so philosophy students are given a 'dumb list' of standard thinkers to read. Bhaskar is usually not on that list.

This means that the story of the ascent of Roy Bhaskar and 'critical realism' is an interesting and unusual one.

'When I started out,' recalls Bhaskar, 'people who had been influenced by my work found themselves frequently marginalised

---

* Interview for *Philosopher's Magazine*, Autumn 1999.
Chris Norris *asked the questions*. Roy Bhaskar *provided the answers, and* Julian Baggini *interpreted the results*.

in academic life. They had extreme difficulty in getting critical realist papers published, and I found myself acting as a sort of one person support mechanism for people influenced by my work. It was helped a little by the publication of books by Ted Benton, Russell Keat and John Urry, and others—and it began to develop an academic reputation. Nevertheless, there was still a feeling of isolation and fragmentation. Then four of us got together—myself, Ted Benton, Andrew Collier and William Outhwaite—in the early 1980s and we would begin by discussing important theses in philosophy and end up by discussing what was wrong with the state of politics or whatever. Out of that was born the *Realism and Human Sciences* conferences movement. From 1983, we had annual conferences, characterised by friendliness and intellectual stimulation, solidarity and great enjoyment. Not really marked by careerism, position taking, fractious argument, but a real sense of comradeship and an idea of the exploration of truth.

These conferences gradually grew bigger and bigger, and critical realism began to take off in the different disciplines—in sociology, economics, biology, even in physics—and it took off in the States, in European countries and all over the world. There were journals, like *Radical Philosophy*, which were sympathetic to critical realism, that published articles more easily by critical realists. And then around 1995, we decided to begin to formulate a Centre for Critical Realism which was instituted as a registered charity in 1997–98. We have our own website and about 30,000 people have subscribed to the Bhaskar list on the internet.'

The story is not just of historical interest. It points to the essentially inter-disciplinary nature of critical realism and its attempt to transcend the artificial borders set up between academic disciplines. It also, claims Bhaskar, reveals a deeper truth about what critical realism stands for.

'I think critical realists are understanding the importance of networking and mutual solidarity. It is still a very radical and somewhat fragmented movement. And I would argue that there are profound reasons for this, because the nature of any society dominated by instrumental reason—by reification, by alienation, by master–slave relations—the categorial structure of such a society will be irrealist in character. Irrealism, of one sort another, will always have the backing, as it were, of the superficial currency of social reality. So critical realists will always be at odds with what appears to be the case in society. So we are marginalised now, by the nature of social reality itself, but despite that we are forming a resistance movement to that categorial structure, in tune and in keeping with deeper categorial structures, which irrealist categorial structures mask, obscure and occlude.'

So what exactly is critical realism? As a theory, critical realism has commitments both to what is (ontology) and what can be known (epistemology). The ontological dimension is the more straightforward. Bhaskar's appears to take a fairly straightforward realist line here. So, for example, he says 'How can we make sense of making a cup of coffee with sugar, except by the notion that the sugar has an independent intransitive existence with respect to our acts of finding it? How can I make sense of my discourse with you, unless I assume that what you say has a sense and intelligibility independent of my understanding of it?'

Rather like John Searle, he makes use of what can be termed a transcendental argument. That is to say, he argues from a starting point we must all accept in order to make sense of experience at all and shows that this requires a commitment to the existence of an independently existing reality.

Bhaskar develops this point by insisting that science requires a commitment to the belief that knowledge increases as we dig deeper into more and more fundamental strata of reality.

I think Marx somewhere observed that the whole of science would be pointless unless there was a possibility of a distinction between essence and appearance—unless there was the possibility that what we thought about natural reality or any other form of reality was wrong.

Therefore, this notion of stratification is already necessary to sustain the idea of critique. The critique of some kinds of understanding or reflection—or the nature of a level of reality, including social reality—in terms of its mis-description of a more basic, deeper or autonomous level of reality. That is essential for the notion of critique or argumentation generally.

Bhaskar neatly sums this up when he says, 'The sort of ontology I was arguing for was the kind of ontology in which the world was seen as structured, differentiated and changing. And science was seen as a process in motion attempting to capture ever deeper and more basic strata of a reality at any moment of time unknown to us and perhaps not even empirically manifest.'

So far, so pretty orthodox realism. But what of the critical aspect? This is where Bhaskar's thought takes an innovative turn. Bhaskar explains.

'Through and through critical realism has been critical of what we can call the nature of reality itself. Not the nature of absolute reality, or the absolute structure of being—to be critical of that is to put oneself into the position of god or the creator of the universe—but rather it is to be critical of the nature of actual, currently existing, social reality, or of our understanding of social and natural reality. Critical realism has always taken epistemologies, philosophical thesis, etc., as reflections of the society in which they are generated and sustained. And as far as these theses are misleading, they point to deep categorial confusions and errors inherent in the very structure of social reality itself.'

Bhaskar's critical realism is therefore an unusual hybrid of commitments both to the ineluctable reality of the external world and a relativistic attitude to our thinking about it. The result is realism, but with an edge. Traditionally, to insist that scientific knowledge is a cultural product went hand in hand with anti-realism. Bhaskar breaks this link.

'There is no conflict between seeing our scientific views as being about objectively given real worlds, and understanding our beliefs about them as subject to all kinds of historical and other determinations. At the same time, there will always be a right or wrong of the matter in anyone discursive domain, which defines the possibility of judgmental rationalism in the normative aspect of science.'

All this, of course, is to simplify matters somewhat. One can get a fuller flavour of the subtlety of Bhaskar's position by considering this detailed account he gives of the relationship between truth and reality.

I argue that truth has four aspects. First, fiduciary—this is, if you like, the intrinsic aspect of science or knowledge—and to say that something is true is to say 'trust me, act on it'. It is quite obvious that we have to have a workable notion of truth to enable us to get around in a world we have only a limited grasp of. This is a pragmatic necessity. The more strongly this aspect can be backed by other aspects, the stronger it is.

The second aspect is truth as warrantedly assertable. This is truth as epistemological. There is no way of getting around the notion of best possible grounds for acting one way rather than another, in a world in which we must act one way rather than another.

Moving now to the notion that lies behind the first two notions, the idea of truth as absolute. To say something is true is to say this is the way reality is. This is absolutely indispensable for any notion of intentional action and hence for any notion we as human beings can have. For intentionality presupposes two things, firstly a belief, and secondly, an orientation to act on the belief in some manner. Without beliefs human beings just aren't humans. So commitment to beliefs as expressive of reality are transcendental features of any form of social life.

Now, what lies behind the truth of a well attested scientific or moral proposition—e.g., the fact that emeralds reflect light of a certain wavelength—is a higher order proposition, the truth of that truth—the reality that generates it, that is, the atomic structure of the crystal, the nature of the wavelength of light that is reflected in a certain way. What makes it true, for example, to say that if Socrates is a man, he must die, is that it is the nature of human beings to be mortal. It is a proposition at a higher level, and it is this higher level truth that grounds the truth of the universal generalisation, the proposition which is expressed in the absolute conception of truth.

'So truth at this higher level just is reality, and it is the reality that grounds or accounts for the mundane realities that we invoke in the absolute conception of truth, and it is that absolute conception of truth that backs our epistemological or social conception of truth. There is no getting away from ontology.

The only solution to all the forms of scepticism that the whole tradition of empiricist epistemology has generated, which encompasses the anti-realism to which you, Norris, refer, is to see that what we're trying to do in science or morality or any other form of life, is to make fallible claims about the world, claims which, if they are true, are true in virtue of the real nature of beings, entities, things—the real nature of the universe quite independently of our claims about it.

It is the real nature of being that grounds well attested, universal empirical generalisations or other propositionalised claims of reality, without which no science, no discourse, no action, or no intentionality is possible. There is no escape from truth.

Critical realism also has a political dimension. For Bhaskar, issues of truth and ontology are inextricably linked to questions of domination and freedom. 'The critical impulse in science,' he explains, 'is one of demystification and the central norm with which I have been concerned recently is that of human freedom. Human freedom depends upon understanding the truth about reality and acting towards it, so it is essential that science and philosophy should be concerned with human liberation.

This takes us into the realm of ethical issues in scientific research. Because we are very far from perfect or free, by which I mean we are far from the full realisation of our potentials, and because we are dominated by a capitalist society in which reification, alienation, dualism, illusion, categorial error are dominant and manifesting themselves in modalities of instrumental reason and a whole complex of master–slave relationships, there must be necessary constraints on generating anything that goes by the empirical name of science. So people have recently, quite rightly, become worried about the abuses of science involved in genetic engineering research. We have very good reason to believe that many increases in scientific understanding will actually be abhorrent.

This raises the important question that we cannot prosecute science in an intellectual or moral vacuum. It may be necessary for morality to correct bad science, but it corrects it in the name of a higher norm, true freedom. And that is guided by the highest norm of all—fundamental truth.

Such a view does not sit happily with the 'third way' politics currently dominant in western, left-leaning politics, as is shown when Bhaskar is asked about critical realism's relation to broader political and socio-cultural developments.

I think this has to be understood in the context in which capitalism has basically won the struggle against actually existing socialism as it was called, and 1989 was indeed a crucial year, in that it marked the decisive victory against Soviet-style socialism. New Labour is just part of the universal accommodation to this fact. Capitalism itself is wreaking havoc on our environment, and quite frankly, unless capitalism is overturned, by a revolution—which will be at once much more peaceful and deeper than the one that overthrew socialism, that will draw on resources and aspects of our being that are at once spiritual and cultural, and set in the context of a programme of feasible transition, done in a non-violent way—unless capitalism is overturned in this way, I can see very little prospect of humanity surviving much into the twenty-first century on this planet.

Such pessimistic thoughts are very much on Bhaskar's mind as he writes his latest book. 'I'm currently working on an exploration of the way in which we can draw on the resources of traditions and worldviews other than those of the west—a book called *East and West*. It has a theoretical component and a component which is more popular—it actually takes the form of a novel.

This is very connected to an earlier answer I gave, for if we are to have the cultural and spiritual resources that we need to generate a true alternative to and a true sublation of the tradition that has given us capitalism, etc. we must draw on the traditions of the east as well as those of the west.

This is linked up to my other feeling that not only has western philosophy drawn on far too restricted traditions, but it has also couched itself in a pretty inaccessible mode. I'm aware of the paradox that I have talked about, human emancipation, but in a relatively inaccessible form! So I'm writing a story, which I hope will be universally accessible, and this will be backed up by theoretical works.

Evidently, Bhaskar has a lot more to say. But will philosophers be listening?

* * * *

Part II: Critical Realism and the Left[*]

Part II: Critical Realism and the Left

David Castle

What is the importance of critical realism for radical politics?

Roy

Critical realism is not designed to support the interests of any particular political tendency or faction. It is oriented to the pursuit of truth and understanding. However, through Critical realism positive values are generated by rational argument which show that capitalism is evil and immoral. We can demonstrate that there is a need for a society which satisfies the fundamental tenets of the Marxian and socialist traditions.

David Castle

What has critical realism got to offer over the dominant intellectual movements of today, such as postmodernism?

---

* Interview with David Castle for *Red Pepper* Magazine, 26 June 1997.

Roy

Critical realism is distinctive from other schools of thought in its concern with ontology or being. This has been continually repressed in recent philosophy. Since Hume and Kant it has been a dogma that in Wittgenstein's words you can only talk about the network that describes reality and not about reality itself. This disables the critical or radical potential of the philosopher's work. It is very important for academics to get free of the delusion that all there is discourse, a delusion which has become common in the social sciences as the scientists have become influenced by post-modernism. Unless one retains notions of reference to an external reality, like nature or the physiology of one's body or the structures of oppression of which we may be unaware, then you have no critical purchase on the discourse. Without a concept of reality the philosopher cannot situate his or her own work. We must remember that philosophy is in society and society is in the natural world, and therefore philosophy is integral to a whole network of forces which it helps produce and is itself partly produced out of. Academics should relate to the social and political movements and structures that exist relatively independently of them but which are affected by them. These movements and structures are increasingly being englobed by a hegemonic capitalism, and unless one can relate to this one is unable to criticise it. It is very easy for postmodernists to get involved in an epistemic retreat in which the world is finally swallowed by the sentence in which you are currently speaking. If no discourse has any concrete referent, then by extension any discourse is as good as another. It ultimately comes down to an absolute relativism in which it is a matter of taste or choice as to what discourse is best.

If postmodernism has a conception of reality at all, it is just as a surface, a flat surface. I think that it is very important to have some conception of the stratification of reality so you can isolate the difference between what I call the real and the actual, or in other words between underlying structures and events. Then you need to assess the relative importance of different underlying structures. Postmodernists claim that this evaluation is impossible. However, while refusing to evaluate elements into a hierarchy, postmodernism lets in some hierarchy through the back door which it then never questions. In postmodernism, language is emphasised at the expense of everything else—economic structures, political structures and other ideological structures which are linguistically mediated but not reducible to language.

David Castle

How does centralising ontology help us move to a critical stance towards reality?

Roy

The critical realist's commitment to ontology is shown in how she or he understands the component categories of the natural or social world. Categories are typically viewed as things that we impose on reality. The critical realist instead sees categories as constitutive of reality itself. Causality is not something we impose on reality. Causality exists, just as substance, space and time are also constitutive of reality itself. However, given that the constitution of the social world is dependent on concepts, we open up the possibility that the social world may be falsely categorised. It can be composed of real categories which genuinely construct our social world, but which are still untrue to underlying structures, or which conceal other truths of our existence. It was part of Marx's critique of capitalism that the functioning of capitalism turned on a series of category mistakes such as the confusion between exchange value and use value, between labour and labour power. These were the mechanisms which hid the generation of profit in the capitalist mode of production. However, these category mistakes were nevertheless real. Money is a false category, but it is very real—we cannot just choose to ignore it. Instead, we can engage in a process of ideology critique—exposing false categories as false and revealing what they conceal—in alliance with all those forces which have been victims of these structures.

David Castle

You said that critical realism does not support any particular political agenda. However, in its critique of current structures it seems to look to a resolution of political problems through a society that is more true to itself, more transparent and more fulfilling. Furthermore, you seem to anticipate this in a form of society that we might loosely call 'communist'. On what basis do you argue for this?

Roy

We should be striving towards a society that is both ontologically simple and ontologically honest. The evils of capitalism—class society, instrumental rationality and the logic of exchange value—are produced through its own contradictions. It is ontologically extravagant. An ontologically simple society would be a society in which people lived in harmony with each other, similar to how Marx imagined primitive communism, although societies of the future will be much more complex and differentiated than this.

The production of an ontologically coherent society requires the universal and harmonious satisfaction of human needs which is no less than striving for universal human emancipation. The chief heiress in the last two centuries of this aspiration had been the socialist tradition. That does not mean that socialist politics have always been right or actually emancipatory, it is just that the programme has been oriented towards universal human emancipation. We have to be very critical of the practice of socialist parties both in the old Soviet Union and in the west. Critical realists may not even subscribe to socialism, they may reject the name or the concept and identify with deep ecology or with feminism or something else. There are disputes within critical realism over whether it entails socialism, which turns on the question of what went wrong with socialist analysis, and how deep these problems are, during the whole history of socialism following from Marx.

David Castle

Many people would see your defence of a society based on the principles of primitive communism as hopeless idealism. There is a widespread conception of human needs and desires as naturally antagonistic, that we will always strive for power over others. We can see this in the popularisation of notions of Darwin's (the survival of the fittest as a natural and inevitable process) or even

Hobbes (where social relations are provisional self-motivated contracts between naturally competitive agents). More recently, of course, Thatcher argued that society as an entity does not exist at all, and that the only meaningful social relation are close personal ones, specifically those of the family.

Roy

To take the example of Thatcher, her view that society doesn't exist, that only individuals and their families exist, is absurd. If you look at the actual practices of Thatcherism then you can see that in fact it built up a strong state and a very strong foreign policy on the basis of a strong government. It was infused with nationalism and it was oriented to the supremacy of monetary structures to make the British economy part of global international capitalism under the dominance of finance capital. This had very little to do with individuals and their families and everything to do with structures that are larger than them. In fact, Thatcherism is a very good example of how capitalism rests on contradictions. Thatcherism produced itself out of a rhetoric of libertarian individual freedom and conservative family values but in fact it undermined both of these through its strict monetarism. It was an ontology full of inconsistency and it ended up being unable to sustain its own existence. It failed the supreme criteria in philosophy: reflexivity. Thatcherism was unable to sustain the intelligibility of its own activities: there was a gulf between theory and practice.

To answer specifically your question concerning the antagonism of needs, I think capitalism generates the illusion that needs are unlimited for all commodities, that we have unlimited wants and desires. This is untrue; we have finite needs. We can be at a dinner table and readily say: 'I've had enough, there is more food than I need to eat'. Indeed, this is the case in the world today. The world is capable of producing more food than we need. To take another example, the set of people who need more than one car is very limited. And indeed, in our daily lives we see that we do in fact have a conception of limited needs: if there were six people around the table and there were only five apples, we know how to resolve the problem. It would not lead to a war of all against all. This misconception of the unsociability of needs is a product of capitalism. It is class structure that has generated poverty. And this is a problem for capitalism, it is not a problem for human beings. The problem for human beings is to overthrow capitalism. If we could tear away this veil of illusion full of logical contradictions and inconsistencies, that is nonetheless still real and oppressive, then we could arrive at a satisfactory resolution of this perceived problem of needs. We would have a society in which we would all be free to develop our powers and opportunities and possibilities and satisfy our needs in harmony with each other and with nature in a sustainable way.

David Castle

I would like to pin you down a bit on the nature of these underlying structures which point us towards communism. Do you follow the traditional Marxist line and believe that behind the illusions of false consciousness the major determining social forces are economic?

Roy

It is not an article of faith that the economic is dominant. Rather, it is an expression of the reality of the world in which we live where capitalist interests and powers are hegemonic. Increasingly, they are by far the most important force governing the structuring of society as it is now, and as it evolves in the future. For the first time we have something like a total world system, which is the capitalist system with the dominant mechanism of finance capital. I think it is no accident that the first thing the Labour government did on arriving in office was to give up control of the Bank of England. That was a recognition that the national economy and the nation state were subservient to finance capital. Therefore economics, in so far as it is the study of capitalism, must move to the fore in our understanding of social reality. Socialists want this to be different. They do not want economic forces and motives and structures to be the dominant ones. They want the free choice of individuals in assemblies working co-operatively to take the future of the societies in which they live into their own hands and to really decide what goes on. Under those conditions, economics would not be the dominant science.

However, even now, economics is not the only structure which produces society as it is today. For example, the media are increasingly important, and have displaced the sites of other objects which themselves were a force in our social reality. If you turn on the television in Cyprus you get the same programme as you would in South Africa or in India or Australia or in the USA. But of course people can intervene and transform these structures rather than constantly reproducing them, though their   vision in doing so will always be limited by how they see themselves as having been formed by very structures under which they live.

David Castle

You have been very critical of postmodernism as a politically disabling set of theories. However, many postmodern arguments have appeared from people on the Left attacking the traditional Marxist model which centralises economics and class. They have asserted the importance of other forces in the workings of oppression—especially gender, ethnicity and sexuality. How do you answer these arguments?

Roy

The postmodern assertion of the politics of identity and difference is in fact very useful. It objects to the homogenising and commandist structures of traditional socialist politics, which are still with us in the new model Labour Party and in the opposition variants to it. It is not good enough to treat all oppressed people as if they were uniform members, male members, of the working class. They are all subject to a multiplicity of structures, and they are at the intersection of a multiplicity of sites of power. By treating everyone as equivalent and interchangeable one is aping the instrumental rationality that was generated by capitalism. Just as the law of exchange value doesn't differentiate between the five pounds spent on this tape recorder, or the five pounds spent on a bottle of whisky, or the five pounds spent on necessary food, so traditional socialism hasn't differentiated between one worker who works for Ford, a male industrial proletariat with a high degree of class cons-ciousness who is a trade union member and is bound into his local community, and a Bangladeshi woman worker in Spitalfields who is not unionised, is frightened, maybe pregnant, perhaps an illegal immigrant, who has got an entirely different consciousness. Neither would recognise each other. This is what the post-modernists stress, and that is the truth.

However, I differ with postmodernists in seeing that the lesson to be learnt is not of ceasing to think in terms of universal structures—the common oppression of a group, the common interests of a group. These two workers are both products of the same system; they have a real identity of interest in overthrowing that system. Rather, we have to refine our conceptions of universal structures. You cannot being them together by asserting the primacy of a traditional model of class over the real interests and feelings and needs of that Bangladeshi woman. You have got to do it by appealing to the commonality of their enemies and then the particularity of their own interests and differences. You have to understand universals as dialectical rather than abstract. To be specific this means that a universal is not a uniformity. To take a different example from natural science, we are sitting in this room but we are not collapsing to the ground; the law of gravity is operating on us, but only as a tendency. Physical laws are universally applicable, but they are underlying structures, which only in particular circumstances manifest themselves as actualities.

We have to think on four different levels. The first moment is this universal moment—which we share with every other human being. As capitalism becomes increasingly hegemonic, this universal moment becomes defined by our relationship to capitalism, our common oppression by capitalist modes of dominance or of reasoning. This is then qualified by the specific mediations that are particular to us as students or teachers or men or women, of being a certain ethnicity, a certain gender, etc. And then there are our own particular world-lines, our geo-historical rhythmics as I call them: the particular history of England as distinct from that of Scotland, Wales and Northern Ireland. And finally there is our concrete singularity, our individuality as a completely unique human being. When Marx said that the free development of each is the condition of the free development of all, he highlighted the singularity of the individual: you can't have universal emancipation unless each singular human being is emancipated.

To return to our Bangladeshi worker, as someone employed by a capitalist firm she has something in common with all other workers: this is the concrete universal. In addition to this, there are specific mediations for her as an exploited woman worker and immigrant worker, perhaps providing causalised and especially cheap labour. Then there are the geo-historical rhythmics: Bangladesh is a country where land is on average only four feet above sea level and if global pollution carries on at the present rate then in ten or fifteen years it could be underwater. What does this mean for her consciousness? And in terms of her concrete singularity, her mother may have just died, or her child may have just died, which will produce an additional sense of hopelessness and alienation. All of that must be accommodated by our model of class.

David Castle

It seems that you are seeing the power struggles along the lines of gender and ethnicity as complexifying the dominant model of class struggle rather than representing fundamentally different sites of oppression.

Roy

I do give a primacy to class. Postmodernists do not. For example, Ernesto Laclau and Chantal Mouffe in *Hegemony and Socialist Strategy* argue for a radical democratic politics which sees a complex political field where no particular struggle can claim dominance. I would like to have both this moment of complexity but also the moment of dominance found in the traditional socialist analysis of class. Indeed, because it is not related to a primary structure the concept of hegemony no longer makes sense in the hands of Laclau and Mouffe. As Lenin and Gramsci used the concept before them it depended on the existence of one struggle being more important than the others, which would play a strategically crucial role. With Laclau and Mouffe it just merges into a general politics of identity and difference.

This is not to say that oppression always takes the form of class. Class is just one manifestation of the broader category of master–slave relationships. For example, you could say that women are often treated as the slaves of men. We are all victims of a number of master–slave relationships. Although capitalism is the dominant structure, the agency will be universal. In so far as we are looking to transform all of society, we cannot base this on a common identity, a common class consciousness. Though awareness of capitalism must be universal, we cannot expect either an immediate identification between individual agents and class position, however defined; of that those agents who satisfy the objective criteria for being workers will relate to, i.e. subjectivity identify with that description. We have to distinguish between the concept of the working class from what people like to call themselves. And we cannot go around telling every worker in America that they are working class if they actually believe they are middle class. We have to adapt our words without losing the validity of the concepts. And that may also apply eventually to socialism. Socialism may become so discredited that we have to drop the word but keep the idea and the ideals.

If we can show people in the world that capitalism is a destructive and evil force, which is destroying the planet, which is unnecessary and increasingly unwanted, and which generates social ills, then people will come together as people, as human beings, to transcend that mode of production. They many not realise they are doing it as workers, because of all the ideology which has obscured that notion. This class consciousness will in fact be a universal consciousness. The equivalents of the revolutionary socialists of tomorrow will think in terms of the crisis of humanity and the crisis of the planet, but they will be overthrowing capitalism for those reasons. So the goal is still the same; the terminology and the mechanisms may be different.

David Castle

You have talked of this 'veil of illusion' produced by capitalism which inhibits people's understanding of reality, and which when taken away would allow people to recognise the desirability and possibility of a truly socialist society. How can this veil of illusion be removed? As analysts and explicators of reality, what relationship should critical realists, and intellectuals more generally, have to society as a whole in relation to this matter? Is it enough merely to announce the true state of things and expect people to change their ways of thinking and being accordingly?

Roy

You can't just produce a grand plan for a new kind of society and expect people to jump on board. You have to work from people's current state of consciousness and approach their problems as they see them: they've got plumbing problems in their homes, or they need an operation and they can't get into the hospital, students can't get grants or their grants are too low. You then tie in these problems and needs with the structures of capitalism and other forms of oppression that dominate them: globalised capitalism, false consciousness, false forms of mediation or stupefying forms of mediation, the ideology of people's unlimited needs. And you make them see the connections between the problems they have in their own lives and the problems that other people have in their lives, so you can bring them together in a coherent joint programme.

However, you do still need a concrete vision of where to go forward, which I call concrete utopianism, the socialist humanist vision of a beautiful social order to replace the antagonisms and the selfish modes characteristic of capitalism. The oppositionist movements of the 60s and 70s which I was associated with thought you could overthrow capitalism merely by mobilising social hatred. This might create a revolution but what would you put in its place? The end has to be prefigured in the means and this requires an ethical change. If you want to produce a society which is based on love and co-operation, then you have to fight for that structure through loving and co-operative relationships. Otherwise there will be an inconsistency between theory and practice, making the new structure inherently unstable.

We can see pockets of concrete utopianism now. Through the LETS scheme people are realising that there can be societies without money. Movements like 'Reclaiming the night' for women shows how we can imagine a society in which we can protect ourselves without armies or police forces (or at least without the oppressive features of these). And you can see how concrete utopianism has played a part in social changes that have worked miraculously. One example is contemporary South Africa. Mandela schooled himself in a different kind of politics while he was imprisoned. He was able to come out as a saintly leader unifying apparently irreconcilable forces and transcending the politics of hate.

We need an end to 'the politics of disenchantment', the politics of Nietzsche and Weber and the politics of social democracy, and which has so profoundly influenced the politics of the Left. We need to produce a different conception of ourselves in the world. The revolution will be nothing less than this: the transformation of our understanding of ourselves and of the whole world in which we live, our situation in the cosmos.

Part Three

En Route from Transcendental Dialectical Critical Realism to the Philosophy of meta-Reality

Chapter Eight

Critical Realism, Postmodernism and the Global Crisis*

I will be talking about critical realism, postmodernism and the global crisis and I will be saying a little bit by way of trying to indicate some kind of resolution to this crisis that I think we all feel we are in, a profound alienation in contemporary society, indeed a threat to the survival of the species on the planet by just introducing some of the themes from my recent book, *From East to West*. But I do want to do justice to the title that you came here for, so for the first part of the talk anyway, critiquing post-modernism. So what is postmodernism? Postmodernism is a movement of thought which is very widespread throughout the world, including India as you know. It is very fashionable, and there are some things about it with which I agree and some things about it which I think are profoundly mistaken but have to be understood and explained in the context of criticising it. So I will list ten general characteristics of postmodernism so we can know roughly what we are talking about.

1. An emphasis on difference, relativity and pluralism.
2. An accentuation on the emphasis of language characteristic to twentieth century philosophy.

---

* Philadelphia, September 2000 and Pune, December 2000.

3. Scepticism about or denial of the need to say anything about the world.
4. The impossibility of giving better or worse grounds for a belief, action (including speech action) or practice.
5. Life is viewed as a pastiche, not a totality; an assemblage not a whole.
6. The failure to universalise or come to terms with such phenomena as global (let alone cosmic) inter-connectedness including the phenomena of globalisation (including the globalisation of postmodernism).
7. The incapacity to sustain an account of change as rational; and hence to topicalise the phenomenon of (individual; collective; global) self-emancipation.
8. Heightened reflexivity, without however a clear conception of self—hence no self-reflexivity or capacity to situate itself.
9. The genesis of a politics or more generally culture, of identity and difference thematising the specificity of particular group interests, and indeed individual ones too, without however sustaining the idea of the essential unity of all human (or more generally just all) beings—that is difference and identity without unity and universality.
10. The germs of a discourse of such phenomena as emotions, a term suppressed in the mind–body dualism characteristic of philosophy.

Let me briefly elaborate on this list. Firstly, it is committed to a stress on difference, relativity, diversity and change. Emphasis on difference in particular. This involves it in a commitment to what in critical realist terms I have called epistemological relativism and that emphasis I think is wholly salutary; in other words I am entirely in favour of that. The second emphasis of postmodernism is an accentuated emphasis on language as the medium and vehicle of social thought and even life. This linguistic turn, making ourselves more aware of language, is also something which is very important and very good, one of the great achievements of the twentieth century. However, I would not want to argue that language exhausts social reality or social life in the way in which most postmodernists tend to do. So I am a bit nuanced, critical about the linguistic turn. The third feature of postmodernism is a lack of ontological realism and in this respect I am very hostile. Basically postmodernists do not like making ontological commitments, they do not believe that you can say anything about the real world and certainly nothing about the deep structures of the real world, maybe platitudes is all. So the third feature is ontological irrealism. The fourth feature is something I am equally critical of and that is what I would call judgmental irrationalism. They do not believe at the end of the day that it is possible to give better or worse grounds for one system of beliefs or practices, and I am going to argue that it is very important that you do.

Fifthly, postmodernism is characterised by an emphasis on life being a pastiche, a medley of different themes with no underlying unity and lacking causal and internal relations between those different parts. And I am against that. Sixthly, postmodernism is characterised by a failure to universalise and even an insistence that you cannot universalise, a lack of universalisability. Even the very existence of postmodernism as a global phenomenon, a universal phenomenon, becomes something that is very different for postmodernists to situate. Why is it that postmodernism has become globalised? They really do not only react against what I will call analytical universality in my talk but they react against any concept of universality at all. I am going to argue in favour of *dialectical universality* and try and explain postmodernism as in part a reaction against phenomena in society and in thought which are analytically universalisable.

The seventh characteristic of postmodernism links them all in a way together and that is the lack of any adequate notions of truth or objectivity. Science tends to be viewed with a lot of suspicion. And the lack of any clear notions of objectivity and truth means that it becomes very difficult for them to sustain the rationality of change; to give an account of how we can change or progress in a better rather than worse direction. So change is, so to speak, an event or a happening which is described from the outside—from an *external,* so to speak, in the worse sense, 'academic' point of view; not the inside, not from the agent's point of view. But when you think about it, we are all agents, we all have to act, and we want to know how, and why, we should act one way rather than another. Choice is as real, and as irreducible, a feature of social life as change.

The eighth feature of postmodernism is a heightened reflexivity associated with its concern with issues to do with language; however, this accentuated emphasis is unable to sustain a clear conception of the self, and it is a conception which is performatively contradictory in that postmodernism cannot sustain and situate its own coherence. In this way it falls foul of what I have called the supreme criterion of philosophy, that is the unity of theory and practice. The ninth feature involves commitment to a radically new politics of identity and difference, closely intricated with the rise of the new social movements, which we will come to see as a reaction against the abstract analytical universality characteristic of modernism. However, what happened here was that postmodernism threw out the baby with the bath water: it was unable to sustain <u>any</u> conception of unity or universality at all, a particularly worrying feature in our epoch of global crisis, when, at all four planes of social being, our close interconnection has become so obvious. The final feature is the beginning of a discourse of the emotions, for so long the suppressed term in philosophical discourse, a term suppressed between the supposedly male domains of mind and body. That is postmodernism in a nutshell.[1]

---

[1] A fuller treatment of postmodernism would of course have to take account of its relationship to, as a specific phase in, the development of the philosophical discourse of modernity, in the way I touch on in chapters 1 and 4 of *Reflections on Meta-Reality*, and my forthcoming *The Philosophy of Meta-Reality*, Volume 3: *Re-Enchantment and the Critique of the Philosophical Discourse of Modernity*, Sage Publications. In terms of the schema that I have developed there, postmodernism is the fourth phase in the development of the philosophical discourse of modernity which was initiated by the revolutionary upsurge around 1968 and is also associated with the rise of new social movements. It has an interesting counterpoint. Whereas postmodernists say 'we are different and there is no way of telling which of us is right or wrong'. The dogmatic fundamentalism that arose around the time of the latest phase of the philosophical discourse of modernity, associated with the collapse of the actually existing socialist societies (in 1989–1991), and the rampant western triumphalism which followed in its wake, says 'yes we are different but I am right and you are wrong'.

So what is critical realism? You probably know roughly but I shall just first list and then briefly comment on five themes or five stages in the development of critical realism.

1. Transcendental realism as a philosophy of science;
2. critical naturalism, a philosophy of social science;
3. the theory of explanatory critique, as a theory of how you can rationally derive evaluative from factual positions;
4. dialectical critical realism, as a theory of dialectic, thematising the characteristic dialectical concepts of negativity, absence and change and totality, holistic causality and internal relationality;
5. transcendental dialectical critical realism, as a theory of the necessary spiritual presupposition of emancipatory projects in east and west alike.

Critical realism started as a philosophy of science which I call transcendental realism and the great breakthrough of this account of science was that it situated ontology, that is the study of being. It put ontology back on the map and critiqued the idea that you could reduce being to knowledge, which I called the epistemic fallacy. It argued for the irreducibility of being and for an entirely different account of being to that which orthodox philosophy had given. It argued that the world was structured, differentiated and changing, not flat, and uniform and unchanging.

The second moment in the development of social science was what I called critical naturalism. This argued against the dualisms and dichotomies that beset the social sciences and to a large extent continue to do so. For example, between naturalism and anti-naturalism, between positivism and hermeneutics, structure and agency, mind and body, reason and cause, fact and value, theory and practice. And it tried to produce a sublation of these dichotomies in a more coherent totality which could show and sustain, albeit under different descriptions, what was right in what the contending parties stressed about social reality without alienating or splitting off that account of social reality from the moment emphasised by the other.

For example structure and agency were reconciled in what I called the transformational model of social activity which saw social structures as certainly pre-existing individuals, but as only existing and continuing to exist in virtue of their ongoing intentional activity, which thereby reproduced or transformed them. So social structures defined a level of reality, relatively autonomous of individual activity, but did not exist independently of it. The role played by human beings was in reproducing it or transforming it. So justice was done to both structure and agency, neither were reducible to the other; and in that way a better position was arrived at, which did not, so to speak, take sides in the dispute; but rather undermined the very grounds of the dispute, showing the way forward beyond the dispute. In the same way I argued that mind and body was a nonsensical dualism, that mind had to be seen as embodied and bodies as minded; and the reason and cause duality was equally nonsensical, for reasons in social life functioned as causes and at the same time were causally conditioned and explicable. I will use a lot of these different moments and developments of critical realism as my talk goes on in the critique of postmodernism.

So the third stage in the development of critical realism was that associated with what I call the theory of explanatory critique. This said that the taboo against talking rationally about values was quite wrong, that we could use the findings of science, and more generally factual statements to rationally inform ethical and political positions. Ethics and politics was not a matter of subjective preference, it was something that could be rationally discussed. So now we can see that critical realism in its development, starting with a concern with science, was moving into a concern with questions of ethics and politics and value.

This was carried on in the fourth stage of critical realism, which was the dialectical stage which began to thematise such notions as absence, totality and so on in a more adequate account of the Hegelian dialectic than Hegel himself had given.

The fifth stage, which is the very latest stage which I am currently stretching and transcending, has seen a further deepening or further radicalisation of this concern with human emancipation and is basically arguing that there are certain presuppositions which could be called spiritual, which is not the same as religious; spiritual presuppositions of liberatory projects in east and west alike—in Marxism, and other western social theory and also in many reli-gious and spiritual traditions. And in my book, *From East to West*, I am trying to show a convergence between eastern and western writers who have been concerned with the project of improving the human condition.

What I will do is just give, as it were, a first level critique of postmodernism and then I will go on to deepen it by situating it in the system of dialectical critical realism as further deepened by the spiritual element. So in this way I will be doing justice not only hopefully to postmodernism but also to the theme of *From East to West*, though I should also say that I am now moving from this concern with taking eastern themes to the west to a standpoint beyond the whole opposition, dichotomy or duality between east and west.[2]

A very simple critique of postmodernism would turn around its failure to sustain ontological realism and judgmental rationalism. What critical realism says is that there is no inconsistency between being an ontological realist, that is believing that there is a real world which consists in structures, generative mechanisms, all sorts of complex things and totalities which exist and act independently of the scientist, which the scientist can come to have knowledge of. There is no inconsistency between that and saying that that knowledge is itself socially produced; it is a geohistorically specific social process, so it is continually in transformation in what I called the epistemological, transitive or social dimension for our understanding of science. Science as a social phenomenon is characterised by relativism, is characterised by pluralism, diversity, difference and change—all features which postmodernists quite correctly stress. The third aspect which is compatible and necessitated by both ontological realism and epistemological relativism that critical realism stresses is judgmental rationalism. This involves the idea that, even though science is a social process and that we know views and opinions change

---

[2] See my forthcoming *Beyond East and West* (Volume 2 of *Philosophy of Meta-Reality*): *Comparative Religion and Spirituality in an Age of Global Crisis*, Sage Publications, 2002. Based on the Radhakrishnan Lectures at the Rabindra Bharati University in Kolkata in February and March 2002.

through time, at any one moment of time there will be better or worse grounds for preferring one rather to another theory, so that we can sustain the rationality of our grounds for choice.

Let us think a little bit about ontological realism and what happens when postmodernists deny it. I have had lots of debates over the years with postmodernists[3] and one of the most striking features is that if you ask them, well, are you not talking or claiming to talk about reality, the postmodernist might say, there is no need to talk about reality, we can just talk about our talk or we can talk about knowledge or about different social practices, we do not need to presuppose a reality which is a referent of those social practices. So then you turn to the postmodernist and say well, what is the status of your own talk, what is your talk? Is your talk real, are you saying something real or is it not? If the postmodernist says, yes, of course my talk is real, then that is fine, at least one object in the world, namely the postmodernists' talk or discourse, is real. And that makes it possible subsequently to refer to it in a future discourse. So if the postmodernist discourse is real then that is the thin edge of the wedge, because at least one item is admitted to reality and then you can talk about the causes or context of that social reality which the postmodernist has already admitted. If, on the other hand, the postmodernist says, no it is not real, then his discourse becomes impossible, because it is not a discourse; discourse is something which has a causal effect. If I was to talk to Pauline over there, I would not be able to have a discussion with her unless in some way she was listening to me and I was having an effect on her. So to deny that discourse or talk is real is to make it impossible. Because discourse, any discussion has a causal effect or else it would be impossible or otiose, redundant, absurd. Is everyone happy with this? Well you can see someone over there is happy with it so this shows that my discourse is having a causal effect. The most general criterion of reality is causality, so without admitting that the discourse is real, there is no way you can get into an argument or discussion and there is no reason to do so—you might as well not listen.

---

[3] Cf my debate with Ernesto Laclau, *Alethia*, volume 1, number 2, September 1998, and reproduced as Chapter 3 of this volume.

Nevertheless this view that in some way we cannot talk about reality is very strong and popular among philosophers. It is what I have called the epistemic fallacy. It is very well captured in Wittgenstein's famous saying that you cannot talk about the world you can only talk about the network in terms of which we capture the world. And other people have talked about the prison house of language. This is a bit like Weber's iron cage. There is no escape from it. What actually happens is if you do not talk about what the network presupposes about the world then you are going to tacitly inherit from some other pre-existing system of thought an ontology which you may really disagree with. So, postmodernists not thematising, not coming to terms with ontology, tacitly inherit or imbibe a positivistic ontology. You can find this in Derrida, in Ernesto Laclau, you find this in places in Foucault. Of course, like all great contributors to social science, they are actually doing or presupposing ontology in their practical investigations, but they deny this in their theory and so they cannot think either the unity of their theory and practice or assess whether they may not be tacitly inheriting some pre-existing ontology.

Let us take an example of this from someone who is not a postmodernist but who is a very vehement opponent of ontology, Habermas. According to one of his variants of critical theory, our understanding of the world is constituted by three knowledge constitutive interests. And his knowledge constitutive interests in prediction and control is actually informed by the Popper–Hempel theory of explanation, according to which to explain an event is to subsume it under a set of universal laws which are conceived as covering laws, which is to conceive them as empirical regularities plus a set of initial conditions. Now that assumption about those universal laws as empirical generalisations presupposes an ontology of the world as flat, undifferentiated and unchanging. So that is tacitly taken into Habermas's account of nature and the world so far as it is subject to our instrumental knowledge. Actually he is very anti-positivist, he wants to say lots of very interesting and liberating things about the social world, but because he has got a flat, positivist ontology of the natural world this will inform the very liberating things he wants to say about our social endeavours.

You can find this time and time again in other writers who are formally critical of positivism but tacitly presuppose a positivist ontology. That is basically what is wrong with the failure to think through and then rationally sustain an ontology—you tacitly presuppose a false ontology which the taboo on ontology disguises or screens. So we also have to ask what is the ideological function of this taboo on ontology that the epistemic ontology screens a view of the world as being uniform. That is something which postmodernists really want to react against. So they are not doing justice to their own intuitions when they tacitly presuppose what they are really fighting against.

So let us go onto judgmental rationalism. What is so important about this? Let us take judgmental irrationalism, the idea that you cannot have better or worse grounds for belief. This was famously articulated by Hume who said there are no better grounds for preferring the destruction of my little finger to the destruction of the world. That is an absurd position. It is absurd in every way because obviously, in any sense the destruction of his little finger is far preferable to the destruction of the world, actually the destruction of the world would include the destruction of his little finger. So it is only a contrast if he is implicitly detotal-ising and taking himself and his finger out of the world and setting the two apart from one another. Another example from Hume: he said I cannot give grounds for going out of this room by the ground floor rather than the second floor. Of course we can give grounds, we know that by virtue of Newtonian understanding of gravity that heavy objects will fall to the ground. Hume knew this, he was not just following custom or convention in always going out through the ground floor door. He had grounds for doing this, grounds which he denied in his formal philosophical theory. So we have once more performative contradiction, the failure of reflexivity or theory to mesh with practice. In short, judgmental irrationalism is false: we do have reasons for preferring one belief to another.

The function of this taboo on giving rational criteria for one ground or another is just to licence convention. It just means that because we cannot give a ground for one belief rather than another what do we do, we just carry on doing what we have always done. So again it is very conservative, it perpetuates in a way the status quo. The real question is, is it correct? First of all, why is it important to have rational grounds for a belief or practice? The answer is because we cannot avoid what I have called the axiological imperative, that is we have to act and the action is not determined. We do actually have free will, we do have a choice, however circumscribed it is by structural and other determinations, we have no alternative but to act and we need to know what are better or worse grounds for our action. So not to provide a criterion for those grounds is very serious because it means that anything we do or say becomes more or less arbitrary. Ultimately rational discourse, not just science but progress in social life and choice, on a daily, moment-by-moment basis, becomes impossible.

Let me give you an example from the philosophy of science which was very important for postmodernism. This was the problem of incommensurability. Most people thought that this more or less proved that you could not have rational grounds for judgment in science. What was the problem of incommensurability? This was a problem formulated by philosophers of science like Kuhn and Feyerabend who pointed out that when a new theory superseded a pre-existing theory, often the new theory had a conceptual structure which was so different from the pre-existing theory that there were no meanings shared in common. If there were no meanings shared in common there was no way in which they could be rationally compared, so it was argued. So Newtonian theory and Einsteinian theory are so radically different in their conceptual structures that you cannot translate formally, in terms of the canons of deductive or any other sort of logic, the one into the other. Does this mean we have no grounds for preferring Einsteinian theory to Newtonian theory? Not at all. Because firstly the very formulation of whether and how you prefer Einsteinian to Newtonian physics presupposes that there is something they have in common, and what they have in common is a common world that they seek to describe, albeit in radically different ways. You do not say that Einsteinian theory is incommensurable with music or with cricket or with chess because no one thinks they belong to the same domain or topic area. In short they do not have a referent in common. So what the formulation of this problem showed was that actually of course Kuhn and Feyerabend, like everyone else, presupposed that Newton and Einstein were actually trying to describe and explain the same world. That they presupposed a common referent. It is very important when you go into linguistics, the study of language, that you do not just have a concept of the sign as being a signifier and signified. The sign is not just a signifier and a signified or meaning, the sign, being the word either spoken or written, also has a referent. So instead of the semiotic duality which stems from Saussure you have what I would call the semiotic triangle. That is any language, any sign system presupposes three terms as a minimum. It presupposes signifier, signified and referent. What the postmodern theorists do is leave out this question of reference. This is the first response to the problem of incommensurability.

All I have done so far is show that the formulation of the problem presupposes that there is a world in common. How, when the theories are so contrasting in their intrinsic, conceptual structures, can you still say that Einsteinian theory is better than another. Very simply you do it like this. You say that Einsteinian theory can explain under its descriptions everything that Newtonian theory can explain under its descriptions, plus some phenomena that Newtonian theory cannot explain under its descriptions. So there is no need for a comparison of the descriptions. If you have a concept of common referentiality then you can just show, which is actually what happened, that Einsteinian theory can explain some theory in its own way that Newtonian theory could not explain in its way. So it becomes a purely quantitative criterion if you like. Einsteinian theory is describing and explaining a greater set, a greater totality than Newtonian theory could do. Now the real world, the actual world that we know (although it may be very difficult to find more than eight or nine test situations) does actually show the superiority of Einsteinian theory, in those eight or nine situations. So that we have a reason for preferring Einsteinian to Newtonian physics. This then shows how the arguments against ontological realism and judgmental irrationalism can be refuted from a critical realist standpoint.

Now let me go a bit further into the development of critical realism. To do this I will take the system of dialectical critical realism. This has four stadia, four moments, four aspects that I have called:

1M – The first moment of ontology,
2E – The second edge of negativity, dialectic and absence,
3L – The third level of totality, and
4D – The fourth domain or dimension of transitive praxis and reflexivity.

At the first level or moment of ontology, what we have already seen is not only the legitimacy, necessity for ontology but the necessity of the entirely different ontology developed by critical realism. This will be a stratified ontology. What critical realism argues here is that not only is ontology necessary so that you are tacitly presupposing it, but also that a correct or adequate ontology is necessary; so if you have a false ontology in practice, in theory you actually presuppose in your causal efficacy a true ontology in practice. So let me give you an example of this. If you were working with a concept which we could call ideology or false consciousness, of laws as being merely empirical regularities, what happens when you apply laws in the open systems of nature is that you are assuming that they will work whether or not there is an empirical invariance. Empirical invariances only obtain in a laboratory. The law of gravity is actually operating on me now although it is not pulling me to the ground. So it is actually empirically false here. But it is transfactually, really true. The engineer in his practice must presuppose the transfactuality of laws. So the philosophical ideology in terms of which he thinks his practice is contradicted by the reality of that practice which presupposes a correct account of reality. Here we have a complex ideological figure of theory–practice inconsistency which is the way in which a false theory presupposes in practice a truth which it denies. This I called a TINA formation, meaning that there is no alternative, there is no alternative but to the tacit presupposition of truth at some level.

A good example of a TINA formation, which will be familiar to you as social scientists and philosophers, is given by Marx's critique of political economy. Here he said that agents in the capitalist world think their world in terms of concepts which actually occlude and deny the true nature of capitalist society which those conceptions actually depend on. So when we engage in exchange, buy a commodity, a newspaper or something like that, that actually presupposes according to Marx the whole basis of exploitation of labour, that is the extraction of surplus value via unpaid labour. Which is the hidden secret of capitalism for Marx. So all the structures of the capitalist society depend on this hidden secret—the extraction of surplus value through unpaid labour. But to take it from a completely different context, this is the tacit pre-supposition of what is false or inadequate by what is true, what is necessary for it, what must be going on anyway. Take an assembly line, what must be going on anyway is that the workers must be free, creative human beings, even though their creativity and freedom may be denied by the structures of capitalist society. Their freedom, creativity and ingenuity are necessary to sustain the production line, to keep it going. Chomsky says this when he talks about our innate capacity as human beings to generate an infinite number of sentences including languages which we will never access. So underneath this, I want to argue in western libertarian thought there is a level in which humanity is free, creative, inventive and I would argue spontaneously loving and compassionate, which is tacitly presupposed, but nevertheless occluded, that is screened, denied and dominated by the false and oppressive structures of the social world we inhabit which are characterised by alienation, misery and ill. To put it in a nutshell, as Rousseau said—this is the summary of the western tradition of libertarian thought—man is born free but is everywhere in chains, in his inner essence he is free, but in his actuality he is in chains. That inner essence is not allowed to manifest, not allowed to express itself in society.

Let us compare that with a Vedic understanding of the world in which most of us live in, a world of *maya*, of illusion. Again we have the same figure, this world of illusion actually sits on, reposes, would not exist without Brahman or pure spirituality. Which it screens and which it dominates in the actuality of our lives. That is to give you an idea of how something from the east also links in with a figure of thought that we have from the west. What I am beginning to suggest is that what liberatory thought is doing is building up to a view of man as being far greater in his potentiality, his possibilities, his powers, his real essence than anything that is ever actualised in our social world. The project of liberation then becomes to shed those unnecessary and unwanted determinations, all those structures, including the structures inside us, which prevent the realisation of the true essence of humanity as free, creative and loving. For those of you coming from a Left-wing tradition, you can take Marx's ideal of the communist society as one in which the free development of each is a condition for the free development of all. This does not only express a wonderful dream. For that freedom is a reality in human beings now and what I want to argue is that the actuality of that dream, this heaven on earth, this utopia, the actuality of a level of (incompletely realised) enlightenment is a tacit presupposition for all the misery and ills in the world that we have. The totality of master–slave relationships, or oppressive relationships including the internalised ones, depend on the free creativity of slaves. War is a horrible phenomenon characterised by violence but it is a phenomenon which is impossible without the human virtue of love. Think of what it tacitly presupposes, think of the selfless solidarity of the soldiers on the front, think of the love and support that sustains them in their struggle, that of their sisters, wives, mothers, daughters, their comrades and friends. This terrible phenomenon war is actually sustained by love. Yet clearly in our society war or hatred or violence or strife dominates love, that on which it depends. So this is the structure of the figure of thought we have here, the suppression by the false of the truth on which it depends and which sustains it.

Let us move on now to the second edge of dialectical critical realism which is the edge or mode or dimension of negativity, absence and most importantly dialectic. I will just say that I think absence is indispensable for any being at all, it is clearly essential for any process or change. Because a process or change is always the absenting of something which was already there and the presenting of something new. The greatest western theorist of dialectic, which turns on absence, was Hegel. Marx famously talked about the rational kernel in Hegelian dialectic being occluded or shrouded by the mystical shell. He said to Engels, in a rather wistful letter, if only I had a few hours or moments, I would love to say what the rational kernel of Hegelian dialectic was, in a few printers sheets, but of course he had arguably more important things to do. So what I have tried to do in my dialectical works from *Dialectic: The Pulse of Freedom* on is to bring out exactly what the rational kernel is. The rational kernel is actually a general learning process which occurs in society, in science, in art, everywhere. It is a process which is driven by absence. What happens is you have a totality such as a scientific theory which is incomplete in some way. That incompleteness means that something is absent from it. That incompleteness generates inconsistencies and contradictions which pile up to the point at which a crisis occurs which then needs to be resolved by transcendence to a greater totality. This is the characteristic pattern of scientific discovery and growth as described by Kuhn and others. I have re-described this in realist terms, but the general pattern is there. You have incompleteness generating inconsistency generating resort to a greater totality, that is transcendence to a greater totality in science and social life generally. And the very development of critical realism is itself a process of self-transcendence.

Now within the moment of transcendence there is a transcendent moment itself, because a new theory can never be induced or deduced from the pre-existing data, it is not a mechanical algorithm. True it only develops to a mind or a community which has immanently prepared the ground, but when it happens it comes as a bolt from the blue, out of nothing, *de novo*, it may come in a dream, as in Crick and Watson's discovery of the double helical structure of DNA, in a moment of rest. This gives rise to a second inflection to the term transcendence in which what actually happens is that in a moment of stillness or quiet or something like that we get the breakthrough we are looking for when we are not looking for it, when we let go, do something different or suspend the search—then (and only then) if it is going to happen, it happens. It is a breakthrough that cannot be mechanically or in any other way, algorithmically, deduced. It is the emergence and emergence always means from nowhere, from absence, through absence of something completely new. Now if you do not accept the idea of *emergence out of absence*, then you cannot have real novelty in social life or anywhere in nature, so it is a very important concept.

I should perhaps just say what the mystical shell is for completion. The mystical shell is Hegel's elimination of absence. This is the way in which at the end of the day, positivity is always restored, so the system ends, as you know, in his political philosophy, which the Left Hegelians saw, correctly, as an apologia for the Prussian state. We have had the theme of the end of history coming up in the west more recently since 1989, after the collapse of what was called the 'actually existing socialist societies', celebrated by Fukuyama in his *The End of History and the Last Man*, which explicitly invokes Hegel. The Left Hegelians already saw that at the end of Hegelian dialectic there was an accommodation to existing reality in its fundamental conceptual structures. But what they did not notice was that accommodation, apologetics, conservatism was already there at the beginning. Because if you look at the *Science of Logic,* it begins with the concept of being and that generates the concept of nothing which immediately passes into the concept of becoming. After that all the concepts of Hegelian dialectic are positive. Whereas what I want to talk about is not just nothing in the sense of indeterminate absence, but *determinate absence*, like the lack of food that drives hunger on, the absence of adequate housing, absence of education, absence of literacy, absence of a fair distribution of income in the world, absence of fair possibilities for people. So you see it is determinate absences which drive the dialectic on in the social process. Without the concept of determinate absence we are not going to see how it is that people, as distinct from abstract conceptual structures, will be moved to real change. I could go on much longer about Hegelian dialectic in another context.

I now move quickly on to the third level of totality. The chief category that critical realism introduces here is absolutely vital for our critical understanding of postmodernism. This is the category of dialectical universalisability. Of course this is not the only category that the third level of totality thematises, nor the only one that is relevant for the critique of postmodernism. For the realm of totality turns above all on internal relationality, and that opens the way to a consideration of holistic causality, interconnectedness, and all the other phenomena which we see manifest phenomenally in globalisation, and the global crisis which we are currently undergoing at all the four planes of social being.

Postmodernism, in its most fundamental aspect, must be seen as a reaction against the logic of abstract analytical universality, and the alienation and reification that goes with it. I have already argued at the level of 1M of ontology, that laws in the real world are not analytical universals, that they do not describe actualities like constant conjunctions of events, or empirical regularities. Rather they must be understood as tendencies, tendencies which apply in their manifold determinations to explain the complexity and uniqueness of particular events in the open systemic world, that is the world outside experimentally controlled closures. However the real basis to the ideology of laws as empirical invariances or universal covering laws (at the domain of the actual) lies in the capitalist mode of production, which has an incessant logic which takes the form of the continuing reproduction of the same. This is the logic of globalising commodification. We can see it manifest not only in the Humean theory of causal laws but in the Kantian categorial imperative which says that the test of an ethical maxim is whether it applies to every case. Of course we know that there are no maxims like this. There are circumstances under which lying, even killing, is right; nor can these circumstances be generalised from one context or one individual to another. Thus it may be right for me to tell x a white lie in a particular context but not y. Just as the real basis of causal laws lies in the tendencies of underlying structures and mechanisms the real basis of right-action lies in the virtue of an embodied personality which is clear and consistent with its ground state. The globalising logic of commodification was mimicked in the practices of actually existing socialist parties and the practice of the states of the Soviet bloc. What all these things have in common is the absence of the ideas of differentiation, geo-historical trajectorisation and uniqueness. Thus just as a ten rupee note does not differentiate one commodity from another, so in the practices of socialist parties no attempt was made to differentiate say one member of the working class (perhaps an immigrant male) from another (perhaps a female agricultural worker). The postmodernist reaction took the form of saying no, we are not just members of the working class, we are not just the same, we are female members of the working class, or we are members of a particular occupation, generation, ethnic minority, sexual orientation or whatever. It was the affirmation of identity and difference which had been eliminated, blanketed out by the abstract universals of the reaction to the logic of capitalism.

Critical realism is very sympathetic to the politics of identity and difference. Where it takes exception is in suggesting that what the postmodernists have done is thrown out the baby of unity with the bathwater of abstract universality. So that postmodernists and those influenced by them—and the new social movements—expressed something of the same logic. They find it very difficult to sustain a concept of the unity of the human race, or all species or all beings, in a situation where our interconnectedness has never been more acute and where a sense of our unity as members of the species, let alone as occupants of ground states within a simple cosmos, been more essential to assert. Quite literally today we stand or fall together. It does not matter whether you are a master or a slave, whether you are an Australian or a Canadian, whether you live in Tokyo or Buenos Aires, we are all bound to the same fate. We can see this at all four planes of social being. This conception of four-planar social being was a generalisation, made at the dialectical stage, of the transformational model of social activity, which we have already seen reconciling structure and agency. What it said was that all social phenomena have to be understood at four levels:

(a) Our material transactions with nature;
(b) our social interactions with others;
(c) social structure;
(d) the stratification of our embodied personalities.

We can see that we are in crisis at all these four levels; and at all four levels we are alienated; and at all four levels we are interconnected, globally. The route of this alienation I would argue lies in our self-alienation, that is our alienation from our ground states, or our most fundamental essential nature. If we were not alienated from our most fundamental essential nature we would see immediately our inter-connectedness with the essential natures of all other human beings and the rest of the cosmos. Of course the globalising logic of commodification has to be nuanced a little bit. It is not just a simple phenomenon, it itself has to be understood dialectically, as a specific phenomenon in its own right. Thus more tandoori chicken is consumed in England than Kentucky fries in India. So it is not a one-way traffic. That would be to make the fallacy of misplaced concreteness.

What then is the categorial schema in terms of which we have to think and explain events and things, including human beings, social phenomena, etc. The minimum unit for understanding anything that happens in the world is the concrete universal. This has four moments:

First we must understand things in terms of their most fundamental universal nature, say in terms of the transfactuality of the laws which apply to them; **second**, we must understand them at the level of those specific differentiations and mediations—the same laws, interpreted as tendencies, will apply to different things in different ways, depending on their circumstances and all the other factors which differentiate them. **Third**, these universals must always be specified in terms of the geo-historical trajectories of the phenomena to which they apply. So one could have a universal, such as human being, subject to all the same mediations, but coming from very different backgrounds or experiencing very different histories, for instance two school teachers in Pune, one an immigrant from Tamil Nadu, the other a local Maharashtrian, etc. After we have taken account of all these three moments there will remain an element of ineluctable uniqueness about any phenomena, any way in which the universal manifests itself in the world. This then is the schema of dialectical universality and concrete singularity. There is no phenomenon, nothing, no event in the world which is not concretely singular and there is no law which applies in any other but a dialectically universal way. This then is the schema which we need to do justice to difference and identity while persevering the idea of the unity of human beings in the context of the global crisis which would engulf us all.

Turning now to the **fourth** domain of transformative praxis. The first thing we have to realise is the truth of five theorems about human agency. First, intentionality is irreducible, and intentionality presupposes the role of consciousness and ideas. We only need talk about a phenomenon as being a human act, in so far as it is the product of intentional agency, otherwise it is just a happening to a human being, like slipping on a banana skin, or catching a cold. (Of course we know that human beings can do things to encourage or avoid such phenomena, but that only shows that the intentional and material levels are in causal interaction.) The second feature is the irreducibility of agency. We have no choice but to act. Whatever we decide to do, even if we decide to abstain from action, this is still a choice and an action. This implies a critique of traditional so-called spiritual thought, which would seek to withdraw from the world of activity by retreating to the monastery or whatever. This may have been appropriate in the past, but in the age of global crisis we live in, such a position is indefensible. The third feature of a social event is that it must be understood in terms of all four planes of social being that I have just described. The fourth feature is extremely important: this is that whatever we do, at some point, at some level, we must just do it spontaneously. I may wonder how I am going to cook a meal, and think, will I do it this way or that way, at some point I just have to do it. We could not do anything in the world unless there was a level of basic, spontaneous action, things we just did. This is profoundly important because it means that ultimately all change in the social world proceeds from self-change. Because if everything we do depends upon our spontaneous activity, then to change at any level of practice in our world, means that we have to in some way change ourselves, our ways of doing things. So this points to the primacy of self-change. However, this must not be misunderstood; and this takes me to the fifth theorem. This is that anything we do will immediately affect all planes of social being. So that although I cannot do anything, except ultimately in the last instance by doing it myself, whatever I do, necessarily myself, I am affecting other beings, other human beings—at level (b), I am affecting the natural environment, i.e. (a), and in some way I am engaged in a relationship with the social structure, i.e. (c), reproducing it or more or less transforming it. So we have the phenomenon of the simultaneity of action, necessarily action by an agent, and therefore self-action and social action, and a dialectic of self-change and social change. The only way we can change society is ultimately by our actions, and if they are erroneous or less than optimal, then ultimately we must change ourselves. But any way we change ourselves and any way we act we will be affecting other human beings and the whole social structure. So there is a natural dialectic between the two.

Recently I have argued that the logic of emancipatory projects is such that they presuppose that we are essentially free, good, loving, creative beings—this is the primary or foundational level of our being, and our social being. That level however is masked and dominated by the social forms that we have generated and we reproduce or transform, many of which are internalised within ourselves in the form of our motives or thoughts or fixations which are contrary to our fundamental natures. This is what is meant by saying that we are alienated at all four planes of our social being, unfree at all four levels of our socialised nature. Supposing it does not matter whether you set yourself a purely personal, individual objective in life or you dedicate yourself to a social ideal, such as ridding the planet of global warming or whatever, the only, and ultimately the most effective, way of doing it, is to be totally clear and single pointed about it. There is however always going to be a problem if what you want is inconsistent with what you essentially are. And if you want to be a millionaire, but this is inconsistent with your ground state, which is loving and compassionate and thinks that having so much money is not a good use of resources, then you will be in conflict. And to have a split intentionality means that you can never achieve any of your objectives. The one level of intentionality that you cannot avoid, that will always be there, is the level which springs from your most fundamental nature. So ultimately you will be forced on a dialectic, presupposing access to that nature (which I have argued we all have all the time) in which you realise that you need to eliminate all the unnecessary and unwanted determinations in your embodied personality, all the aspects of heteronomy, to be an effective agent in the world, whether you are setting yourself an individual or a social objective. When you have eliminated these heteronomies, you will become inevitably more clear, and more aware of our inter-connectedness, you will become more loving, more creative (or we could put it the other way around, you would be ridding yourself of the blocks on your natural loving, creative nature) and be a more creative agent of social change. And this will inevitably take you to a commitment to the goal of universal self-realisation, or ushering in what I have called a eudaimonistic society, that is a society which corresponded to an ideal which was expressed by Marx in the words that the free development of each would be the condition of the free development of all; that your happiness and flourishing would be just as important to me as my own. And in fact unless we have this ideal, at least in practice, we will never succeed in being free ourselves, because we are so bound up together. We are all aware of this in the case of things like smoking. If someone smokes in the room this affects everyone. But we should be aware of this at a global level now, following events such as those that happened on and issued after 11 September 2001.

Of course without the categories of independent reality, the capacity for rational judgment and choice, the understanding of the world as being punctuated by negativity and a sense of dialectic, the idea of universals and particulars as being subject to the norms of dialectal universality and concrete singularity and an understanding of the dialectic of self-change and social change, embedded in a view of human beings as beings with a ground state in terms of which they are inter-connected with all other beings with their ground states on what I have called the cosmic envelope, it is very difficult for the postmodernist to cope with our contemporary global crisis. Moreover, it is difficult for him even to understand the phenomena of the globalisation of postmodernism itself. How is it that everyone is affected by and even adopting postmodernist attitudes everywhere. Isn't this a dialectical universal, not just a local belief system. What I am arguing then is that postmodernist man or woman presupposes a realist man or woman in practice and that the realist man is a man constituted by a dialectic of co-presence, in which an essential, true or alethic man or nature sustains all the heteronomy that is co-present within him; and that that ensemble, that compromise itself sustains the compromises, or what I have called TINA formations, in society at large. At least critical realism can set the agenda, show what we need to understand and overcome our global crisis. This is quite simply the disemergence, the shedding of all the elements of heteronomy in our world today, at all levels of social being. And this practice begins here, right now, with each individual with everything they do.

Chapter Nine

Left versus Right Brain, Creativity and Emancipation*

I suppose the motivation for making this presentation here was that this is a women's university and traditionally the distinction between left and right brain is associated with a distinction between the male and female or men and women. I think that there is something in that definitely, but one should not immediately identify left brain with men and right brain with women. So, I will do this in two parts. I will talk about the characteristics of the left and the right brain and then I will look at how this relates to women's activity, women's labour, women's oppression and women's emancipation in the context of an orientation to universal human emancipation and indeed ultimately universal self-realisation.

Actually I think what you can say is that the left brain reflects certain features, which are very fundamental to our society. I will be very critical of the limits of left-brain thought. In arguing for the right brain I will be arguing for the need to supplement the formal analytical logic associated with the left brain with a number of right-brain characteristics which I will go into in a moment. At the end of the day what I would like to see is these

---

* SNDT, Mumbai, December 2001.

two hemispheres integrated and synthesised; so that everyone, men and women alike, should be able to think in both a formal analytical mode, and in a right-brain, creative, practical, intuitive way. In fact both ways are necessary in order to be able to operate computers, information technology, and even spontaneous fluency in language. But even more, both are necessary ultimately to do anything at all.

I do not agree with all the normal characterisations of the differences between left and right brain. I think language actually comes from a point of intersection of the two hemispheres, so that really, although you can do a lot with the right brain alone, and you can do a bit (although not so much) with the left brain alone, language and linguistic fluency, communicative fluency, many of the skills which women possess and perform so well, actually already display the kind of synthesis I am arguing we all have to achieve.[1] And in arguing thus for the compatibility and synthesis of these two kinds of mental functioning, you can say that this is a sort of argument for showing how women can be the leading edge in the struggle for human emancipation. When I say that what I mean is that some aspects of women's activity today are pre-figurative of the kind of features which will be necessary at a universal level in an emancipated society of the future. But you cannot just abstract those features and extrapolate them into an emancipated society. What we have now in the case of women is a kind of punctuated pre-figuration of aspects which must be realised in the future, if indeed the species is to survive. I do not want you to think that I am condoning the context of women's activity today. The struggle for women's emancipation is a vital part and that is why it is a punctuated pre-figuration. It has got to be the sense in which women today embody aspects of the society of the future, has to be punctuated by the total abolition of all oppressive relationships or what I call master–slave hierarchies.

---

[1] When you do empirical studies you find that often boys at a young age will be better at mathematics and abstract reasoning, but women will almost always be better at communication; they actually flow from the point of integration between the two hemispheres.

Let us look at some of the features of left and right brain. Now what I want to argue is that the left brain thought actually mimics and chimes in with the philosophical discourse of modernity. It is left-brain thought which is reflected in that discourse and that discourse itself reflects the logic of our society and the globalising imperialistic logic of the capitalist mode of production. We are dealing with a nice synchronicity or set of resonances between left-brain thought, the philosophical discourse of modernity and the logic of the capitalist mode of production. There is one further term I want to add to that, and that is the globalising logic of capitalism itself produces a very crude and materialistic society. And a certain sense of materialism which I am going to define. The radical way I want to move is to show how the body of philosophical thought with which I have been associated, critical realism, actually displays a spiritual element, a level of spirituality which is presupposed by all theories and projects of human emancipation, for example by Marxism—which must actually pay attention to this element of spirituality without which we are not going to have the universal revolution which we need to save the human species on this planet. This seemingly little simple perhaps academic contrast between left and right brain is actually going to be very important.

The first thing I want to do is distinguish this contrast between left and right brain from some other contrast. From the contrast between the discursive and the intuitive intellect. All these things shade into one another, but that is the second distinction. And the third is the contrast between analytical and dialectical reasoning. We will see why that is important in a moment. The fourth is between sentential and iconic thought. That is thought which thinks in terms of words and thought which thinks in terms of pictures. The fifth is the distinction between instrumental and non-instrumental modes of reasoning. That is between conditional and unconditional or some other mode of reasoning. The sixth feature is the distinction between reasoning and behaviour which displays attitudes of attachment, of possessiveness, of manipulation and unattached activities and relationships. All these are nuanced differences, so that though they cannot be read one-to-one, there is a clear sort of family resemblance between the aspects of the left brain and the right brain. The seventh feature is between an ethics which is based on virtues, that is an ethics which is based on the idea of cultivating good human beings, virtuous human beings, who will act rightly from the nature of their hearts. This is an ethics of virtue versus what I will call an ethics of rules. This is an ethics where people behave rightly only because they are told to. Only because they have to conform to a certain set of rule systems. Virtually everything we do in our life is constrained by rules, laws, bureaucratic or financial dictates.

How lovely it would be if we could just all be spontaneously good, and there was no tension between what we wanted to do and what we were being forced to do or what was right. And most of us can feel this tension in every move we make. It is very important philosophically and politically that that tension exists. So the eighth formal proposition that I want to bring out is the distinction between dualistic and non-dualistic modes of thought and activity. The left brain is typically dualistic, is typically oppositional and thinks in terms of binary oppositions whereas the right brain is non-dualistic, synthetic, holistic and it is convergent. It is concrete in a way which the left brain is abstract. Let us discuss a bit more some of the features of the left and right brain and then we will look at how important these distinctions are.

The first thing is that the left brain is sequential. Only one thing, you can only do one thing, think one thing at a time. It is a whole sequence of binary oppositions or choices. Yes or no. There is no fuzziness. Then it is a process which is carried out entirely in thought. It is a symbolic process carried out entirely in thought. What does this mean? It means verbal thought, the right brain is non-verbal which is why I have said the faculty of language, and in many cases, what women are doing, or spontaneously do or are forced to do by the nature of the society in which they were placed is to synthesise these two aspects, these two kinds of mental functioning. So the right brain is non-verbal. The right brain is imaginative, visualising, picturing. Actually language involves the synthesis and in some way the transcendence of the opposition between these two brains. Ultimately we need all of us to understand and fully utilise the powers of both aspects of our brain, that is both brains or both hemispheres of the brain;

they are not even to be thought of as two horses, two stallions which should pull in the same way so that they should not be opposed to each other, rather, they have to in some way be transcended. What I am going to argue for is that actually we do spontaneously in our daily life transcend the oppositions of left and right brain at a level which I am going to call the supramental level of consciousness.

The new concepts that I am going to introduce really are those of the levels of the *ground state*, which is our innermost being, the *cosmic envelope* which relates us to everything else in the whole cosmos and in particular the notion of *transcendence* and *transcendental identification*. This is where, if you like, the overlap with spirituality comes in. And I am going to put, if you like, the basic features of what the new synthesis or new transcending philosophical position should be and then articulate it in relation to those polarities and those aspects of left-brain thought, the philosophical discourse of modernity and the globalising logic, particularly of the capitalist mode of production. Let us then talk about transcendence. Because I was talking a moment ago about the way in which in language we do not only synthesise but in some magical way we transcend the opposition between the verbal and the non-verbal. We transcend it verbally, but when we are fluent we can communicate in a non-verbal way as well as a verbal way. We have the expression 'body language'. We can intuitively feel or read someone's face. This concept of transcendence I would like to make the key concept in my talk today.

Let us look at a few senses of transcendence. For one sense in which one thing can be said to transcend another is just a simple sense in which it surpasses or over-reaches another. Particularly in science we have a completely non-spiritual, or you could call it a-spiritual, concept of transcendence in which we talk about one theory transcending or overcoming the splits or oppositions within another in a way in which Einsteinian theory overcame aporia or contradictions within Newtonian theory. And that is very familiar to people who look at science as a process. Because characteristically what happens in science is that any particular theory that you formulate will have some kind of weakness; this weakness will be an absence, some sort of incompleteness in its depiction, characterisation of reality. This absence, either a level of depth or a reach of totality that the theory has not included within its existing structures, will eventually get to a point where it generates contradictions and crises. This is well known from Kuhn. This is the period of revolutionary crisis. But at some point someone will come up with a theory which transcends both the contradictions and the old theory. So that is the relative sense of transcendence. Now this transcendence also will include the synthesis of what was best in the old theory, but under the new descriptions— so generally the world will be re-described but the truth that was contained will be preserved.

Now moving on to the absolute concept of transcendence we can ask where this new theory comes from which is the moment at which positive contraries generating the contradiction are transformed into negative sub-contraries, that is consistent descriptions of the world. This moment is a moment that cannot be achieved by induction or deduction, or by any procedure known to formal logic. So it has to come from the unknown, from absence, out of the blue, from nowhere—it is an emergent, real, novel feature. Let us see how emergence out of the blue happens in science. The first thing to note is that it does not happen to just anyone. It happens always as the irruption of a transcendent cause onto immanently well prepared ground. Thus, who had the brilliant idea of gravity? just that scientist who was most thoroughly immersed in the subject matter. So this moment of creative imagination that Newton had when he discovered gravity is the first concept of transcendence, particularly associated with creativity—it is really emergence from nowhere. Again I am not saying it is ontologically nowhere, it comes out of the blue. And we can go a bit later to ask whether there is a sense in which we can actually say anything about where it comes from, because surely something cannot come from absolutely nothing, but we will leave that as a puzzle for the moment. That is the first concept of transcendence, as the emergence from nowhere that is necessary for any novelty or change.

The second, and now we are on more familiar ground, is the sense in which you become one. Transcendental identification: you become one with something else which you know, or of which you had no uncertain descriptions. This is a different concept of transcendence. And this is transcendence as transcendental identification. What is important here is to realise that most thinkers in the spiritual traditions of both west and east have only looked at transcendental identification as identification with what is within. Transcendental identification with oneself. One reaches oneself. One reaches a point of non-duality, you are completely one with yourself. For example in meditation or in prayer. But of course we all experience other forms of transcendental identification. I can be absorbed, engulfed in a picture, a walk in a sea, if I listen to music or listen to bird song then I am one with the bird song, I actually become one with the bird song. This is transcendental identification taken out of a spiritual context. You can think for a moment whether you have ever experienced this. This is transcendence <u>into</u> something, rather than <u>onto</u> you. So actually I can become one with this pencil or one with myself. In the case of becoming one with myself I retreat from the objective world, totally into subjectivity until in a state of what is from the point of view of thought, in emptiness, I am just one with myself, totally to do with myself, and there is nothing outside me. Or I can become one with something external to me. Here what happens is my subjectivity goes completely into an object. The Zen Buddhists, for example, have a tradition in which you have to become one with something which is not particularly nice, or not necessarily beautiful. We all may feel we can become one with a beautiful rug or a beautiful symphony, but becoming one with a corner of the room, this would be a task, or becoming one with this pencil. We might feel that we could become one with a tree, but can you become one with a fence, it is more difficult perhaps you might think. But actually becoming one, transcendental identification is absolutely essential to any form of social life. Because when you hear me and understand me then you become one with an aspect of me. You become one with my speech, with my thought. And unless you became one with each other in your daily life then you could not do anything at all. So this capacity to transcendentally identify with another being is essential to any social life. What I want to argue is that at a cosmological level, its most fundamental form is *love*.

There are two other kinds of transcendence, transcendental identification, total unity with one's context, with no sense of duality. The third sense is transcendental identification with the activity you are doing. This is transcendental identification in non-dual activity. For example, the footballer who is focusing entirely on his movement of kicking the ball, or the cricketer who is focusing entirely on hitting the ball, just like the cook who is focused entirely on what he is doing, or the driver who is focusing entirely on what she is doing, then she is totally at one with her object her context. There is no duality, there is transcendental identification with the activity, this is focused, single-pointed, activity. This is activity which is not split. Any activity which is split, for example by attention to the result or consequence of the activity, or split by being concerned with something else, by not being here and now in the activity, by being somewhere else or some other time, will be dualistic activity. And dualistic activity will always be split because actually it is not clear what you are trying to do. Because if you are not totally here now and you are somewhere else, where is your intentionality? Where are you as a subjectivity if you are not totally here now, but you are partly here now, and partly at lunch, or partly back at home sleeping, or you are thinking only about how this is going to help you achieve better grades in your exam or advance your professional career, or you are thinking, if only I had been focused on what I did yesterday I might have been better at it, even that is to split your intention. This is the nub of Krishna's advice to Arjuna when he said do not think about the results, the consequences, just be focused on the activity. And the whole Vedic critique of attachment and the Buddhist critique of craving, the critique of desire or its inverse form, fear, the critique of attachment as attraction and attachment as repulsion is really based on a critique of activity which is dualistically split.

Actually we all know that it is possible to perform non-dualistically split action. How do we know this? Well, if you just thought about doing something and thought about how you were going to do something then you would never do anything. Ultimately you must just do something without thinking of doing it. That is ultimately all action reposes on a level of infrastructure of basic or spontaneous non-dual action. That is action which you do not do by doing anything else, you just do it. In that moment of non-dual action then you are just totally focused and you do that spontaneously, you just do it. Ultimately all action, any form of life, must depend on non-dual action. You can think about how you are going to make the meal and what ingredients you are going to put in, but ultimately you just have to cook. This is true even of thoughts. If you are thinking about what you are going to think about at some point you just did not think, you would not be able to think. It is also true of language, of understanding. You may wonder what is he saying, but at some point you just have to stop and just do it. So we are all skilled performers of non-dual action, we are all skilled performers of that form of transcendental identification.

There is a fourth form of transcendental identification which is transcendence with, that is when you are part of a team. Sometimes you will be so at one in your movements, your interactions, that there will be no duality, no split. For instance, sports is a very good example of this. Perfect footballers will be playing, not the whole time, but at least in part as if they were one. Similarly cooks. People who get to know each other will anticipate each other's moves. That is the fourth form of non-duality.

All this really is beginning to make transcendence seem quite a central concept but also quite a non-religious one. I am not going to say irreligious because obviously it does come into religion as well. But we are taking it out of any association with a special place or a special object. We see that transcendence in the sense of emergence out of the blue is essential for any form of creativity. Creativity is doing something which has never been done before. Something original. And in this sense it is a necessary feature of any human action, for no two situations, and therefore no two responses to them, can ever be completely the same— so however much creativity is suppressed, it can never be eliminated. Then there is transcendental identification which we must have in order to understand each other or to do anything in life. That I am associating with love. Then there is transcendence in the sense of transcendental action, that is non-dual action which is essential to agency. Creativity, love and agency (including holistic agency) are the three features of human life that I would particularly like to foreground today. They all involve different but overlapping forms of transcendence.

How does it then relate to a further concept of transcendence or kind of transcendence that we might have, that is when we talk about transcendental consciousness. All these forms of transcendence I have been talking about involve a form of transcendental consciousness in the sense of non-dual consciousness, but you may want to argue that the mind and our being is so structured that there is a level of consciousness which monitors, as it were, all our other quotidian everyday acts. So *transcendental consciousness* will then be the *monitor*. And what we will be trying to do for example in a state of meditation would be to reach that point of transcendental consciousness. Rather than using the terminology of transcendental consciousness I want to use a different sort of terminology for talking about the self. For here we looked at three features—creativity, love and right-action—which are things people do. So now we have to ask: Who are we? What are we essentially? And the extraordinary thing is that most of us are not who we think we are. Most of our self-conceptions are based on mis-identifications, mis-I-dentifications. We mis-identify mainly with our ego, but also with our minds or our careers, or our particular achievements, or our desires, or our possessions, or our problems, or our issues. There are actually three important conceptions in our normal sense of our selves.

First of all there is a sense in which the self is the ego. What is the ego? This is something, an I which is separated, cut off and in opposition to all other I's and opposition to social and natural forms generally. This I has a sense of itself as entirely separate from the rest of reality. This ego is essential to the philosophical discourse of modernity, essential to capitalism, essential to most of our existing social institutions. Because a lot of things in our society presuppose an isolated subject. So we say that someone possesses something else; possession is a very good example because when you actually possess something then you have to ask what is that peculiar relationship between you and that possession? How does a car that you possess actually relate to you, does it really relate to you from any deep ontological level in a different way from anyone else. This concept of the ego I want to argue is an illusion. There is no self which is separate from other selves and the object world. We are not separate from the rest of the universe. We are intrinsically connected with it.

There is another sense of the self which is not an illusion and that is a sense in which we are all embodied personalities. As an embodied personality I am clearly differentiated in space and time from Lakshmi, because she is over there and I am here. Now we can have this sense of being embodied personalities without having the sense that we are separates. We can have the sense that there is no separateness between us but we still have to recognise that in the physical world we are physically distinct. The point of physical distinction is characteristically the point of agency. This is the point from which I must act. This is the only point from which I can speak, I cannot speak from Lakshmi or from you. I can only speak from myself, so the embodied personality must be real.

What is the embodied personality? The embodied personality definitely has a mind, emotions, feelings and it definitely has a physical being. In fact it is the physical nature of our embodiment which defies our separateness and gives a degree of validity to the sense of the ego that we all have which is part of the logic of capitalism and our society. We are at least tripartite beings. We have mind, emotions and bodies. What is interesting from the point of view of our topic today is that the philosophical discourse has really only concentrated on the mind and body. It is not really bothered about emotions. And this of course reflects the sexist and chauvinist structure of our society. Because men think that they have the better minds because they are better in left-brain thought. Men think that they have better bodies, but you can ask them, when was the last time you had a baby? Is not that as clever as digging so many tonnes of coal? The idea that women do not have such good minds is terrible. Our emotional nature is really very interesting because this is probably the most important part of our being to get a grip on. Because what really drives us are emotions. Fear, love, hate, jealousy, possessiveness. Possessiveness, we cling on to something, we regard it as our own. Then in some way, any action which is done in a possessive way will obviously be a non-dual action. You can also see the critique of dual or split action as linking up very much to the critique of possessiveness and attachment which are two things very familiar from the discourse of the east, the spiritual discourse of the east. This neglected field is actually absolutely central. If we have got three aspects of our embodied personality, is that the end of the matter of the self.

Well clearly it cannot be because actually it is not clear at all where your embodied personality begins and ends. What is part of you? Is your being a philosophy or sociology student part of you or not? Are your parents part of you? Certainly your genes are part of you. In your genes you carry the physical imprint of the past. You carry your ancestors around with you. Actually when talking about emancipation we also have to free ourselves in some way from our genes. We have to be free of everything, everything that we could inherit. Not just our circumstances, not just all our wrong attitudes, our possessiveness, not just everything which is so intrinsically related to capitalism and all the other oppressive structures in our society. But also we have to be free from our genes. Coming back to the question of what we are. Buddhists have for long said that the sense of the self as an embodied personality is going to be relative because where the self begins and ends, how it is constituted, what sort of relations we take into account, whether we include the causes and the effects, that is all going to be somewhat relative and perspectival. But one thing is certainly clear. Some embodied personalities are freer and more empowered than others. There is a sense in which our qualities and powers change and develop over time. So I would not go so far as some Buddhists and say that the Buddhist sense of self is also not real; all you can say is this sense of self—the self as embodied personality—has a transient and slightly fuzzy character to it. We cannot be too remonistic about it because what we centrally are in the world is embodied personalities.

There is a third aspect of the self which I am going to call the transcendentally real self. This is that state which underpins our embodied personality. This is what I am going to call our ground state. Let us just consider how we might argue that we do have an essential or inner nature. This is something very deep and profound about human beings. First, before I argue this—

because we know that some religious traditions have always said that we have something very deep within us—let us see how some secular thinkers actually presuppose something very similar. Marx says the communist society of the future will be a society in which the free development of each is a condition of the free development of all. That means your development, your growth, your fulfilment matters as much to me as my own. That is a stunning critique of egoism and that is a beautiful idea which means that in some way we must be, there must be a level of being actually now within us even though it may be obscured by an awful lot else which we actually are. Which could develop, flower into being those beings who could sustain such an ideal. Such an ideal that your own development, everyone's development was an important condition, was the condition of your own. This obviously presupposes the potentiality of our becoming such beings. We must have that potentiality within us. How could you argue that this potentiality is actually real and connected up with some other features of the world? You could argue by looking at us from the point of view of the universe. Critical realism as you probably know has a view of the world as being structured, differentiated and changing. In respect of its stratification what we have is a nested series of levels of being which are emergent powers or properties of more basic, deeper levels of being so we can see the stratification within me. We can see this as revealed to science. For example we explain the overt behaviour manifest by tables and chairs in terms of their molecular structure and we explain molecular structure in terms of atomic structure, and we explain atomic in terms of electronic and ultimately quantum mechanically structure, which seems to be a limit that contemporary science cannot get beyond.

What we can say is that there is something essential and ultimate in being which is also ingredient within us. This ingredient would be innermost being or our most essential nature because it would be that aspect of our being upon which all other properties of our being depended. We could not get angry unless we had the ground state properties which made anger possible. Some of these ground state properties I want to argue will be quite surprising, we cannot do anything without creativity, love, action, spontaneous action. That is the basic idea between, evolved in the idea that we have a fundamental or innermost level of being.

How would this level of being relate to other aspects of being? Exactly the same argument, as we are part of the universe there is something essential to the universe which must be ingredient in us. That argument applies to all beings. So everything which is within our cosmic totality must have an essential ingredient within it. It would not be a universe, one universe, unless there was something which actually all these elements in the cosmic totality made it one universe. What is it that makes it one universe? The easiest way to look at it is to think that the universe is characterised by what I call the cosmic envelope. So we must have a most basic state and everything in the universe must have a basic state and the envelope which encompasses all these most basic states or the ground states of every being I would call the cosmic envelope. What is outside the cosmic envelope we know nothing about. How the cosmic envelope came into being or how it will end we know nothing about. What we do know is that through our capacity to transcendentally identify we can identify with other aspects of the cosmic envelope. So I can become one with you just in speech. You do not have to feel that I become one with the whole of you but I become one with one aspect of your being. So that when you are listening to me there is no sense of separation between what I say and what you hear, in that moment we are one there is no you as distinct from me, there is no split or duality and there is no ego either. So as I can become one with you in sound, so I am one with sound; and as I can become one with sound, so I can become one with a rose, a tree, a pet, so I can become one with any aspect of being. This means that the cosmic envelope must be implicitly characterised by the capacity for transcendental identification.

This means that the cosmic envelope, even if items and beings emerge as a process of time, even if, as according to modern evolutionary theory, from inanimate matter, in the big bang so that you had helium then you had hydrogen and then gradually millions of years later you had the planet earth, physical matter, and after that vital matter, organic life and after organic life consciousness. Because I can transcendentally identify with anything

in the cosmos, no matter how material or brute, the consciousness which I experience is somehow magically endowed in everything else and that consciousness must have been there implicitly
at the beginning. And of course there is no other way in which
we can make sense of evolution unless we suppose that consciousness was implicit, enfolded at the beginning of time. Consciousness somehow magically endows us with the capacity to transcendentally identify with other beings in the universe.

All we have to say is this cosmic envelope is implicitly consciousness. The idea of matter, mind as having emerged diachronically over time out of organic life and out of matter is quite
consistent with the idea that consciousness was enfolded or implicit in matter potentially. What happens when you look at a
plant and become one with the plant is that you identify with
that plant in consciousness, consciousness must be implicit in the
plant for you to become one with it. My words must be already
implicit in you for you to become one with what I am saying.

To use a more text-book kind of example, Newton discovered gravity. What happens is that you, as a teacher, have to explain gravity to your student, but there comes a point when the
student just has to see it. You cannot force students to learn something, they just have to at some point see it. If you are a teacher in
logic, you can endlessly go on trying to prove a theory in logic on
the blackboard. If you say to your student do you see it, and they
say no, then you try something else. But at some point the student will not get it until he just sees it, he just has to see it. This
capacity to transcendentally identify with what you are being told
means that every discovery, every creation is in a way for the person who is learning it for the first time also a re-discovery or a re-
creation. Every student has to recreate when they understand gravity as Newton's insight. We cannot exaggerate the enormity of
this insight. We see a stone falling from the sky, we think the
cause, the momentum of falling actually requires a tremendous
turning upside-down to see the earth as pulling objects to the
ground, and you can try to do this; it is difficult to try and think
of objects being pulled to bodies, bodies as attracting. Or think
of the break that Copernicus made when he, instead of viewing
the sun as moving around the earth, viewed the earth as moving

around the sun. While the heliocentric theory was known to many different traditions long before the European middle ages, it was certainly a discovery for the European middle ages. If you think about it, it is a dizzying concept. It is absolutely dizzying. How difficult is it to do that. We all seem to do that very easily now, just accept it. But think how difficult it was initially to have that conceptual, make that conceptual change. What this suggests really is that learning is always a matter you have to see for yourself, you have to see, feel, understand it. And actually learning or knowledge which is not part of your innermost being, which is heteronomous, something stuck in your mind, which you have not completely seen, absorbed, taken into yourself, such knowledge is not real knowledge. When you fully understand physics you can just do physics. When you can fully understand a language you just speak it. While you are learning it then you have to remember the rules of grammar, when you are learning driving you have to remember which way to turn the wheel when you are driving backwards. Yet to an experienced driver there is no problem. You think you may be able to remember when as a small child you first tried to tie your shoelaces. Think how difficult it is sometimes to have to relearn in life: how difficult it must be for someone who is ill to have to move a muscle.

Once we have acquired a knowledge, an understanding, then it must become part of our being. So we can now map out a kind of subjective dialectic of discovery. To learn anything, to understand anything first you must see it. This suggests that we have, what I am going to argue for, the primacy of the standpoint of self-referentiality. But what I am also going to argue for is that this necessarily entails a commitment to universal self-realisation. So there is nothing egoistic in that. I teach you something and I can only get so far unless you see it. That brings out an aspect of truth within the Platonic theory of anamnesis. Because what Plato said was that basically knowledge is recollection. All I am saying is not that knowledge is recollection but the potential for it must be implicit. It must be contained, enfolded within you. If you did not have the potential to see it, it could not be actualised. The actualisation of the potential to see it is the stimulus created jointly by your teacher and your hard work, your stretching of your concepts to get yourself into a position to see it. So that moment of 'I see it', is akin to Newton's moment of discovery of gravity. Re-discovery. What kind of potential did Newton discover in the universe? He discovered, this is my conjecture, the alethic truth or innermost being relative to the laws of physics which had been discovered at the time of the truth of the truth of the next run or level of reality. He actually just saw it. That gravity, the concept of gravity would be on this worldview an implicit potential within each of us. We see how easily we see it now. For Newton it was very difficult. And Newton by an extraordinary effort got to the point where he reached transcendental identification with grav- ity. He actually became one with gravity. That is my conjecture. This would be a way in which we could acknowledge the epistemic transcendence of gravity for Newton, the way in which it came out of the blue, with this ontological immanence. The way in which, though it was out of the blue for him and out of the blue for knowledge, it was actually something which was a real feature of the world. So scientific discovery, the discovery of something objective, will just be the discovery of the innermost truth impli- cit in that level of being that you are already very close to. You cannot begin to understand gravity in a way that physicists do unless you are already a master of the first six grades of physics. You can say that Newton was a path breaker in that he went through those six grades for us. Now we have all formulated and regimented it and it is very easy for us to make that re-discovery of gravity.

So gravity had to be something not only out there, it had to be something in here; but actually what was happening in the moment that Newton discovered gravity was that he became one with the alethic truth, that is the real truth, of gravity. And in becoming one with gravity he was able to produce a scientific revolution. All I am saying is that the truth of gravity was already implicit within him. This takes us back, of course it must have been, but he had to dig very deep in an objective way down into the innermost reaches of his being to reach that truth. If you want to accept that line of reasoning then you can say perhaps it is not so absurd to claim, as I have heard some people claim, that you can find many truths on atomic structure in the Vedas that actually were there because people reached deep enough down into their being, even though they could not communicate it to anyone else, in meditative or far down meditative states. That remains a possibility. Who knows what went on when Pythagoras or Plato were teaching. Just to go through what would happen in the case of a dialectic of learning. You have this truth, you suddenly re-discover it for yourself, of gravity. Then you must make this truth part of your being. So long as it is not part of your being, so long as it is something heteronomous you cannot act in a non-dualistic way with it. When you see it only in a non-dualistic way, it stands a chance of being spontaneously right. Non-dual action is spontaneous action. Any dualistic action will have a split intentionality and cannot at least be spontaneously right. If it is right, it is only right if everything else happens successfully or just correctly as it should.

So far I have argued for the importance of transcendence of the ground state, of the cosmic envelope and for transcendental identification. If we are to do anything, if we must ultimately do it spontaneously, another way of looking at this is, if we are to do anything then ultimately we must do it. Is there any other person who can do it. Ultimately, we are the point of agency. All action has to be related back to the self. The only way you can change the world is by doing something. This does not mean that your vision has to be restricted. I argue that the ego, the sense of your own self as separate was an illusion, but the only way you can bring about a better society is by acting. And when you are acting you are doing something on yourself. You are not doing something on anyone else. Your action may have an effect on someone else but you cannot change anyone else. You can only change, effect change from the point of your action. This is one of the core theses of the primacy of the standpoint of self-referentiality which in ancient Greece in the western tradition, which derives from ancient Egypt through ancient Greece, is called the hermetic tradition.

Ultimately you have to test every truth for yourself. The only way you know what is right and wrong is by testing it in yourself. What I am saying is that it is actually the only way you can act. You cannot act through someone else. If you look at our manipulative instrumentalist reasoning it is all directed at trying to make someone else do something for you. You tell your functionary but how does he remain your functionary. Only because his circumstances are such that he feels he must do what you say. If he stopped feeling that then he would not be your functionary. You may have the most wonderful insight into the need for evolutionary change. How do you communicate that to other people? You could only do it by acting in the best possible way, be the most forceful communicator yourself. You cannot get someone else to communicate for you. So that as you become more free of all your sense of egoism and all the elements of heteronomy, all those things which are inconsistent with your ground state, your personality, your embodied personality will expand and grow. And when you no longer have a sense of ego, a sense of your own separate identity distinct from the rest of the world, then you will not be treating the rest of the world in a manipulative, instrumental way but you will be entirely oriented to the emancipation of other beings just as much as your own.

This standpoint of self-referentiality is the only standpoint which is consistent with an orientation to the good society, the eudemonistic society, that is the global and universal revolution. When you realise that you are not separate from the rest of the universe, then you can adopt the standpoint of no ego, and when you understand the primacy of self-referentiality then you will inevitably be attempting in your right-action to materially embody, practically engage and work for the social realisation of everyone else. Not for a moment could you accept the goal of individual emancipation. Individual freedom. In fact if you look at individual freedom, what could this possibly be. If I really am separate from you then individual freedom is an illusion. The only freedom can be universal self-realisation, universal freedom. If I have no ego then how can I be liberated or free if you are still unfree. This gives a rationale to the idea of the Bodhisattva. The idea that he is not just giving up his freedom for others but that he has no sense of his own freedom. He has no ego to liberate. He is just an expanded personality who is working through what he must work through physically here in the world, as an embodied personality with physical, emotional, mental and supramental powers, for the realisation of all beings. There is no incompatibility between commitment to universal self-realisation and what seems to be the most subjective position you can have, that no one else can liberate you, you have to do it yourself, and you cannot impose freedom or emancipation upon anyone else. Freedom cannot impose on anyone else, you cannot emancipate anyone else. You can unlock the prison doors, emancipation in that sense, but ultimately the prisoners will walk out of the doors. Ultimately all you can do for the whole of society, every being in society is to unlock the doors, they have to walk out. This theory then is one which implies a commitment to total universal self-realisation.

Creativity then is the emergence of something new. How does this come about? Creativity, the emergence of something new, actually is a feature of every genuine human act. How impossible it is not to be creative. Imagine on a factory assembly line, which seems the complete opposite of creativity, what tremendous regimentation it involves to stop people being creative. It is extraordinary. We can generate a fantastic critique of the institution of organisational structures of our society just by looking at how creativity is suppressed. But a factory line cannot keep going, your computer will not work unless you are innovative, creative, you can adapt immediately, spontaneously, intuitively to the situation that is wrong. The workers keep the factory line going and they do it in a spontaneous, intuitive, non-dual way. That is their spontaneous creativity that the logic of our social systems deny. If you think about it repetition is really impossible because the repetition is always the production of something new. When you repeat something it can be very very boring but actually what you are doing is changing the status quo, changing from what it would have been otherwise. Creativity is essential to change and is implicit in every transformative human act, let me relate this back to left versus right brain. I will just say a little bit about love and a little bit about agency. Creativity is the emergence of something new out of the blue, but something which must be implicit in the creative agent.

Love is a basic attractive, binding, healing, totalising force in the universe. How is it that the most horrible things we know, if scratched hard enough, are actually sustained by love. What could be worse than war, violence between armed bodies of men. What does war actually involve? It involves solidarity of the soldiers at the front. That is the full manifestation of love. It involves the support and sustenance of their sisters at home. If you scratch any emotional situation you will find there love. Even to take an example from Plato, using it in a slightly different way from him, a gang of robbers could not stay together for a moment unless they showed some degree of solidarity. This is the developing, nurturing, shaping force in social life.

Spontaneous activity we have always seen is necessary for anything else. We can look now at five cycles of creativity which are involved in everything, anything, any state of being, anything that happens in the world.

First you have being, which is implicit. Then there must be the moment of becoming. These are all mapped out as moments or stadia or systems of critical realism. The first I have called ontology, which just means thinking being, and then we have to deepen our thinking of being to encompass being as a process, we have to think being using concepts of absence, think being processually, think being as involving change. The third thing when we are thinking being in a concrete way, is to think being as being bound together; we have to think being holistically as a totality, and I would argue that the primary and binding force in the social world is love. The fourth level of thinking being, we are not only thinking being processually, as involving creativity and emergence, process and change, we are thinking being holistically as a whole, the fourth moment which we think being as involving transformative agency. That is as involving making, doing, and objectification. When you perform an act you send something out into the world. The ideal here at the level of agency would be to get your actions absolutely right so that what you send out into the world correctly reflected your intentionality so that your intentionality was fulfilled. This cycle has a fifth level which is the fulfilment of intentionality in the world. If your intentionality is not fulfilled in the world then you have a choice: you either return to the task and try and fulfil it in the world or you move on to something else. If your intentionality is not correctly reflected in the world and if you do not let go or release your intentionality then it will still be in you whatever happens. .

Let me show you how this works. Supposing I have the intentionality, or someone else has the intentionality to hit someone else in the world, that intention to hit someone else will actually, whether they succeed in it or not, bind that other being in transcendental identification; what happens is that I become one with someone else. Or, we could argue from the standpoint of self-referentiality that I must also be that other. That other, that gravity that must be implicit within me, therefore what I would hit or teach, you must also be implicit within me. So the hitting of you actually is also a hitting within me. This is how *karma* is not something speculative but actually entailed by this ontology that I am mapping. You are co-present in me, therefore whatever I intend to you, will be within me. Because you are actually in me, and so that will return to me. The only way it will not return to me is if I let go unconditionally and in a completely unattached way—I just give it to you. If I try and tell you something and I hope you will learn or understand what I have told you, and I do not just give it to you unconditionally and spontaneously, then this wanting to have an effect on you will still remain within me. If every act you do, you just totally give completely, unconditionally and spontaneously to the world, then there is no way it can bind you because you have lost all sense of attachment. You are the world, remember you are the world, this is true, absolutely true, there is no individual ego, we are all bound up with other aspects, other beings in the world, and all other beings in the world are implicitly one within us. What you have to do is reach a point where whatever your act, your intentionality will be fulfilled, and you will have no sense of desire or attachment to the result. If you have an attachment to that result, then that will be in you in one way or another.

What would it be to be in such a state of non-attachment? This would mean that you were at one with your ground state, this would mean action flowing spontaneously from you in the best possible way. Then being at one with your innermost being you would be maximally sensitive to the whole of the universe and you would act from the only point of agency you know, which is your physically embodied personality, but you would act from the perspective of the whole totality. Acting from such a perspective, your inner submissiveness to your ground state, your clearing of your embodied personality and all mental, emotional and physical aspects which could mean blocks on your action, then you would just be an extension of your ground state and you would just immediately and spontaneously be at one with the rest of the universe, and act in a maximally coherent, compassionate and creative way.

There is an old question. Someone says they go into a lovely state, and they go into a state of unity with themselves. If you think you are in that state of non-duality then you are not, you are actually in a state of thinking non-duality. If you think you are meditating then you are not meditating, if you think you are in a state of non-transcendence then you are not. Now we all have to talk, we are operating in a dualistic world. All the structures of contradiction and oppression and alienation are a part of this dualistic world. We can be oriented to the transformation of this world but we have to be in this world. The old standpoint, the standpoint where we could opt out of this world is no longer possible. This may have been feasible 2,000 years ago or fifty years ago. Today it is not feasible. We are all so inter-dependent and inter-connected now and the planet is hurtling to a position of global crisis, there is no way you could claim to have a sense of no ego and not be in this world. The average height of Bangladesh is 4 feet above sea level, so if present ecological trends continue, in fifty years there will be no Bangladesh, and that will be true of all the islands. We have seen from the events of the past couple of months how bound together we are. The acts and reactions of a few dozen people have hurtled the whole world into crisis. These include governments. Who actually knows any government which is really constituted in a fully democratic way? But we do know that what a few people decide in politics on some whim or other affects us all profoundly. At a structural level we know that we have chronic economic problems alongside our chronic political, social and cultural problems. Even our lives are becoming shallow as the logic of commodification and reification really takes hold everywhere. In this situation, how could you claim to be a person who had no ego, a person who was enlightened, unless you were in this world? You have to be in this world. You can have an orientation to the transformation of this world but the only way you can achieve this orientation is by actually effecting it in some way from the point of agency with which you must act.

There are five theorems in relation to action.

First, we must act. We cannot not act. That is what I call the axiological imperative. So even a person who thinks that by going on a retreat they are abstaining from action, they are also acting. Secondly, our action is intentional. We must take subjective responsibility for our intentionality. Unless our intentionality is completely pure then there is a chance that our intentionality will not be fulfilled. The purer our intentionality the more likely it is that it will be fulfilled. Does this intentionality not have to be in a dual-state? No. Because just like knowledge you can have the intention to liberate the world but you do not carry that intention in your head. Just like I do not carry the knowledge of Greek or some other philosophy in my head, it is in me. Just like your knowledge of driving or cooking is in you. The third feature of action is that at some level it must be basic and non-dual. So what I am arguing for really is that we expand the zone of non-duality in our lives. The fourth feature of action is that it always takes place in the context of (and the fifth feature is that whatever I do always affects) four planes of social being.

First of all it always involves and affects material transactions of nature. Then it always involves and affects our social interaction with others. Third, it always involves and affects, reproducing and transforming in some way, a social structure, and finally it always involves or affects the stratification of your embodied personality.

So the philosophical standpoint from which I am talking has clear implications along all these lines. We know this in terms of our material transactions with nature, in terms of the instrumental reasoning that is used by man, or in terms of the social systems that he has created and he himself sustains. And let us not think that social systems are things out there. Social systems, like capitalism, are not just out there, they are also in here, inhering in us in our daily activity, so that we unwittingly reproduce or sustain the very structures we deplore. We first have to disconnect them from within us before our actions can be maximally feasible outside. So long as you feel greed, lust, possessiveness within yourself, and you are fearful or proud, then you are the ideal functionary for capitalism. Even if you feel anger, anger is a defence against pride, and the pride is something that capitalism depends on—the pride of everyone just to get a job for a job's sake or just to get a wage to keep up with their neighbours. All these negative emotions you see are part of the logic of these social systems. Only by operating from a point which is as clear in terms of thought, in terms of feeling and physically, and which is going to be unblocked by heteronomous determinations, can you be a good agent of social change. The best thing you can do is to strive to be such a person as an embodied agent in the world, because you must act in the world. So this is arguing for a form of spirituality in which if you like transcendence or meditation becomes a part of daily life. It is not something removed from daily life. In fact if you still want to call it by that name it is your practice in daily life. And the practice is one of transformation.

If you doubt this for a moment you just scratch beneath the surface of some negative emotion and you will find love there. Love cannot do any harm. You have some problem with a situation, then just think creativity. Think creatively, be creative about it. If you do not think you are creative then just scratch anything, scratch your routines, you will see how creative you are in sustaining routines. Often you may get to a point where you will see that the mind itself is a trap. And this is the point where you transcend the mind and the mind is an instrument and you suspend thought and 'unthink'. When you get to the point where you can use the mind and unthink at will then you will be in a maximally creative space. That is the sort of space you will be in when you are in your ground state. When you get to that point then you will immediately and spontaneously, be maximally creative in the world. Similarly when you get to the point where in your emotions you feel nothing but love, joy and happiness then you will be maximally effective in the world. This does not mean that you behave in a soppy way. The best way of loving someone may be to tell them the truth and that may hurt. This does not mean that you see it as being revolutionary. The best way of loving people may be to transform structures, but this does not mean that you never kill. The best way of transforming a structure may be to shoot someone, though I am not saying it is. If you see two people fighting each other, then showing love does not necessarily mean that you abstain from the conflict. So love does not imply any particular action. It is consistent with a lot of different behaviours.

When you are in your ground state or moving towards it then you will be embodying within yourself the ideals of the three traditional paths to spiritual enlightenment: the path of knowledge, the path of devotional love and the path of action. Because you will be engaged in action.

There is nothing which I have said here that necessarily involves god, nor does it mean that you cannot believe in god. All it means is that you are committed to action for your own freedom and self-realisation and the freedom and self-realisation of all other beings in the universe. And you can be so committed in a completely secular way or you can do so on the basis of a certain set of religious beliefs and engaged in particular religious practices. Nor does this involve any prediction of what is going to happen in the future, because if you look at it any prediction would not be particularly bright. But it does involve themes that all emancipatory projects must presuppose for these projects to make sense. Which gives us hope. If you look empirically at the way the world is going then there is no hope. But let us look at it another way. The world, capitalism, the structures of oppression, evil, violence and hatred could not survive without our good nature, our love, our creative work. The totality of master–slave relationships depends entirely on the creativity of slaves. The ugly, false, vicious depend entirely on the true. It could not exist for a moment without the true, the beautiful and the loving. Nothing could be sustained. We could exist without the social structures that are oppressing us. They could not exist without us. So they depend on us because we not only represent, we are the essential ingredients of the universe. We are at the basic, fundamental level of the universe, we have the power—that level which I have called the cosmic envelope, the strength of the binding force of the universe—embodied within us. Remember capitalism and all those terrible social systems that oppress us, including those which we have internalised as our angers, hatreds and greeds, which repress us internally, they all depend on our freedom, our creativity, our love which is our greatest strength and on our sense of equity (or true equality which is respecting the differences between us all), and our inherent capacity for right-action. And they could not survive for a moment without us and our powers. So let us take strength from our realisation of this strength (i.e. power) which our strength (that one-way dependency) gives us.

Chapter Ten

The Philosophy of meta-Reality: Identity, Spirituality, System*

In his new book, Reflections on meta-Reality (RMR), *Roy Bhaskar claims to articulate a new philosophy that transcends critical realism, while preserving its insights. And indeed it proceeds by immanent critique of critical realism, thereby extending critical realism's systematic attempt to think being.*

With the demise of historical socialism and the rise of bourgeois triumphalism in the late 80s and the 90s, the deficiency, absence or lack Bhaskar has pinpointed in the discourse and practice of critical realism and the Left in general is that insufficient attention is being paid to the spiritual dimension of human life, with the consequence that the Right is hegemonic in that area. So he self-consciously set out to remedy this lack, embarking on 'the spiritual exposition of being'.

Bhaskar's previous book, From East to West (FEW), *offered 'a theory of the necessary spiritual presuppositions of emancipatory [. . .] projects', adding a fifth aspect (5A) to the MELD schema as a further transcendental and dialectical development and deepening of his system, introducing or extending notions of ultimate alethic truth or god*

* Part 1 of interview with Mervyn Hartwig, London, May 2002. Also forthcoming in *Journal of Critical Realism*, June 2002.

at *1M; creativity and transcendence at 2E; love at 3L; spontaneous right-action and cosmic consciousness or enlightenment at 4D; and fulfilled intentionality or self-reflexivity at 5A itself.*

RMR *both systematises and develops what was initiated in* FEW. *Its basic line of argument is that a non-dual world or ultimate zone of being underpins and is co-present in an occluded way in the dual world of alienation and contradiction in which we live, as a condition of its possibility, and that this requires a new philosophy of identity for its exposition. Realism about this world, about transcendence, thus entails the self-transcendence of critical realism itself, which is a philosophy of non-identity or duality. Bhaskar calls this non-dual world the cosmic envelope (in which the deepest natures or ground states of all beings sit and are connected), describing it also as Bohm's implicate order of pure enfolded being, of pure potentiality, of 'Platonic anamnesis', involving 'a level of consciousness beyond thought itself'. Other key figures, elaborated from* FEW, *are generalised co-presence or synchronicity and the inwardness of being (everything is implicated or enfolded within everything else); and transcendental identification in consciousness between entities and beings within the explicated or become dual world we inhabit.*

Mervyn

In *FEW* you distinguish (i) absolute being, characterised by identity from (ii) relative being, characterised by non-identity involving duality and union, and both from (iii) demi-real relative being, characterised also by non-identity but involving dualism and alienation. The new book largely drops the discourse of the demi-real and runs together, on the one hand, identity and union, and, on the other, duality and dualism. What's going on? From your perspective the evil and ignorance of the dual world within which we live is, as you said in *FEW*, 'a sort of grand illusion', but as you also keep insisting, illusions are only too real causally. This double aspect is precisely what the figure of the demi-real is designed to capture—like mirages, illusions are real in causal efficacy yet remain illusions because they have no real object. So why (largely) drop the figure of the demi-real, along with the distinction between duality and dualism? Are you saying that critical realism, as a philosophy of non-identity, is now only regionally applicable—appropriate only for the study of master–slave-type societies—but that we need to invoke the identity such a world presupposes both fully to explain and to move beyond it?

Roy

You are absolutely right, I do say that this transcends but preserves critical realism, and it transcends it in a very radical way. It can be thought of as having been arrived at by taking realism about transcendence seriously. I'd like to talk a little bit about transcendence; in so far as the position in *RMR* constitutes a real break from and development beyond *FEW*, it involves understanding the absolutely foundational role the non-dual and transcendental plays in our life. Because most people who have talked about transcendence have regarded it as being something that is rather unusual or recondite, something that we have, say, in a magical moment of union with god, union with our higher self, or perhaps which we capture in a blissful experience of listening to Bach or Beethoven.

The non-dual plays a triple role in the new philosophy I'm developing. Firstly, we have to see the non-dual—whether it is consistent with our ground states or not—as a necessary condition for all social interaction and human agency. Secondly, all social interaction and human agency, whether non-dual or not, is unilaterally dependent upon the non-dual level of our ground states, which constitute the most fundamental level of our being and connect us through what I call the cosmic envelope to the rest of the universe. Thirdly, if we go deeply enough into any non-dual moment, that is into moments which are constitutive of all our experience, even the most quotidian or routine sort, we find, amazingly enough, that it reveals the properties of what the Vedic tradition called 'bliss consciousness of being' (*sat-chit-anand*); or what has been called 'suchness' (*tathata*) which is also 'emptiness' (*sunyata*) or the Buddhist 'void', but which is also the rich Buddha-nature in everything; so that in each moment of our experience, if we really go deeply into it, we get a taste or anticipation of the absolute, the ground state, or 'heaven'. Another way of putting this is to say that, if you go deeply enough into anything, you will ultimately find its existential source in a ground state on the cosmic envelope, and in the non-dual state of transcendental identification with its ultimate existential base you will be, in your ground state, at one with its ground state. So the three moments of non-duality, which I have been differentiating, are then all brought together.

The most radical thing I am saying here is that transcendence and transcendental identification is a ubiquitous feature and a necessary condition for all social interaction and all human agency; that, unless we were in a non-dual state, I cannot understand what you are saying. In that aspect of reality in which I understand your question to me, we have transcendental identification. I immediately identify with you, I am in a non-dual state. It is not a dual state. When someone is watching television they immediately follow it, they are not in a dual state. When someone is performing a basic spontaneous act, they are in an immediate state of non-duality and we cannot do anything at all unless at some point we just did something immediately, spontaneously, basically. And then, of course, as complex beings, we can do lots of other things too in virtue of our spontaneous basic acts. What I am saying is that society couldn't function, and we couldn't communicate, or do anything at all, unless we were in non-dual states. That is the first aspect.

The second aspect concerns our ground states, which are characterised by qualities such as, corresponding to 1M, our implicit human potential and freedom; corresponding to 2E, creativity; corresponding to 3L, love; corresponding to 4D, right-action; and corresponding to 5A, the fulfilment of our intentionality. Now the important point here is to see that we can't do anything in our social activity that does not make use of or depend upon these ground state qualities, such as creativity, love and right-action. We cannot do anything at all except creatively. There cannot be a social situation which was not underpinned and characterised by love. We cannot say that someone had performed an act at all, even if what he did was something absolutely stupid and heinous, unless it was, at some level, a spontaneous right-action.

The third aspect, which is not really very well developed in *RMR* (but will be in the forthcoming books, particularly *Beyond*

East and West[1] and *meta-Reality*[2]), is that in which, if you go into the fine structure of a non-dual moment, you will see that it is characterised by some remarkable qualities, and if you can stay with these, they give you a kind of pre-figuration of what society might be like. And that is really extraordinary. In a way, in each moment of our life, if we live, experience it really clearly, fully, we have a little taste of heaven. Of course, it is occluded and dominated by hell. So these then are the three aspects.

The first feature depends upon the fact that we can't do anything at all unless we are in transcendental identification, unless we are performing at some level transcendental acts. But these need not be consistent with our ground states. Consider someone who is doing something really terrible, like shooting someone else, or beating someone up. That can be a non-dual act, and in that sense it is transcendental, but it is not coming from their ground state. The second feature then pinpoints the fact that the robbery or murder or whatever, which involved that non-dual component, still couldn't have been possible without at some level being sustained by his or someone else's love, solidarity, compassion, creativity. Normally robbers are very creative people, and they also have to be loyal to their own kind. If you take the most regimented actions in capitalist society, you will find that there is a level which is, so to speak, below and underpinning the level of the extraction of surplus value in Marx's theory, which is unpaid. Consider the role of women's domestic labour in the reproduction of labour power. Or the sense in which it is not a part of Andrew's 'job description' here to make the coffee. But he does. And similarly it is not part of his job to kick the computer, but when he has to, he does. And this sort of thing is necessary for any production line, in any office, in any household. There is a level at which we have to act spontaneously, unconditionally, effortlessly, in the moment and without thinking.

---

[1] Roy Bhaskar, *Beyond East and West: Spirituality and Comparative Religion in an Age of Global Crisis*. Sage: New Delhi, London: Thousand Oaks, 2002.
[2] Roy Bhaskar, *meta-Reality: The Philosophy of meta-Reality, Volume 1: Creativity, Love and Freedom*. Sage: New Delhi, London: Thousand Oaks, forthcoming.

Mervyn

Nonetheless we remain dual beings embodying both duality and dualism.

Roy

Precisely. The thing is, we are almost all dual beings. What does this mean? This means that in addition to our ground states, and qualities which are consistent with our ground states, we have lots of heteronomous qualities which block, constrain, drain our ground states. This highlights the importance of the idea of the TINA formation. This really seems to me to be central to all emancipatory projects.

The idea in any emancipatory project is that there is a level of being which is basic, primary, good, natural, and that that level of being is occluded and dominated by a superstructure which constrains it. That's what I think every emancipatory theory claims—that we are in conflict, we are in contradiction with ourselves. It is not only our fault as individuals, because society is like that too; we, as heteronomous individuals, reproduce or transform a heteronomously constituted social form. Now, the extraordinary thing is that, if you look at the amount of energy we actually put into keeping all our neuroses, addictions, oppressions and self-oppressions—that is, our heteronomy—going, it is just not worth the candle. Because all of that—all the blocks and oppressions—have to be sustained, kept in place, by the energy, intelligence, love, creativity and our capacity for right-action which flows from the ground state.

So the obvious question is: why don't we get rid of all the bullshit? Because, for anything we want to do, we'll do it better and be better off without the constraints on our ground state qualities, which block and impede our activity in the world. For we need those ground state qualities anyway, even if we want to do something like rob a bank. Suppose we decide to do something which we know is really counter-productive, we will have to utilise and drain our creativity and energy even more just to sustain that counter-productive act. So I believe that the natural state of being is our ground state, and if we were in our ground states we would all flourish. For there is no contradiction, rather mutual entailment, between the goals of self-realisation and collective human emancipation, or even more basically, universal self-realisation. Even becoming a little bit clearer, a little bit freer, in yourself enables you to act a little bit more coherently, clearly, socially.

Putting this in a nutshell, there is only one thing we need in life, and that is to be clear. Whatever you set out to do, whatever objective in life you have, that will set you on a dialectic in which you will ultimately come to see that the only objective which is sustainable is to be a being who is consistent with their ground state. Because if you're not, you will always have a split intentionality. Your split intentionality will mean that you have unfulfilled intentionality. Your ground state and its intentionality is always there. You can never eliminate the intentionality of your ground state, it is the one thing you can't lose. And you'll be a split and unfulfilled personality so long as there is anything within you which is at odds or in contradiction to your ground state and its intentionality. What is your ground state's intentionality then? This is your *dharma*, what you essentially are, and are, so to speak, meant to be, how you would flourish effortlessly, as the sun shines without trying, or an acorn, if we let it, grows effortlessly into an oak. That is the model of how you could be. Putting this another way, you can never out-perform your ground state. You will always be unhappy unless you're in it, but when, how you are as an embodied personality is at one with your ground state, then you find that you grow enormously, expand, flourish.

Mervyn

[Our ground state is basically, then, our essential human nature— Marx's 'species being', what you called in *Dialectic* 'our core universal human nature'?]

Roy

[Yes, that's right.] When you're in your ground state does this mean you're free? Well it means there is nothing in you which is a result of your intentionality that is blocking you. But of course there are a lot of other things in the world outside you, which are still blocking you, so you immediately fight to remove them. And part of that fight will be to aid and empower the struggle of all beings everywhere, to get rid of their heteronomies and those emergent strata, the social forces and entities and systems which are blocks and constraints for us all. Nor am I saying you first become realised and then engage in social action—because at each point you are engaged in social action. I am completely opposed to the idea of the 'beautiful soul', the idea that you can retreat from this world. Let's take an example. If someone has a problem with their jealousy, what good is it their going on a retreat and spending six months working on their jealousy, when there is no one there to be jealous of. They have to work on their jealousy on the site, with the people they're jealous of. We work on ourselves while we're working in the world and this entails a critique of both traditional religiosity and traditional politics. For politics, political action without self-transformation is useless, and believing that you can become a perfect or realised being without acting in this world is delusory.

I think it is important to say here very specifically what we have to lose to become enlightened or realised. First we have to lose our ego, because, being in our ground state, we would see that our freedoms were indivisible. Secondly, we need to be intellectually more generally mentally clear, that is have no fixations, no prejudices, no preconceptions; in a way everything that we know in-built into our being, so that our minds are as free, clear, empty, flexible and creative as possible. Thirdly, we have to be emotionally clear; and this is a very difficult one to work on because most of us have problems with one or more emotional states, anger, jealousy or whatever. So no ego, a clear mind, a pure heart, and then, fourthly, a healthy and energised body; that is, we need to be as well balanced and healthy as we can. But there's a fifth condition, we need our 'psychic being' to be clear too, that is, free of all traces and residues of the past, which include *karma* from our past in this life and, if we believe in them, our past lives; but also our past in the form of the residues or scars of our experience buried in our unconscious—we need to transform our unconsciousness into consciousness, and, like our *karma*, clear it, release it, let go of it; get totally free of our past. Indeed, you could say that ultimately we need to be free of our genes, our genetic endowment too. When these five conditions are satisfied we'll be a *realised* being. But it's very important to appreciate we still won't be *free* so long as there is heteronomy outside us which constrains our action; so ultimately we can only be free in activity, only fulfil our ground state potential in a society in which everyone is free. There is thus a direct link between my own freedom and everyone else's.

Mervyn

Are you partly getting at what Kathryn Dean seems to be getting at in a recent paper[3] when she says:

> dichotomous conceptions of social relations as well as the dichotomies of individual/society and structure/agency are of sociological and therefore political significance only in highly differentiated and contradictory cultures such as that of capitalism. A critical realist account of subjectivity must deconstruct these dichotomies to show that the 'social' is in the strongest sense intra-psychic and that it is the specific 'social' of capitalist cultures which produces the individual/society and structure/agency dichotomies. For this reason, I can't agree with critical realists such as Archer and Bhaskar who insist on maintaining these dichotomies.

I take it that you're now not insisting on maintaining those dichotomies—far from it. You presumably don't agree that the social is just intra-psychic in slave-type societies, but perhaps you envisage that it will be in post-slave ones? You say in *RMR* (p. 113) that social structure is both out there and in here, inherent within us—in post-slave society it will be entirely within us?

Roy

There are two points, the point about critical realism generally and the point that Kathryn Dean is raising. The thing is, I think critical realism is all its five phases as I periodise it, and of course you can break it up in different ways and you can go into the

---

[3] 'Capitalism, psychic immiseration, and decentred subjectivity', *Journal for the Psychoanalysis of Culture & Society* 5:1, Spring 2000, pp. 41–56.

microstructure of these phases and the different ways in which they could be developed—that is absolutely valid. On the one hand, it's the best account we have of the world of duality. The best account of what we have to get rid of to be realised, to be enlightened, to be free, to be living in an eudaimonistic society. The best account of our obstacles and our blocks.

But there is another side to it, which is the non-dual basis of that world. And this has not been theorised by critical realism. Nor to my knowledge has it been theorised systematically and adequately by any other philosophy. One could, of course, take Vedanta in India. But there would be two things I have to say here. First, the world of duality is not an illusion; it contains illusions, but they are causally efficacious realities which constitute and block the fulfilment of our intrinsic potential. Secondly, Vedanta and other traditions have placed great emphasis on practices such as meditation, and even given the impression that the route to enlightenment is to be achieved through meditation, and that everything else you need, all the other virtues, will flow automatically, so to speak, from good meditation. This gives a very misleading picture. For the point of enlightenment is defined by the shedding from your embodied personality of everything which is inconsistent with your ground state. As and when you are shedding, you are gradually able to embed your embodied personality in your ground state, and your personality becomes saturated with the qualities of your ground state in an unalloyed form; qualities such as love and creativity, which are manifesting and expressing themselves anyway, are now allowed to develop and flourish freely, and your consciousness is suffused with the properties of the transcendental consciousness of your ground state. As you move into your *dharma*, everything will become for you more effortless, more spontaneous, you will have more energy, tend to get more things right, etc. But you will still be living in the world of duality, and so your *dharma* won't be realised, your freedoms will be impeded by things outside yourself, and your intentionality can't be fulfilled or perfectly expressed. Redefining the goal of enlightenment as shedding focuses on the embodied personality which is what needs changing, transforming. Your ground state is fine. Of course it's wonderful to have beautiful meditations. They can energise you and help in many other ways, but what you have to do is become a better, which means clearer, person in the relative phase of existence. Meditation can allow you to access your ground state, but according to my way of looking at things we're accessing our ground state all the time. We, that is our embodied personalities, can achieve transcendental identification with our own higher, innermost being, i.e. our ground state, in meditation, inaction, in removal from active life, but the definition of an enlightened being is someone who is in a non-dual state in the relative phase of existence, that is in ordinary life.

This redefines the goal of enlightenment, and no-one has put it exactly like this before. The goal is to shed everything within your embodied personality which constrains, blocks and gets in the way of your ground state qualities and hence your feeling of total solidarity with all other beings. In the first instance this solidarity will probably be mainly with other human beings. Of course this doesn't mean that you'll treat each human being in the same way. The way you behave, the way you manifest your unconditional love in relation to other beings, will depend on the concrete singularity of your relation with them; thus if someone had given me their child to look after during this interview I wouldn't treat them in the same way as I'd treat you. Non-judgmentalism is very important here and it goes hand-in-hand with the fact that we all have unique ground states, concretely singularised, specific *dharmas*. One of the features of the philosophy I'm presenting in this book is that it applies concepts such as dialectical universalisability and concrete singularity, which were initially developed in relation to the relative world of duality, to the absolute world of non-duality, which I'm arguing is its basis and condition of possibility.

So we have this idea of critical realism as being the best account of what we have to get rid of. But then we have to know what sustains it, and that is what the philosophy of meta-Reality does. So we incorporate, we retain all the critical realist moments. And this is quite in line with my understanding of the history of critical realism, because in the very first phase there was, for example, the idea of laws being tendencies, the transfactuality of laws; that is retained in the second phase and the third and the fourth and the fifth. You don't give that up, there is still a distinction between the transitive and the intransitive, that doesn't go; it's just that now the distinction between knowledge and being has to be theorised within being, and similarly the world of duality, structured in terms of our concepts of non-identity, has to be inserted within what I call rich concepts of identity. These are differentiated concepts. You see, people have thought of identity as being punctiform and even spiritual philosophers have called it that. Actually, if you are in unity with my words now, or any word, or a television picture, you are in unity with a whole. It is not punctiform, no example of transcendence that I've ever heard of is without differentiation. Similarly with development.

Mervyn

I want to ask why you drop the distinction between union and identity in favour of identity? Why isn't constellational union still the appropriate concept instead of identity? And why doesn't this shift to identity end up leaving you where it left Hegel—unable to sustain real negativity and open totality?

Roy

I do in this book actually use the idea of philosophy of meta-Reality as being the constellational unity of duality and non-duality.

Mervyn

Sometimes you say identity and sometimes you say unity, previously you would have strictly said unity rather than identity.

Roy

This is a very important point, because when you perform any simple act, for example, read the newspaper, you are in immediate identity. So union is too weak. But unity also has its place because, when we are living in a eudaimonistic society, then we won't be identical. You'll be different from me, but we'll be in unity. Your ground state is different from mine, that gives you a different *dharma*, a different set of qualities, a different set of potentials, from mine. You will value our diversities. And so we need concepts of unity as well as identity. Duality is a very important concept for the philosophy of meta-Reality because it is precisely that which we are trying to eliminate or reduce.

Let me align two sets of distinctions. The distinction between the demi-real, the relative and the absolute; and the distinction between the oppositional or antagonistic dual, the non-oppositional (non-antagonistic) dual and the non-dual—and in particular the contrasts between oppositional dualistic activity and non-oppositional dualistic activity and non-dual being. As a realised non-dual being, you will be engaged in oppositional dualistic activity, struggling to eliminate heteronomies and unfreedoms which affect you and exist in the world of which you are a part. When we have a eudaimonistic society, or more generally, cosmos, then there will be no non-dual beings, but you will still be growing and developing, differentiated from other non-dual beings, and still employing dualistic modes of activity, including obviously dualistic thought and discursive language, talking about things, learning about things, etc. As a non-dual being you will recursively embed your new experiences and knowledge into your non-dual being, and as such you will be expanding in an open and, in principle, infinite way. Such a world will still be a relative world in the sense that it will be finite, governed by physical parameters and laws, you will still physically die, etc. And of course you will be engaged in dualistic activity, as part of the process of living and developing and flourishing in a eudaimonistic but relative world. In such a world there will be no demi-real, and no oppositional dualistic activity. But, in the world in which we are living now, the demi-real defines the categorial structure of the relative phase of existence. So you could say that the demi-real dominates the relative and is the form in which the relative dominates or emasculates its absolute or non-dual basis or ground. I hope this clarifies the sense in which the concepts of the demi-real and the relative retain their validity within the philosophy of meta-Reality.

Mervyn

So we need both identity and union, but does that hinge on this notion of an unmediated connection between minds, direct mind-to-mind causality? I find that very difficult to accept. I accept that you and I understand each other directly now, but I am very aware that there are all kinds of physical causes going on.

Roy

Certainly there are physical conditions, but in that moment in which you understand me or in that moment at which you follow a play on television there is no separation, no duality, no opposition, but immediate, direct understanding or following or listening, and so on.

Mervyn

There are still many brain states going on here.

Roy

But we're not talking at that level, I'm not arguing that there are not physiological conditions for transcendental identification in consciousness, but in that moment, they are as irrelevant as the weather or the position of the planets in the sky. Let me put it like this. When you're listening, you are not thinking; you're listening. As soon as you start thinking, you are not listening. When you're listening or when you're looking, you're just listening or looking and that's all. When I'm listening to you there is no ego, no duality, no separation, in that moment there is identity and not just unity.

Mervyn

We're not self-conscious of it, we're just doing it.

Roy

That's right. Of course, as an embodied personality you're over there, but notice that the moment you stop focusing, the moment you stop listening, that's when you lose the plot. This applies to whatever we do. So really the most important thing in life is single-pointedness and clarity. And when you are single-pointed and clear then you are in a non-dual state. Now, of course, we can't be in non-dual states all our life, so we have to have a new conception of our being as rich and differentiated, such that we can—because we all have to—perform non-dual actions. We all have to think, to reflect—is this the right thing to do, do I really understand Japanese, am I really understanding what Kathryn Dean is saying? But I can still be a non-dual being by recursively embedding that within my non-duality, and I am of course performing a dual action.

To answer Kathryn Dean. Once we view our embodied personalities within what I call four-planar social being—this concept was there in *Scientific Realism and Human Emancipation*, but was only really fully developed in *Dialectic*—we have a much richer understanding than that provided by my efforts to transcend dualism and dichotomy in *The Possibility of Naturalism* (*PON*). Some critical realists are still, it seems to me, fighting on the battleground of *PON*; so reconciling and re-articulating the relationship between structure and agency (e.g. against Tony Giddens) is still very important to them—and it is important. But I agree with Kathryn Dean. I think society is in here, and that really makes it a lot easier, it makes the task of transforming society much easier when we realise that what ultimately keeps the whole production line going is our desires, our greed, our vanity, our selfishness in failing to see that there is another way in which we can collectively satisfy our egos.

Mervyn

You want to say society is just in here?

Roy

No, that's why I've got four-planar social being. Actually when we act *in-here*, at the dimension which I call (d), that is of the stratification of our personalities in the conception of four-planar social being, we're also simultaneously acting *out-there*, at all the other dimensions of four-planar social being, that is potentially at the level of our material transactions with nature, at the level of our social interactions with other people and at the level of social structure. And I'm also saying that there is no other way in which we can act: on the one hand, we can't act in-here without acting out-there; and on the other hand, we can't act out-there save by acting in-here—that's the only point of our agency in the world, we can only act from ourselves, necessarily.

Mervyn

She actually said that society is in the strongest sense within yourself.

Roy

She has made the point that we internalise social forms and I agree with her. The thing is, a master–slave relationship is at once out-there and in-here. One of the things about this philosophy is that, although we inwardise, we don't collapse externality. They didn't understand this in India, because in India there is a long tradition of inwardising everything, uncompensated by retaining or developing adequate conceptions of the outer, the not-self. And this is, in a way, reflected in Indian philosophy, in the very centrality and wonderful ambiguity of the concept of the self, on the basis of which subjectivity spreads outwards to encompass the totality.

As you know, Kant had this dictum that the starry heavens are out-there and the moral law is in-here. I am not too keen on the 'moral law', the ethics here is a virtue-based ethics. But the point I want to make is that the starry heavens are not just up there, they're also in-here, enfolded within us. And they all said, oh, that's great, my starry heaven is different from yours. But hang on a moment, the starry heavens are also out-there. In other words, capitalism is also out-there, it's not just in your head. You have to work on it out-there. Global warming is not just an idea, it is a reality. A reality of course produced largely as a result of the ideas that humanity has had and objectified in its technologies. But still a reality out-there.

Mervyn

As we've seen, you argue that 'realism about transcendence leads into the transcendence of realism itself in a "new, more totalising worldview"' (as is the way with immanent critique). You claim that, in shedding duality, we shed the semiotic triangle, i.e., the distinction between the signifier and the referent, and the signified and the referent, achieving an immediate identity of meaning and being (reality is immediately meaningful) and of value and being or the sacred and profane (things are intrinsically right or wrong). So we have the re-enchantment or re-spiritualisation of reality. The world is of course always already enchanted—it's just that we denizens of the demi-real don't see it: the modernist ideology of disenchantment, which says there isn't any meaning or value in being, masks it. When we shed the mask, we see, and our powers to see expand. This seems a wonderfully attractive notion for our times, and a very big and bold thought, but I have at least one big problem with it.

It seems to entail that we lose referential detachment and hence the intransitive dimension. Does this mean that in eudaimonia we shed realism itself, retaining it only for the study of the past? What are we left with—presumably not irrealism—just realism about everything as usual, but with everything now in the transitive dimension as 'existence' and 'essence' are brought into line by absolute reason? Such that a generalised hermeneutics and semiotics will provide the appropriate methodologies rather than realism (and you have a brief section on this)? Also, you had previously argued that referential detachment is a necessary condition for specifically human being, so again, are you now saying that it is only applicable regionally? But if it doesn't hold in eudaimonia, how could we even talk about anything? (Existential intransitivity was previously a necessary condition for discourse itself.) Indeed, how could we have anything to say to each other?

Roy

You're absolutely right. Referential detachment and realism will always be there, and that's something I insist on. Because, when we have a eudaimonistic society, we'll want to grow and develop, we won't stop using our minds, we won't stop using language, we won't stop referring to things. Even for me, when we talked about identity and unity a moment ago, I will be physically separate, I will still be an embodied being, and you'll be different from me both in your ground state and your physical spatio-temporal distinctness. This will be the end of pre-history. We'll have fantastic challenges, we will want to expand our minds, and we will talk about the basic things without constraint. So it is getting rid of the constraints, everything we do will be consistent with our ground state, and in a eudaimonistic society every being would be free. Because as long as some being is not free then your intentionality cannot be fulfilled in so far as your intentionality depends on them. This is the most important thing to realise. I don't know a philosophy that has said this in quite the same way, quite so clearly, that when we are in a eudaimonistic society this is the beginning of real challenges and the beginning of real history. We'll use our minds and our linguistic abilities, we'll use our capacity to refer, to much greater effect. I'm not saying we are not embodied personalities. I'm saying underneath and underlying our embodied personality there is something more important, our ground state. When you get rid of all the blocks within your embodied personality which actually precluded it from growing, and you're only at one with your ground state, because your ground state is sustaining it, your embodied personality will then expand, it will soar. So this is very much within the conception that Marx had, and of course we'll always use language, the domain of realism never goes. The domain of referential detachment never goes, but referential detachment is underpinned by non-dual immediate identification, and if we weren't in a non-dual state now we couldn't be talking about anything. This talking about anything is sustained by our talking. And in just talking we are in a non-dual state.

Mervyn

You say, memorably, that the philosophy of meta-Reality espouses 'a spirituality within the bounds of secularism, consistent with all faiths and no faith'. Is this agnosticism in relation to the existence of god? (You say in one of your lectures that you honestly don't know what lies beyond the cosmic envelope.) Or are god and the divine just metaphors for the cosmic envelope, for the intrinsic cosmic structure of possibility? Or are you saying something stronger than this, that there's a divine purpose or plan (whose realisation in an open world is however up to us)? But if that's the case, how is it that we have a secularism albeit a spiritual one?

Roy

What I'm saying is that I think I can prove that at the end of the day, whatever you want in life, you have to reach a point of self-consistency with your ground state, and that will take you to a position where you desire and fight for the self-consistency of all beings with their ground states, in recognition that every ground state will be different. And all these ground states are connected by the cosmic envelope. That ideal is, I think, implicit in all emancipatory projects. You can also find it in all the religious traditions if you look, at least little bits of it. If you take a very transcendent monotheistic religion like Judaism, it's still arguably there in a subtle way. One of the books coming out soon is based on lectures I gave in India recently on comparative religion and spirituality.[4] I think there is a remarkable unity within religious traditions. Religious practices I honestly have got very little sympathy for, but if someone finds a particular religious practice helpful, that's fine. Similarly, if you look at most libertarian or socialist projects, you will see they eventually presuppose something pretty close to the position I am articulating here. So where does god fit into all this? The thing is, if someone wants to say god is the cosmic envelope, that's fine. If someone wants to say, OK, I agree with everything you've said, and I can find this also in my religion, but there is something beyond the cosmic envelope which is the cause or creator of the cosmic envelope, that too is absolutely fine with me. There may well be a cause, and there may not be a cause, the point is really, if you like, this is a minimal programme, a programme on which all people who want to see a eudaimonistic society, or achieve any objective in life, or ensure the survival of the planet, can all agree. And they can still go on being a Muslim, do their five sets of *rakats* a day, or be a Christian, Hindu, Sikh, Buddhist, or whatever. It doesn't really matter.

---

[4] *Beyond East and West*, op. cit.

It follows obviously from what I am talking about here that they shouldn't go around slitting each other's throats, and certain forms of political practice are completely wrong.

Let's take the case of the collapse of actually existing socialism. The immediate producers were never in control, and at some stage, despite the fact that the immediate cause might have been capitalist encirclement at some point, the whole project of transferring power from the bureaucracy to the immediate producers collapsed. At some point the project stopped being that of building a different kind of society and instead became a matter of producing a society which would do capitalistic or consumeristic type things, like build motor cars or go to the moon, better than the Americans. Now while the Soviet bloc was importing a western technology which had a built-in incentive, a monetarised incentive, for creative innovation, they could do far better than the west. And that is why, in the 60s, it looked as if they were going to overtake the west. The first space ship was a Soviet one, and were the Americans worried! The strange thing is that in 1989 the so-called realists in international relations theory, led by people like Kissinger, had persuaded everyone that the Soviet bloc was here to stay. Well, of course, what had happened is that no-one in the Soviet Union really knew how to handle a computer, they were all drunk before eight o'clock in the morning, there was nothing in life for them to live for, except possibly American pop music or a holiday by the Black Sea; at some point, the lie was exposed. There was no source of dynamism intrinsic to the Soviet bloc. Gorbachev tried to produce it, and what a result. He was a really great man, the main effect of it was the opposite, of course, of what he intended. So little creativity, so little love, had been allowed to be expressed under actually existing socialism that those who came through were nearly all westerners—a Russian Orthodox Church fell out of the cupboard, that was the only institution that had somehow kept going. And then, when they got to the west, or the west got to them, they realised that now they were living in a much more insecure society, and they started realising that they had lost many things. The root cause of the collapse was the failure to do the socialist thing, the failure to observe the third thesis on Feuerbach, that if you want to educate society, if you want to transform society, you have got to educate and transform yourself. That is the basis. We can't just transform an objectified reified social structure without transforming the human beings, and once you transform the human beings, once you unleash their ground state qualities, you'll find they have tremendous creativity—actually their creativity was manifest in things like chess that were kept going.

Mervyn

Qualities which a modern atheist will think have nothing to do with god or anything like that.

Roy

That's fine by me. The thing is, you could say there is an argument for god that goes like this. If you look at all the parameters etc., they have to be so precisely attuned to each other that it would be the most extraordinary accident. But I don't agree with that argument at all. You could say, for Mervyn to be Mervyn, just imagine what would have to happen. For you to have turned out exactly like you, the chances would be astronomical. In other words, anything that happens in the world is always going to strike you as a miracle, so it's an absolutely absurd argument. For all we know, there may be at a parallel level thousands of universes which are working with other parameters, and we don't know that's not true. So if someone asks me, well, is god up there or not, surely you can tell us, I say really I don't know. All I know is that it is possible and arguable to talk about a level of unity which is perhaps beyond self-realisation and beyond what, to use Christian terms, would be called the establishment of the kingdom of heaven on earth—that is when everyone's realised, everyone's self-realised, that would be like a communist society, and that's the condition Jesus has in mind when he says, look, I'm going to join my father, you go and establish the kingdom of heaven here on earth. That meant he is becoming god. What would that mean? In secular terms that would mean that it was possible, perhaps, for a human being to become one with the cosmic envelope. At the moment I don't know, but that would be what I call god-realisation. You can imagine that as an ideal, but it would still be within the bounds of this ontology.

Mervyn

Some critical realists just couldn't accept that.

Roy

That's fine, but it is conceivable that a being can set themselves a task of becoming one with the totality. For having the totality enfolded within them, which I'd say we all do—we all have that potential—we may actually become one with the totality. The totality is implicit, enfolded within us. In principle, we can make what is implicit explicit, and if everything (the totality) is implicit, in principle, we can become the totality or *its* ground state; that is, we can become one with all elements of the totality which are not inconsistent with the ground of the cosmic totality, the cosmic envelope. We might then conceive god as the *shed* totality, i.e. the totality minus that which does not reflect or fulfil, or that which is in some way inconsistent with, its ground. But it is the argument of *RMR* that everything is in the *process* of becoming one with its ground state; and this process is inevitable, irresistible and ultimately irreversible. We can only delay the end of unity with our ground state and, projecting a bit further, the end of unity with the ground of all ground states (god-realisation); we can never 'surpass' it. We can never do better than our best, but in the end we will and must just be our best.

I would not want to debunk the idea of becoming one with a totality; I don't want to say that's impossible, but we have a long way to go. If it is possible, we would have a long way to go to even start to comprehend it. And if you really ask me, I think if we become self-realised beings we've done very well, but we have to do even better because we have to radically transform the social matrix and the natural matrix in which we live so that we can fulfil our potential and our promise, which depends on everyone else being free, because we are all so interconnected. And I can't see that a spiritual being like Jesus or Buddha or Gandhi would have adopted a different approach. We are actually in crisis, and it's more important than ever to be socially engaged. As far as I know the Buddha never talked about himself, he didn't tell anyone what *nirvana* was; he said, look, if you go chasing transitory things, if you chase your cravings, you're going to be unsatisfied. There is something beyond that which is open to you, and when you are in that state you can be fully abundant and you won't need anything outside yourself.

I think you were at a talk where I spelt out Eckhart's formulation of the ideal state, which is to 'have nothing, know nothing, want nothing'. What that meant was to be empty of anything in your personality so that it is completely clear, so that it can really expand and grow. Of course at any moment of time you may be learning something, but when you learn it, then it becomes a part of your being and doesn't clutter your mind. This is very important. Let's take education. There is a conflict in educational theory, right at the centre of it, which we all know from our own experience, because teachers say to their students, don't revise before an exam, and students always do. So who is correct? Both are. The ideal would be that you fully knew your subject so you didn't need to revise; but in actuality the student doesn't fully know his subject or is not sufficiently self-confident, so he can't take the chance of not revising. But, really, when you know how to drive a car you don't think twice about it. When I say something about critical realism you probably don't have to think twice about it because you're familiar with it; I don't need to do notes for a critical realist. Now, it's a good idea, before you give a talk, just to warm up. I'm not denying this; when in his prime the long-jump marvel, Carl Lewis, used to just do a few runs a day to keep warm, that was it. We actually had a choice whether to do this interview spontaneously or for me to see the questions, but it is much better to do it spontaneously because everything is holistic. When you're listening to me now, this is holistic, we're at one. Of course, you have got to think about what's happening in terms of the interview that will come out eventually, and is it all going according to form, but it's better than it would have been if I'd seen your questions before, because I'd be thinking, oh, I haven't read that book.

Mervyn

You say we are at one but then what does it mean to say that we actually become each other?

Roy

The extraordinary thing is that, when you understand my words there is no separation, no duality between us, and no ego either, nor does the past come into it, nor the specificities of our bodily differentiations.

Mervyn

In that respect, but there are all sorts of things in which we differ.

Roy

Of course, your kidneys and your brains are distinct from mine. But look at this, if you allow your concentration to slip, if you split your intentionality, then we can't be at one, then you are a divided mind. When you are focused, then you are at one with what you are focusing; it could be playing football, or I could be playing football with myself, when I am totally focused: imagine David Beckham.[5] He is practising his free kicks, there's no one else there, but he's perfectly at one with his activity, and that's how you become proficient at anything. If we want to achieve our potentials as human beings, then we should try and be in that state as much as we can. And that goes for social change. If we want to change the social structure, we should try to be at one with our practice, and of course in unity with our comrades or colleagues. That doesn't mean that we agree about everything, of course not; just at that moment, in that struggle.

Mervyn

I can identify with David Beckham, but I can't play football like him, I can't become David Beckham.

---

[5] An English soccer star whose play exemplifies spontaneous right-action. With only a few weeks to go to the soccer World Cup, currently being contested, he famously broke the meta-tarsal bone in his left foot.

Roy

This is interesting. I must just say one thing, the day after he got his injury I went into the newsagent and Tony Blair was saying there is nothing more important in our society than David Beckham's left foot! That's the level of our political leadership! But let's put this the other way around. I don't know whether you'll watch the World Cup on television, but most English people will, they'll be identifying, and they'll be one with David Beckham's right foot, when we're losing 1-0 to Argentina and there are two minutes left to go and this is the last chance really to get back in the game and go through, everyone will be one.

Mervyn

One of the things I personally find truly impressive about the book is the multiple articulation and re-articulation of your system along a range of dimensions, with everything ultimately driven by the central concepts of absence and transcendence, such that we come to see in the end that, as in your system, so in the world of which it is a part and seeks to grasp in thought, everything is in open process and inter-connected. All this is nicely resumed in the book, as indeed it has to be, because exposition of transcendence produces an expansion of the critical realist ontology at every one of its moments. The articulation and re-articulation occurs

   (i) internally, both diachronically and synchronically, in relation to each of the moments of the MELDA schema;

  (ii) externally, in relation to the main moments of the philosophical discourse of modernity and associated socio-economic forms—again proceeding by immanent critique, and contextualising each moment in relation to a world-historical event (this contextualising is something you haven't previously done very much, so it's particularly good to see);

 (iii) vertically, in relation to the ground state properties of will (1M), creativity (2E), love (4D), and fulfilled intentionality or reflexivity (5A);

 (iv) mimetically or recapitulatively, in relation to the creative unfolding of being as such (cosmogeny) which is in turn reflected in the historical process of self-realisation (phylogeny, history), and in turn again in the development of the embodied personality and the psychic being (ontogeny and—if reincarnation is true—the odyssey of a soul over many lives). As we 'unfold ourselves in an ever-increasingly universal way', mimicking cosmic creation in cosmic consciousness, so does your system.

I personally find this exhilarating—in the sheer range and interinanimation of its many moments, the system seems to me a thing of great beauty as well as a very handy instrument for understanding and changing the world. But, as you know, systems and grand narratives, like god, have had a bad press of late, and the new book can only add to the concerns of those who take this view because it produces a vast expansion of the previous ontology. What is your response to those who say that you elaborate 'a theory of everything', or that you deconstruct western metaphysics, only to reconstruct it, leading to 'an extreme complication, multiplication, explication' of 'precise and rigorous distinctions';[6] that you yourself are a victim of the speculative illusion which subsumes science into philosophy, if not into mysticism, that you have become a master scientist or builder rather than an under-labourer for science?

Roy

Well, if we start at the last point. Supposing I have an enemy I want to defeat; the more I know about him, the more I can become one with him, the more I'll be able to eliminate him. Judgmental rationality is certainly preserved. Supposing you're listening to me, and I'm listening to you, and you have a conception of what the ground state is and I have a conception, and these conceptions are different—or you have a conception of what truth is and I have a conception and they're different—what's the problem? You're a different human being. If you want to understand my conception, then you should really try and get into me, and at the end of the day, if you don't agree with my conception, that's

---

[6] Heikki Patomäki, *After International Relations: Critical Realism and the (Re)construction of World Politics*, Routledge, 2001, p. 6, citing Derrida.

fine. That's absolutely fine. It is up to someone else, and this is where the system bit comes in, because ultimately—extraordinarily enough—life is about consistency, reflexivity. The basic thing that's wrong with Hume is that the moment he says something like, well, it's not more rational to go out of the second floor window than the ground floor, you know that he is not at one with himself. Why? Because he always goes out through the ground floor, and of course he has got a very good reason. Everyone is unique. Marx understood that, and I think probably—well I'm sure—that Jesus and Buddha, and Socrates— other great beings with different systems of thought—they understood that. If you understand that everyone is different, then you don't try and impose your own way of life on them.

That is why I'm very opposed to moral rules as such because, supposing I'm killing someone: to kill can pretty well normally be wrong for all people all of the time, but for some people it may be the only thing they can do now and they'll have to do it. In the famous example in the Bhagavad Gita, Krishna tells Arjuna, pull yourself together, you are a great archer, be focused on what you have to do and don't worry that you're going to shoot and probably kill your kin. Put that out of your mind. You are here to participate in a war which you have decided is correct, if you wobble you're not going to fire the arrow straight at this heart which is what you've got to do, that is your *dharma*, that is your life. If someone came in here and jumped at you or Andrew with a nasty bat or something, I only hope I'd jump up and stop them. So this is about having the virtue of courage, and that stopping the intruder can be done with love. Afterwards, when the guy had calmed down, if the context was right, we might get talking and I might ask what was bugging him. He might tell me that he is having a problem with his wife, then I try and get into him and help him and hopefully he will never do that again. But just in that moment I have to act like that.

Let's take Kant's categorical imperative. If you say something like never tell a lie, according to Kant, this is only right if you can universalise it. I might say to Kant, well look, I want to tell a white lie—suppose someone's had a haircut, had all their hair shaved off and they looked terrible and they say, 'don't I look great?' I say, 'yes', because there is no way they can put their hair back on, that's a white lie. According to Kant if you accept that once, then the whole system breaks down. Because we would be telling lies the whole time. But that's absolutely not true. There would be a good reason for telling that lie, intuitively that is why we call it 'white'. A good reason which certainly would not vitiate the fact that one normally wants to know and tell the truth. But even this is not so simple. For how you tell the truth depends on who you're talking to. The truth for you is going to be more subtle, more sophisticated than for someone who doesn't know as much. At any level one has got to accept that everything has to be concretely singularised. What is virtuous for you now depends on where you are in your embodied personality, and at the end of the day we want your embodied personality to be completely in line with your ground state so that you can achieve, fulfil, any objective you want in life. And you will. Those objectives will be such that they will basically be creative and loving, you will be a wonderfully expanded personality. But you will be different from me because you are a different human being.

Mervyn

That's fine, but there are social constraints and impediments— not just at the level of the concretely singular, but the general; one of the best lines you ever wrote I think was when you said 'capitalism is founded on a lie', but when you get to that kind of assertion, how is that reconciled with epistemic relativism, with you saying in effect, well, it's only a provisional opinion given where we're at in history? What some critical realists seem worried about is that if people take 'capitalism is founded on a lie' at face value, then people will react really confidently on that, and this gets us into absolutism and non-relativism; that's what the issue is in concrete terms.

Roy

The thing *is* capitalism is founded on a lie, and we must transform it. I think it is obvious and demonstrable that we can't have a truly spiritual or fulfilling or eudaimonistic society with it— or even a society at one, consistent (organically, dialectically, develop-mentally) with itself. Note once more the importance of reflex-ivity, the unity of theory and practice. And importantly unity between the idea of *consistency*—rich, differentiated, developing, organic consistency—and *clarity*, in the sense of being clear and unconstrained by anything at any level of one's being inconsis-tent with what one most essentially is; and between consistency, clarity and *commitment* to total transformation, transformation of the totality, the whole.

The idea of truly spiritual consistent modes of existence, or a eudaimonistic society, or even self-realisation or fulfilment, with capitalism is rubbish. Now, you *can* work towards being a totally cleared being in society, now as you are, and you can become a realised being despite capitalism, but you can't fulfil your intentionality, you will never fulfil your potentiality. And because you are realised and clear you will be struggling really powerfully, not necessarily in the conventional ways, to undermine that system. There is no way that we can have eudaimonia, there is no way that even a single individual can fulfil their intentionality, achieve the fulfilment of the ground state qualities, in our existing system. We are not monads, and for me or you to achieve our potential, everyone has to be free. We have to stop the planet going down the plug, no more 9/11's, no more follow ups to 9/11. I am not making a particular political point, but no more chronic Third World debt; it has all got to go, total transformation. I would argue that I am on the Left, that I have always been on the Left, and I do not cease to be on the Left, but we have to think through a lot of our political practices much more radically. And actually, once we understand this spiritual dimension which is there within Marxism, we have a good basis to build on—emancipatory thought which is there actually within the practices as well but was not allowed to be completed; in other words there was great heroism, the Stakhonovites were fantastic, they were truly heroes and probably the whole system can only keep going because of the kind of selfless love and solidarity that they have. But it was in terms of the lie, it was in terms of the lie that they were building socialism. That lie was exposed. The lie of capitalism will be exposed. People will see it, people will walk away. They will. I am much more optimistic in a peculiar way than I was a few years ago, just because of the history of revolutions; every revolution has been unpredicted and a kind of spontaneous mechanism, a spontaneous seeing through: ah, there's a deeper level, we don't have to do this, to keep well we don't have to have capitalism! Sooner or later people will know this.

Mervyn

One of the concerns within the movement is that people find it very difficult to understand or accept your notion of ontological or alethic truth and morality, such that you can be so sure of the truth of your positions.

Roy

One of the things would be this. I say that, when Newton discovered gravity, he became one with the alethic truth of gravity, and that is an extraordinary thing to say; he was in transcendental identification, if you like, with gravity. Nowadays, when we learn the theory of gravity, we find it very easy, that it is actually within us. It was actually within him then, but given where critical science was, it was a great effort by a great mind to reach it. This may sound a little bit Trotskyist, but we are all standing on Newton's shoulders. Everyone knows that once a discovery has been made, it becomes much easier for other people to re-discover it, re-create it, make it their own. Thus it is much easier for children to use computers than it is for their parents. There is a species-specific learning, culture-specific learning. These are some of the things we all intuitively know, which the theory of co-presence can begin to help explain.

So gravity is part of our common sense now, it is an alethic truth enfolded within us, but which has been so awakened and utilised by humanity for the generations following the moment in which for the first time Newton became gravity, that gravity is something that we can all become, quite easily, when we learn it. And this is what we mean by saying that gravity is part of our common sense now.

Mervyn

One day we will see things differently again.

Roy

There is nothing wrong if every student has a slightly different conception of gravity as long as they understand basically what it is, that is absolutely fine. If you put it in the context of their total epistemic package, their take on gravity may always be slightly different from everyone else's. I don't see a problem there. It's like we can communicate in English and we've agreed that we have to be one for each other to understand what we're saying. Your understanding of what I'm saying may, in your total context, be different from what I'm saying. It doesn't matter. In that moment we understand. When you go home—I'm not saying this will happen, because I think our understanding is pretty close—at the end of the day, if your take on this conversation is a certain way, and my take on it is another way, you go on, you be free, and we have had a great conversation. Because I know this interview is intended for critical realists, let me say people have often asked me which is correct: books like Andrew Collier's or William Outhwaite's? And that is what a deep idea should do, it should have infinite possibilities for development. So I don't want us all to be the same epistemically, any more than in terms of all our other qualities.

Mervyn

But this is bound up with ontological diversity and pluralism?

Roy

There are two aspects to this. If we go a little bit beyond reality to the ideal of truth, then the alethic concept of truth, you can say, how could it not be valid—how could we live in a world which was not constituted by truths? What would we be doing? Such a world would be a subjectivist—a huge subjectivist—illusion. It would mean, really, that there would be no constraint, either within me, or outside me, or on me doing anything. As soon as you introduce the idea of a constraint on your potentiality you have to have the idea of alethic truth, that that constraint is truly a constraint on your potentiality. In other words it is truly a constraint. And then you have to have a theory of that constraint, and then a theory of getting rid of that constraint, and then a theory of what you are and why you are constrained like that, and I'm saying we are all essentially unique bundles of intelligence, creativity, love, capacity for right-action. All different. In Bengal they never identify two tigers that are exactly the same. We are like that. That does not mean we can't be one. The development of your individuality is just as much an objective as the development of my own.

Mervyn

It is perhaps unfortunate that this has all become obscured by the dominance of an extreme form of epistemic relativism today.

Roy

That's right. The truth of things is that there has to be real truth, there has to be alethic truth, otherwise we'd already be empowered, we could do whatever we wanted to do; but of course we can't, we're blocked, we're constrained, we're confused, and we have to get rid of that. The very important point is that, when you've got rid of it, there will still be truth, there will be endless truths for us to discover, we won't give up on truth, on language, realism will still be there, there will still be a place for all the theorems of critical realism. It is that we will have got rid of all the blocks and constraints within ourselves and the major blocks within society, which we ourselves produce and sustain, such as capitalism, and all the other terrible forms which can all be analysed in terms of master–slave relationships. But the biggest master–slave aspects of it are those we carry within ourselves.

The thing about systems is that it is fine for people not to have a system if they don't like it.

Mervyn

Many people nowadays are very suspicious of philosophical systems.

Roy

If someone understands that, really, they can only achieve anything in life by being clear and focused, and that ultimately they won't get anywhere unless they come into consistency with their ground state; if they're listening to what I'm saying or looking at some-thing or doing something and doing it clearly, then they will reach a point at which they will be fighting for the freedom of everyone else, all other beings. And then they do not under-stand ontology in their heads but they do in their action, and that is fine. My idea of a philosophically enlightened being is consist-ent with someone who does not read, who has never read any of my books; if he's acting in this way, that's fine, brilliant. But of course you and I are living in a very intellectualised world in which we are all engaged, you can see that, particularly academics, we all have a system. Derrida has a system, Foucault has a system, I don't know a single academic who doesn't have a system. They may have the most rotten confused system, that is the whole point. If you're going to be an academic, if you're going to be an intel-lectual, you get the best system, you get the most coherent sys-tem—you get a system, unlike Hume, that you can live with. You can't live with Derrida's system: *il n'y a pas de hors-texte* (there's nothing outside the text). What does this mean? Oh, of course! It's just a metaphor. Why do you need that way of saying things? You don't. And now Derrida has discovered religions, he has dis-covered god, he discovered Marx a few years ago—that was a bit late wasn't it!

Mervyn

Some people who read *Dialectic: The Pulse of Freedom* would wonder how you would make sense of what you were doing before that.

Roy

Everything is inter-connected. As I understand the history of criti-cal realism, it started off by trying to rectify absences within exist-ing problematics, the glaring absence of the concept of being at the time I wrote *A Realist Theory of Science*. Then from that mo-ment on it was engaged in a double dialectic, because it was en-gaged with things outside itself but at the same time was in the process of self-transcendence, until you go to the time of *Dialec-tic*; and there I had to say well, sorry, I've left out something—actually I was working on the concept of negation and absence for ten years before I got on top of it—and that is determinate absence, and that is what drives dialectic on, and now I can make sense of everything I've been doing, and now I can make sense of the possibility of human progress. And then, of course, everything since then does fall into a dialectical schema, and that takes you right through to the realm of non-duality. I might have stuck at a very primitive level of non-duality, and thought, oh, this is fantastic, I've discovered that non-duality is absolutely central to human life and existence; and then someone would say, does that mean it is absolute in the sense that you can't go any further, and how can my non-duality be any different from your non-duality? So then I had to say, this non-duality is rich, differentiated and developing, and your non-duality can be different from mine, and that is fine. Then that also involves the critique of identity. So if I had just accepted an empiricist's or an absolute idealist's concept of identity and identification and unity, that would have been terrible. So now we have got a new kind of identity theory.

Mervyn

You need to spell that out in print somewhere.

Roy

This level of identification is only part of the social story. The greater part of it is difference, non-identity, but it is underpinned by identification. But even identification gives the wrong model unless you have a new concept of identity, a new concept which is rich, differentiated. You see, practically everyone thinks of transcendental consciousness as being empty, but actually when you are in transcendental identity or union with something like some music, it is fantastically rich and complex. You are one with it, but you are one with a tremendously complex whole, and even when you're listening to my words, or I am listening to your questions, I am at one with a tremendously rich complex whole. We have had arduous preparation for this, you can say that the whole of our life has been building up to this! This is a nice point, you see, this is an example of synchronicity, because I just said something which sounds very mystical. You asked about science and mysticism. Now the characteristic feature of the mystical experience is its non-duality. People achieve or think they become one with god or maybe a saint, maybe Jesus or whatever, it doesn't matter. In the more classical eastern traditions, take Hinduism, they become one with something very abstract, or at the same time they can worship and become one, they are really devoted to Krishna and at the same time they are one with Brahman, which is an abstract absolute. So again I do not see a contradiction or difference here, but the characteristic of the mystical experience is normally understood as being—probably you have to add this here—non-dual identification with something to do with the sublime. Now everything you do in science involves single-pointedness and clarity. The moments of greatest inspiration in science, when we're not thinking inductively or deductively, we suddenly have, on the basis that we've already worked for, an idea from nowhere—that is the stroke of creative genius.

Mervyn
Why do you say that ideas come from nowhere?

Roy
Well you see a new theory, a new concept, can't be induced or deduced, because if you could take the canons . . .

Mervyn
Imagination?

Roy
Yes, that's fine. So the imagination, where does the imagination come from? Where does the truly innovative, imaginative idea in the imagination come from? Where does the beauty in the metaphor come from? When I say something really poetic, something really magical—'as light as rain', that's a cliché, but probably in a particular context it might be beautiful. Where does it come from? If you said 'as light as rain' in the streets of Delhi or Kolkata, they would know what you mean.

Mervyn
They would have experienced it, would have felt it.

Roy

Yes, it is over 40 degrees centigrade. OK, but just in that context it was a new idea. I don't know where it came from, you never know where it comes from. The most wonderful thing in life, particularly if you're intellectual and a scientist, is that you do all your thinking, all your experimenting—you read, you work, you study, and then you *un*think, you suspend thought—and then it happens. That's when it happens.

Mervyn

A new idea then comes from the beyond, beyond the given and beyond the immanent?

Roy

Yes, but it only comes if you've done all your homework. So it's like a reward. Some people don't have to work very hard for this reward. Consider Mozart. We have all seen *Amadeus*, so we know that everyone would be enormously jealous of him, but think of creative minds at school, they're squashed. Really, we all know that there is a real problem, the individual child has to be nurtured and probably we're all potential Mozarts. There was something flukey, some wonderful combination there, but we can all be Mozarts in our own domain, that is what I truly believe. Or take Schubert—Schubert was so prolific that he could never afford the paper to write, so when he went to a restaurant he wrote on the serviettes. Where did it come from?

Mervyn

Basically the scientist and the artist and the mystic are doing the same thing?

Roy

Exactly, the scientist is a mystic . . .

Mervyn

A practical mystic?

Roy

Absolutely. Someone who sets out to be non-dual just to be a mystic without being practical will never be a mystic—they will be a parasite on the rest of society. It is a wonderful thing to go out as a Buddhist monk with your begging bowl, we all understand that, and at the end of the day, if you don't get any food, well, that's part of the culture and you won't grumble, and then you're a non-dual being. But basically we're talking about a bygone era; you can't be religious, you can't be spiritual, without being engaged in the world today.

Mervyn

So the scientists are practical mystics, but nonetheless you yourself say that philosophy needs to be consistent with science in the long run. There's mysticism and mysticism, for instance, the 'anything goes' mysticism. How is this emphasis on the mystical moment in science consistent with your early emphasis on science and the underlabouring role of philosophy?

Roy

Science has very strict protocols, so your mystical experience has to be communicable to other people, and if you suddenly see DNA in a particular way for that to be scientifically valuable, it has to be insertable within the problem field. There are people who have analysed ancient Vedic texts; you can do the same thing with Ancient Egypt in terms of numbers. They have a fantastic understanding of numbers. But the point is, to stick with the Vedas for a moment, they knew that there were other planets beyond Saturn, and they knew what atomic structure was, but there was no-one to communicate this to. I'm not sure actually whether that's true or false, but science is an institution in which you have to be able to communicate your truth, and it has to be consistent with what is already known. Now what is 'already known' may contain a lot of false things. So it does not mean that the totality as it is constituted now is right, it may be completely wrong, and your little insight may be only half a per cent of what counts as knowledge and that may be right, and the 99 per cent may be wrong. However, you are not going to get anywhere in science unless you make an effort to gradually pull the rest of it into shape. You go with your half per cent, and you try and get it consistent with 5 per cent, then you get some funds and you're able to go on, 10 per cent, 15 per cent, and I daresay revolutionary thinkers like Freud—the Freudian programme, the Darwinian programme—all started like that, this guy is crazy, then gradually, gradually it became an orthodoxy. Everything has to be consistent at the end, because if there is a weakness, a flaw anywhere, then it is going to crack. It's like we can't have a eudaimonistic society so long as we have terrible social systems such as we do now, which oppress women, which oppress workers. Let us be very clear, oppressing workers is oppressing everyone. And oppressing women is oppressing everyone.

Mervyn

What some critical realists also want to know is: you started out with an emphasis on science and on the role of philosophy as an underlabourer for science, and being opposed to pure philosophy, in particular what you call the speculative illusion, now you're no longer just doing philosophical underlabouring.

Roy

Yes and no. At that time when I was stressing the underlabouring work, I always said that we can be critical of the practice of the scientist, but in terms of my philosophical ontology: so we can see that the socio-psychological analysis of science was not being scientific. Now it is actually not being scientific to suppress human creativity even in science. This does not mean that we go back to Feyerabend or anything like that. Science has probably developed very good protocols, and it is our understanding of science that has to be transformed. Actually scientists rarely think in accordance with the canons of formal logic; they only think logically when they have to prove a theorem on a blackboard or write up a research book, otherwise they are always thinking dialectically. Now the vital component of the process of dialectic is this transcendental moment, or rather the moment of transcendence in the transcendental moment, when a new concept emerges, irrupts, containing the seeds of a whole new theoretical worldview—and that moment cannot be described in accordance with any set of dialectical rules, techniques or tricks: it just happens.

So this, if you like, is inserting a transcendental moment into the dialectical process which is science and philosophy, and at the end of the day it all has to come together. At the end of the day you will see artistic inspiration in science, and you will see scientific endeavour in art, a lot of our dualism will completely have to go. Now to make sense of this intellectually you do need ontology. If you want to call that a system, everything has to fit together. But it is an organic whole—it is not a formal logical whole, it is not a system in the bad sense—it is more like an acorn growing into an oak. That it's the only kind of consistency I believe in. So critical realism, up to and going into the philosophy of meta-Reality, is a whole, it is a gradually developing tree. And there are further branches.

What I wanted to say, really, is that this has very radical implications, because (talking about truth) the old traditions of religious and political practice were all based on the fact that the leaders or authorities possessed the truth. There was a certain caste, there were priests who knew the truth, and you had to go to the priests, or to the political leaders, who were there to tell you what to do. Well, now I'm saying, actually we don't need those mediators, we can all be in touch with our ground state, no one owns the truth. These are very radical positions in terms of the history of politics and in terms of the history of religion. At the beginning of *RMR* I cite a little paean to, not so much the ordinary man, but what we are all ordinarily able to do in our everyday life. Just realise how wonderful it is. And then the task of doing exceptional things won't seem so extraordinary. When we realise how brilliant we are. Take how brilliant women are in the domestic sphere at bringing up kids. In this respect, men have to be as women, even in their daily life. It is really an extraordinary thing, but women's domestic labour is uncommodified—that is a mark of demerit in our society. But it is spontaneous, unconditional, holistic, it has many aspects which actually prefigure the sort of society I want to see. So this is very characteristic of dialectical progress. You can sometimes find something which looks very backward that is really radically progressive. Many feminists will say, well yes, there was a great campaign about twenty years ago that domestic labour should be paid, it's fizzled out now I think. But actually, that paradigm is there, that non-commodified role is there—formally within the reproduction of labour power through domestic labour—but actually it is there sustaining all the other commodified roles.

Mervyn
That's necessarily true.

Roy
Absolutely necessary too. Spontaneous, unconditional, effortless, it couldn't be otherwise. And that is a ground state quality. It is just that most of us are also paid for what we do, and we forget about all the things that we do freely and give freely, and actually, when you look at it, we only need to eat so much and we can function. It is an extraordinary thing, because we think we can't function without a system, but actually the system only functions because of us. We keep the money system going. Development economists have found that contracts in the Third World never work, never clinch in the market, they are always done as a result of negotiations outside the market, so you do not have the invisible hand of the market, you have the visible, or almost visible, handshake. That is how the money system works. The money system does not work according to the rules that economics describes. It works as a result of informal social transactions. Take great moments in history or great opportunities that have passed by. There are lots of ways of interpreting what went on in France in 1968, but there was a month when De Gaulle was ready to abdicate. He was waiting, the students were waiting for the Communist Party to take power. But although the workers and students were actually in control of the streets, nothing happened, no-one took power, because they all thought that someone had to take power. But being actually in control, they could have kept production going without waiting for the Communist Party. And of course the Communist Party, true to the spirit of Yalta, did not take power. So after a month De Gaulle shrugged his shoulders

and it was back to business. But that was a wonderful opportunity, and such will occur again. I think the so-called problem of social regulation is not really a problem. Because actually social regulation only occurs in virtue of the *unregulated*, free, spontaneous realm of activity, which can do very well without the regulated bit.

Part Four

Explorations within the Philosophy of meta-Reality

Chapter Eleven

Educating the Educators—Or, Empowering Teachers*

*R*oy Bhaskar is a very well-known philosopher who founded the theory of critical realism, an internationally acclaimed theory. Roy Bhaskar wrote his first book when he was 20 and he will share with us his reactions at that first time. There is a long list of books he has written, starting with Philosophy of Science, including discourses on social science, Marxism, emancipation and many other topics. In due course we will all get a chance to get to know Roy today. I think it is really fortunate that we have Roy with us. In one sense it is nice to have a well known philosopher, who has combined east and west, who has challenged many theories to celebrate the anniversary of our foundation. But in another sense it is also nice to have him as someone who shares our concerns. I have not only asked him because he is a Professor, who is used to talking to academics and giving very many lectures over the world; but also because he has his own radical views about education and experiences of them which we would like him to share with us today. When he asked me whether I wanted to work with him, I asked him whether I had to take an exam before he appointed me—and I asked him what the criteria were for passing the test. But

---

* Talk on the seventh anniversary of the foundation of the Rewachand Bhojwani Academy, Pune, 17 February 2002.

he asked me what I thought he should be doing. I told him that we want more complete, more down to earth theories, and in his own famous new concepts such as ground state and cosmic envelope, we are getting that closeness to practical concerns which I feel now we need.

First of all I must congratulate you all on seven years of a wonderful radical achievement. I have known Lakshmi for about fifteen months and I know this school is very important to her. I know it is set up on very radical principles and I have read the brochure, met some of the products, and they are lovely—the products, not the brochure, though the brochure is lovely as well! I am very honoured to be here on this auspicious occasion. With this lovely grouping here, I would like to say only a very few words, indeed I would prefer us just to have a discussion. However I also know that I would not be doing my duty if I did only that.

I suppose you could say what I am going to try to do now is to talk about education and my experiences and your experiences. I want to bear in mind this thought, a very timely thought, that Marx had when he asked—in his third thesis on Feuerbach—who is going to educate the educators, who is going to empower them, who is going to transform them? And when you look at the practice of actually existing communist parties we can see that the leadership had not transformed themselves, that the educators, the so-called educators or the would-be transformers had not educated, transformed and changed themselves. So in a way this is a very good lead into my own talk today because what I want to talk about is a kind of dialectic between self-change, self-transformation which you can say is a typical eastern approach, if you like a typically spiritual approach, in which the emphasis is on self-change, self-development and self-improvement (or perfection), and the western approach, in which the emphasis is on change outside the self, transformation in the rest of the world. It is typically this-worldly rather than other-worldly; it is at its best altruistic, outward going, concerned with doing things for other people rather than the self which remains unexamined and so unchanged.

Now actually I think there is no inconsistency between these two approaches. I think that if you are truly spiritual, if you really have no ego, if you really love other people, then you must be engaged in activities of practical transformation in the world. So real spirituality for me is what I call practical mysticism. That is very down to earth, and that is entirely engaged in putting yourself in the service of the cause of human emancipation, in fact universal self-realisation. That is the only spiritual approach that I can see is truly spiritual, that is of course the approach of all the great spiritual teachers. If you look at Jesus, Buddha, it does not matter. But it is also interestingly enough the approach which is implicit in western and secular theories of emancipation. Now if you take the ideal from Mahayana Buddhism of the Bodhisattva, he may be the most realised human being but he will postpone his own enlightenment, his own bliss, his own *nirvana* until the realisation of every other being in the world. That is very similar to the standpoint of Marx—and Marx was an atheist—when he said that in a communist society the free development of each would be the condition of the free development of all. In other words, your well being, your flourishing was the condition for my own. It was as important to me as mine. In other words, it is no good my being free, it is no good my being the most fantastically improved and perfect person, if you are still miserable and unhappy. That is also precisely the standpoint of Buddhism. And if you go into it deeply enough, at some level, this is the standpoint of all great religious and also even political inspirations and aspirations. So that is where I am coming from, that really there is no contradiction between spirituality and radical social change. No contradiction between self-improvement and therefore education in the broad sense and commitment to transformation of social structures and the emancipation of all.

Once you get to that point where you feel that you are really oriented in your life to collective human emancipation, ultimately universal self-realisation, then you want to know, where does this outcome come from, how do we bring it about? The thing is, the really important thing to understand is, that you can never emancipate anyone else. Emancipation cannot be imposed from without, emancipation always comes from within. So you are going to go through a dialectic. How does this exactly work out? Starting say from a spiritual inspiration, you want to have a political experience, you want to be in this consciousness that will take you to commitment to radical social change. Then when you are committed to radical social change you will ask yourself, how do you change people, and you will find that any attempt to force emancipation from outside is false, it is heteronomous and it will not work. Only individuals themselves can free themselves, emancipation cannot be imposed from without. All the failures of utopian projects, secular projects of emancipation come down to not taking seriously enough the principle of self-referentiality. This is very important for education, to sketch out this dialectic of spiritual development and radical social transformation.[1]

Let us come back to the point that nothing happens without the individual. We are all involved in education, most of you are teachers or counsellors, so how do you actually teach someone something. Have you thought about this? Supposing I write a proof in logic or mathematics on the board and I say, well, you see if p implies q and p therefore q, do people understand that? If you do not understand that then you have to invoke a meta-theory and you have to deduce that theory from another theory.[1] If you do not understand what I am saying then my effort at teaching is hopeless, useless. At the end of the day teaching, which is a dialogical relationship, always depends on the subject gaining a new perspective, just at the point he/she gets it, 'ah now I see how you do it'. This is true even of applied skills like learning to drive a car. A lot of people who start to drive do not know how to reverse, they do not know which way to turn the wheel. It is difficult, but suddenly you get the hang of it, or suddenly you get the hang of how you speak French. If you are looking at a painting, ah now, I thought it was a duck now I can see it as a rabbit. This is the gestalt involved in all acts of learning and education. Without that you cannot teach anyone anything at all. So it is always the self, the subject who has to understand. You cannot impose understanding on them, they have to bring from within.

---

[1] You have to say for example, if P implies Q, and P then Q; and P therefore (because if P implies Q and P then Q), Q. Does this help?

So what is the condition of this, it is an extraordinary condition. The condition is it means they must already know it. Because if it comes from within they must already have the knowledge and this is in fact nothing other than Plato's theory that all education is anamnesis, that what you are doing is bringing out something that was implicit, enfolded, potential within them, you are actualising it, making it explicit, but unless it was there, you could not have that 'ah', that 'I see it', that *coming together* when the pupil understands what the teacher is trying to say. So the primacy of the standpoint of self-referentiality is not only important for emancipation, it is just as important for education, which is our main theme today.

Once you see how important it is, then you can say how do I get these people who are just where they are, who are maybe concerned with the little things, nothing to do with collective emancipation, nothing to do with making the world a better place, how do we get them there. So we come to another level of our dialectic, at this level you can see that any objective, it does not matter how stuck a person is in life, if they want to fulfil that objective there is only one route. The one route is single-pointedness or clarity, coherence and purity. Most failures in life at any level stem from confusion, stem from not being clear about what you want. So supposing a robber wants to rob a bank, and you are his counsellor. The first thing to tell him is to be clear about what he wants to do—tell me, what do you want to do; rob a bank, then if he is single-minded about it, fine; but then you might want to say to him, why do you want to rob a bank, do you think it will really make you rich. Then you can take it back a step further, at whatever point you take it to, the criterion for successful action, the criterion for achieving your goal in life is single-pointedness, clarity, coherence and purity.

Now wherever you start, as you become more coherent, clear, pure in your mental, emotional and physical being, then you will find you start to manifest some beautiful qualities. These are the qualities that Lakshmi referred to, which I call the ground state qualities of human beings. These are qualities of freedom, qualities of endless creativity, these are qualities of love, right-action, these are qualities that fulfil intentionality and without these qualities the extraordinary thing is that we could not do anything at all. And you might say this is very extraordinary: are you telling me that under all this mess, and tremendous confusion, all this sort of bundle of compromises that we are, there is nothing other than pure creativity, pure energy, love, freedom and even knowingness? Yes, that is what I am claiming.

Let us first of all make this consistent with some themes in secular thought and then let us look at it in our own way. Just to say this is not my idea, if you look deep enough every theory of emancipation, every theory of realisation makes this claim, that ultimately human beings are fine, they are absolutely fine, there is nothing wrong with them, they are beautiful. Even in their individuality, especially in their individuality—for no two human beings are the same. We all have a unique *dharma*, we are all very special. But we are all absolutely fine. Some people have even said that we are all enlightened already. It is only this mess that we have on top of it which stops us realising our enlightenment.

Anyway, coming from the west, Rousseau said, we are born free but everywhere are in chains. What he meant was that the human essence is such that we are free, that we imprison ourselves, or rather the society which we sustain (and are ultimately responsible for) imprisons us. Chomsky, the great contemporary linguist, says that we have at birth the innate capacity to learn any language, the capacity to generate an infinite number of sentences, no matter how few sentences most people may actually generate. We have the capacity of endless creativity. If we were sitting here in Japan we would not be talking in English, we would not be talking in Hindi, we would not be talking in Marathi, we would be talking in Japanese. We all have that gift, that capacity at birth. What I would say is you take a social phenomenon, say drudgery in the office or on the shop floor—these are male examples, we will come to typical female examples—on the factory floor, how could a production line, the most uncreative, the most alienating, how could that keep going for a moment without the spontaneous ingenuity of the workers on the production line. Even an office could not keep functioning if you only observed the rules. You have to show spontaneity, ingenuity to keep even the most mechanical systems going. How do you get your computer going? You give it a little kick: if it gets naughty, then you just have to put it in its place.

Or if you take a social development like war, what could be more horrendous then war, but how is a war sustained? At the end of the day, it is sustained by the selfless solidarity of soldiers at the front, the support, sustenance and love of their sisters, wives, daughters back home. How is even that bank robbed: without that solidarity, that trust between the robbers, the action would not be successful. But there is also a further point. How could you do anything in life unless you did something right. Whatever I am doing, whether I am convincing you of my argument or not, I am at least uttering some words correctly, that is a right-action. So what I would do is challenge you to find any human situation which does not repose on these ground state qualities of freedom, creativity, love, right-action or fulfilment of intentionality. These are the bedrock qualities of human beings.

What I want to say is that the project of education, the project of enlightenment, and the project of universal self-realisation are all the same, or all turn on a single matter, and this turns on eliminating the heteronomy, eliminating everything which is not essentially you. And in that process of eliminating everything which is not essentially you, you will automatically be working towards the elimination of everything which is not essentially everyone else. This is not an individualistic approach, because it presupposes what I call, and this is one of the few technical concepts I will use here, four-planar social being. It presupposes that every event in social life has to be understood in terms of four dimensions. In terms of our natural exchanges; our material transactions with nature; in terms of our social interactions with others; then in terms of our relationships with the social structure. What is the social structure? Social structures are things like languages, economies, political forms. Clearly we do not create them at birth, we inherit them, but we play a vital role in their reproduction. Because what we do, and what they could not exist without, is our intentional activity. And it is in virtue of our conscious intentional activity that social structures, unwittingly, are more or less reproduced or transformed. For example, take the social structure of capitalism, or commercialism, call it what you like.

How could this function for a moment without greed, without desires. You go to the west, to America, go to Europe, England, it is not sufficient to have one car, you have to have one car per person—it is not sufficient to have one car, you have to have two or three, or as many as four, five and six! And the result is that where I live, or mainly live, around England and south east England the roads are congested. Two people, next-door neighbours, will both drive a car to work, instead of doing the sensible thing which is to share. They may work in next-door offices, and may even park their cars next to each other—though they will have tremendous trouble parking and it will take them a long time.

Now let us consider the impact of the social structure on the fourth dimension of four-planar social being, which is the stratification of our personalities. What is it doing, it is making us irritable, bad tempered, this reproducing of a structure which can only produce more and more of the same. Radical innovation, innovation for qualitative change, innovation which takes into account internal relationships, external economies, qualitative, non-quantitative considerations which pay attention to the environment—this kind of innovation, our social system knows nothing about. Then consider its impact on the second dimension of four-planar social being, it is spoiling our relations with each other. Because after you have spent ten or twelve hours in your office and in your car and then go back home and there is your wife or husband whom you immediately have a row with and then your children get upset and then you hit your children or something even worse and then you feel terrible, then you sulk, and then you wake up with a headache and the endless cycle repeats itself. So all these four dimensions of social life interact.

The question really is not where do we start, because what most people who do not really understand this kind of spiritual approach properly think that the spiritual being is not doing anything. Now this may have been appropriate in a different time and age, and perhaps there is still a role for some beings to not be in society, but I would argue that we have to say that today everyone has to be in society because we are globally inter-connected, we are in global crisis. We are fast reaching a point of no return. We are like a car that has lost control and heading towards a cliff, we are five feet away from the cliff, we are travelling at 50 mph and we have got five seconds to make the change. It is like that. The height of Bangladesh is four feet above sea level. This is a terrible thing for in twenty-five to thirty years it will not be there, nor will any of the islands in the world and England too will look very different. The rate at which global warming is proceeding is so rapid that we have to do something about it now. But not just that, take our interactions with each other, and the way we reproduce the surface structure. And without going into rights and wrongs, we now know, after the events of 11 September, how the actions of a few people could destabilise the whole of the world. And then a few actions of politicians and political leaders who accentuate this destabilising. At a political level we are in a terrible state. At an economic level there is chronic debt, chronic Third World debt, chronic crisis, and yet we are living on a planet of abundance. We have potentially everything we need. So whatever the merits of going to a retreat, or going into a monastery in the old days, today to be a spiritual being, to be concerned with the realisation of the divine on earth, you have to be a practical being, and you have to participate in society. And that means willy-nilly, that <u>whatever you do, you will be acting on all these four fronts simultaneously.</u>

Whether you like it or not you will be engaged in a process of social change. Either repetition and reproduction or transformation and change. Because everything that happens in society happens only in virtue of intentional agency. Intentionality is irreducible; agency is irreducible; agency at all these four dimensions of planes and effects is irreducible; so whatever you do is going to affect the world in this multidimensional way. But then also, you cannot not act. You must act. If you abstain from acting, that too is an action is it not? That is an action, that is a choice. Also at the end of the day you will have to act spontaneously, at some point you will act spontaneously. This is very important. If you just imagine that you are trying to do something. Supposing I am trying to pick up this glass of water. Well, I might think what is the most elegant way to do this. I can do it this way or should I pick it up this way, and so on. But at some point I just have to pick it up. And then I think well I wonder how I should follow the argument, I wonder what I should say next, but at some point I just have to say it. It is the same when cooking a meal. This is the spontaneity of human action. At some point we just have to act. When we act spontaneously, our thought does not come into it, we are not thinking. It is something that flows from our innermost being, we do not plan it, we do not premeditate it. Of course we can learn it and acquire it, that is skill, but when it happens it is just spontaneous, it is unconditional, it is a gift. It is a gift, we are not asking for anything.

Now we will move on from men in a way to women. This is a double-edged sword. If we look at women's domestic labour, it is not respected or recognised by the capitalist economy, it is not paid, it is not part of the commodified role; with domestic labour the woman does not sign a contract with her children, it is unconditional, non-contractual, it is a spontaneous gift. In a way that is a beautiful thing. If we are to have this vision, this vision in Buddhism, in Marxism (only of course the best, that is true of everything), if we are to realise this vision, we have got to have these qualities, unconditional spontaneous behaviour, unthought behaviour but effortless behaviour, exhausting but still effortless and joyous. Not only that but holistic as well, because the women typically will know how to balance the interests of one child against another, when the husband is coming home, when the neighbours will pop in. There was a UN report produced a couple of months ago which basically argued that if men carried on 'husbanding' those resources, being in charge of resources, then there was no future for the planet. It would be down the spout in fifteen to twenty years. But if women took their modes of domestic economy and employed them globally, nationally, in power, then there was a real future.

This asymmetry between women's typical, unconditional, spontaneous behaviour, this asymmetry and the reified alienated world of men is, to repeat, a very double-edged one. But the asymmetry is there and in the characteristics of women's domestic labour there is what you could call a kind of punctuated prefiguration of what we must have universally in the future. But it is not only something we must have universally in the future, we also do have and must have it, at least partially, now. And, men to be men must in this respect be as women, and they are women. When the wife is not there, the man will parent spontaneously and joyously and in a well balanced and sharing household, then the male will actually take joy in discovering the women within and being it.

And of course women, for their part, will engage in long chains of mental reasoning. You may think you are not be good at arithmetic, but come on, it's fine. You can enjoy it. There is even room for chess. When you think of chess (there is room for chess, and room for what I am talking about in chess—in fact there couldn't be chess without it) or the labour of Newton in working his way towards his great discovery of gravity or of Einstein working his way towards the discovery of space time. Well what happens? When it comes, it comes from nowhere, this flash, out of the blue, it is something which cannot be induced or deduced, it comes from the transcendent, from the beyond. Take the most refined, exceptional, take the most quotidian, ordinary, acts. In either case these are spontaneous, these are gifts. The gift of discovering gravity was a gift from nature, which the universe, god (you can call it what you like), the cosmos, gave to Newton. But it was a gift given to a specially prepared mind, because the mind had toiled ardently, arduously, prepared itself exhaustively. You can say that mind, Newton's mind, was so at one with the area of gravity, the whole physical field that we now know as gravity, that when the moment came, the moment when the creative inspiration came, he was gravity, he was one, in that 'eureka' he *became* gravity. This was a non-dual or transcendental moment.

Just before we go back to this, let us follow this example of the child who is learning something. So it seems in a way the child must already know it to learn anything. Now when he has this eureka, this, 'I get it, I see it', it is very similar to what the scientists or the artists have when suddenly they know they have done it. Everyone has it. When you have mastered a skill, when you have built the skill into yourself and just clinch it, it is a new gestalt. So in all processes of learning or creativity you will find there are four characteristic moments. First the emergence of something out of the blue, somewhere, somehow the child suddenly sees it, or Newton sees it and gets it. Or you understand a picture, or understand how to interpret a book or understand what a philosopher is saying. Now I see what he is doing. That is the basis. Then with this understanding, the knowledge is still heteronomous and you have to continually keep it in mind. Actually, as a philosopher, as a poet, or as a writer of any sort, you often find that you get an idea and then it's gone. So the thing is you have got to write it down, externalise it. That is the second step. And then of course when a child or anyone else is learning something they have to gradually make it part of themselves. And this is an extraordinary arduous process but also a process that can be very enjoyable. This is a process of formation, of shaping, plaing, you apply, you get to see how the computer works, what you can do with a car, what you can do with a language, and then at some point you just know it. Then you have in built the knowledge.

So it is a dialectic. The knowledge was there implicitly already. Then it was awakened by something from outside, came to consciousness, but you were not in control of it, so you gradually had to master it, make it one with yourself. Then when it is one with yourself, it is not outside you anymore. At this stage you can be spontaneous. Then you can engage in objectification, that is action, that is making things in the world. So every cycle of creativity has these characteristic moments, the lightning flash, the inspiration; then the creation itself, involving externalisation; then the shaping, formation, the gradual deep re-internalisation; then the making, the production of objectification of something new. The fifth component of the cycle of creation is seeing whether what you have made reflects your intentionality. Does that express the internal impulse that I had, or not. When it reflects your intentionality then the cycle of creation is perfectly complete.

Now this is in fact the cycle of cosmic creation. All cosmologies have the same characteristic formula, from nowhere, out of the blue, there may be seeds, it may be something which comes and goes but something emerges. Then there is the phase of creation, it stabilises. Then the phase of shaping, formation. Then it is objectified. And then it fulfils or fails to fulfil the intentionality of the creator. Every human act mirrors these five phases of the cycle of creation. So every human act, including especially every act of learning, mirrors if you like the creation of the universe. And at the end of the day what we want to do is to fulfil ourselves. Find our reflection in the outside world. When will this be? This will be when we are fulfilled and that will only be when every human being is fulfilled and then that would be finally fulfilling or completing the initial impulse.

So corresponding to these five phases of the cycle of creation, critical realism, or the philosophy that Lakshmi mentioned, has engaged in the re-thematisation within western philosophy of ontology, that is the theory of being. Because I was invited to share my experiences at school and at college, and I will if we have time, I can tell you that when I was an undergraduate you could not say anything about the world as such in western philosophy, it was a prohibited, a taboo subject. That was the first step in critical realism which was just thinking being. The second step was thinking being as a process. The third step was thinking being as a process and as a totality, as a whole, holistically. The fourth step was thinking it as all those things and as incorporating transformative, self-conscious, potentiality, self-conscious transformative human agency and reflexivity—that is our capacity for the unity of theory and practice. And then the fifth stage was to think being as in some way fulfilled, as in some way free, as in some way realised.

This is the stage that I am now developing, in which I would like to bring in new spiritual concepts, or put them in a slightly different light. But let us see how we can apply them to education. So just going through those five phases in the cycle of creation you can see that they correspond to five moments of human action, a moment of will, a moment of thought, a moment of feeling, objectification and the moment of finding fulfilment in your objectification or not. They correspond to those five domains of the successive enrichment of being and they correspond to various ground state properties. These are fundamental characteristics of human beings. So the first would be freedom, the second would be creativity, the third would be love, the fourth would be right-action and the fifth would be the capacity to fulfil intentionality. Now most people think that the spiritual is something very far removed from ordinary life. And they would associate the spiritual quite rightly with concepts like transcendence with non-duality.

What I want to say is transcendence and non-duality is the underpinning, is the ground level of human beings and we are all familiar with it, in fact it is going on here all the time. Philosophers have had a wrong concept of being and of agency, not only materialist philosophers, but even spiritual philosophers have had a wrong concept of non-duality and transcendence.

So let us go into this a little bit because I want to argue that our goal as educators, self-educators, is to be a party to a process of being and creating and helping beings help create themselves to be non-dual beings in a world of duality. Let us look at transcendence. Something which is involved is obviously identification. There are two terms which are separate, so there is me and you, or there is a state of consciousness you are in and a state of consciousness that you seek to get into. In fact these exemplify two very simple paradigms of transcendental identification. One is when you lose your sense of objectivity, you lose the object in a subject–object duality and just become one with yourself, deep into one with yourself, then that lovely bundle of creative energy or bliss or contentment or peace. That is one paradigm. The other is when you lose your sense of subjectivity and go completely into something outside yourself. This is when you become engulfed in a picture, inspired by music, you lose any sense of separation between yourself and the notes.

Now the extraordinary thing is that transcendental identification is essential for any human communication or act at all. Unless you were at one with my words in the simple sense that you understood at some level what I was saying, then I would not be communicating to you. If you say hello how are you, then the other person has to understand 'hello, how are you', and in that moment of understanding, there is transcendental identification. If you are watching a film, you lose your self, if you concentrate, focus on the film, you lose your sense of separateness from the film. When you are reading a newspaper, how could you understand a sentence in it unless you were one with that sentence? You couldn't. The moment you cease to be one with the sentence you are not reading it, you are not listening. You become completely one with the act. So this transcendental identification, or transcendence in the sense of breaking down the duality between subject and object, is something we are familiar with in every aspect of our social life.

However, it is not only that; non-duality is not only a characteristic of states of consciousness; it is a characteristic of action because when you spontaneously know how to drive a car you do not think about it you just drive it. When you spontaneously know how to drive or to speak, you just drive or speak, you just spontaneously express yourself. When a baby is crawling by you just pick it up, you do not think about it, you just do it, in a non-dual way. Everything in life, every action you perform has an element, and is sustained by that element of non-duality. That element you touch something with is your ground state or something which is consistent with it. So we are all very familiar with who we essentially are. Then there is a fourth aspect to transcendence. This fourth form of transcendence is when two people work so perfectly together as a team that there is no sense of separation. You can find two people who cook together, one anticipates the move of the other, or two footballers or two cricket players in perfect unity. Again, a group of musicians must be in this state to produce anything. Have you ever thought how odd it is how so few people actually bump into each other on the streets in India, or anywhere else for that matter. There are so many people, so little space, there is so little calculation. This is magical, the synchronicity that stops people from bumping into each other. So this is the fourth kind of transcendental non-dual state we must be in to do anything. So this state of non-duality that spiritual philosophers have talked so much about is something that we are very familiar with in our everyday experience.

Now a lot of philosophers think that because it is spontaneous it is not structured. Now that is not true. Because when you have unity with a whole, a picture, then of course that unity is structured. When you listen to the music, the music has a holistic structure, you are at one with a whole. Our concept of unity, of oneness, is far too simple, oneness is not punctiform, is not a point. Oneness is a whole. When you have oneness with oneness it is a whole with a whole. It is two wholes, meshed. To have transcendental identification is consistent with—*do just come in and everyone just join the whole*—see how nice, how beautiful, synchronicitous, coherent, timely nature is because this leads into my second point that transcendental unity is not only consistent with non-punctiform, differentiated wholes, is the way in which a beautiful picture or sequence of music is differentiated, but it is consistent with development, so you can expand and grow. Supposing you are perfectly realised, perfectly enlightened: that does not mean that you know every skill. If no-one has taught you Japanese, how are you expected to know it; if you decide to learn it, you might learn it faster than other people or you may not. So you go and acquire it and you build that skill into your unity. In the process of building that skill which is external to you into yourself, you remain whole all the time and you embed, you recursively embed, that new development into yourself and so expand. So we can be non-dual and growing beings. People have always thought that when you reach the absolute then that is the end. Actually the absolute is only the beginning, all the rest is free development, growth, expansion.

It is important also to appreciate that saying that I am in a state of non-duality is not to say we are the same; we can have uniquely differentiated properties, this is very important for education. Actually when you approach enlightenment then you have no sense of a personal ego, so this point really does not matter very much to the enlightened being. But it is worth noting that every *avatar* is the most uniquely defined being, every Buddha is different, every enlightened being is uniquely different, the more creative, the more of a genius you are, the more expanded you are, the more unique you are. But you do not have a sense of your uniqueness because you do not attribute your uniqueness to an ego, you do not 'own' your uniqueness any more than someone can 'own' the truth. Your uniqueness is a manifestation of the cosmos, you are just happy, privileged to be a point at which the cosmos can fulfil itself. The really important point is that each of us in our ground state is unique. And understanding this uniqueness and respecting difference is consistent with non-duality because I can become one with you. Supposing we are arguing about which team plays better at hockey, you may say Holland I may say Germany. We may understand what the other is saying so we have transcendental identity as a condition for the argument, but he has his point of view and I have my point of view. This is a way in which two people can be non-dual, one can be a gifted artist, the other can be a gifted scientist. One can be and esteem, love their identity as an Indian, as a woman, as a Maharashtrian, as a hockey player, and the other can love their prowess as a basketball player, as Jewish or whatever. And they can both be non-dual beings. So we have non-duality consistent with the holism, differentiation, with development, with identity-in-difference.

The last point to appreciate is that non-duality does not mean that you stop fighting. The best warrior has total identity with the enemy, completely understands the enemy. I know as a philosopher—we could go (as Lakshmi was suggesting) into my battles at school and so on—but I know as a philosopher that I cannot really critique a false and mystified system of beliefs until I totally absorb it, am totally at one with it. So the best general is the one who has done his reconnaissance, the one who completely understands his enemy, he is totally at one with his enemy. But he is not only at one with the enemy because he is going to fight back and kill and remove his enemy. We become one with the other, not in order necessarily to agree with the other or to be the other permanently; but in order to eliminate the other. So we have to understand what are the blocks, the constraints, the checks on our own emancipation, what are the blocks, the constraints, the checks on the emancipation of all people, all beings everywhere. We have to become one with them. We have to totally understand them to eliminate them, that is these blocks, constraints, forces. This means that the spiritual being is also a warrior, but he is a warrior at peace with himself. This is the beautiful thing, and when Krishna said to Arjuna—do not be upset at your *dharma*, what you have to do, for you have to understand the soul is immortal, and it is your *dharma* for you to kill your enemies, you just focus on your action, do not worry about the consequence—he was telling him, you can be a man of god and fight. That is what we have to do. The extraordinary feature of action is that at a first level it is at once a gift from the universe and an offering to the divine or to nature, to our fellow human beings, whatever it is that we love. At a second level, it is a transformation of the world. And at the third, it is a struggle, part of a process, the practice of emancipation.

At this point I will end up and say that all this really is possible because of some very beautiful features of our ground state and our connectedness in it. Which means that in a real sense, a sense which is very difficult for most people to comprehend, you are not really different from me, but you actually are me. Sure, you are different as an embodied personality from me, but you are also enfolded within me, you are part of me and I am part of you and therefore your pain is as much my pain. When I fully understand this, raise my sensitivity to a level that I can feel it as my pain then your unfreedom is as much a curse, a blight on me as my unfreedom. Then I cannot stop struggling until everyone is free. This is the ideal. The freer I become the more my action will move in the right direction.

* * * *

Your words were like music to my ears.

Roy
Everything is a holistic performance; my words were in unity with your response.

It is a real pleasure to be here, I feel very much one with you and your project, but can you say something more about experience?

Roy
I think that experience is a double-edged sword. On the one hand it is a window on the world, so we learn from it. And then at the same time, as and when we learn, we have to let go. It is a very extraordinary thing to have to say but it is true. As long as you cling to something, someone you have had a bad experience with, it will imprison, impede and hurt you. Then what should you do? Imagine that you have a lovely jewel box there and this bad experience is something like a rock coming at you, you pluck the jewel

from the rock and put it in that jewel box; that is the learning, the rest you let go of.

Suppose someone has done something terrible to you, you just let it go. Of course you will be wary of, you will be sensible about that person. When I say that love is a ground state quality and that we should—and (to an extent) do—love unconditionally, that is not expecting anything in exchange for it, I am not saying that you should go up and embrace everyone. No, you would not go and embrace someone who was going to put a dagger in your heart, so that is the learning, that is the jewel from that person. What you throw away is that you do not feel that everyone who comes up to you is going to try and throttle or suffocate or abuse you. It is very sensible for women not to go out in the streets in New York at night, or sometimes in London. It is a terrible condition, but it is very sensible. What you do is you learn from that, you do not have a feeling of paranoia haunting you the whole time, you do not dwell on it. You just know it, you build it in, you let go, you are free, you feel it and then you work to transform the situation that makes that action necessary. So you work to get rid not of that rock but the source of all rocks.

That is the teaching, the diamond, the jewel that you plucked from that rock, that has been given to you. Everything in life is like a gift, you say thank you, yes, thank you for teaching me, now I have got to be really careful where I go in Brixton, I have got to be really careful and I have got to work very hard to make it safe for women to walk in the streets in New York and London at night. It is terrible, that is the learning but you do not hold it within yourself. Our minds should be completely free. Actually there should be nothing in our minds. If there is something in our minds, then we are not free to do what we need to do, what is best to do. You cannot learn. It is an extraordinary thing but if you have something in your mind you cannot learn. If something is fixed in your mind, if there is anything in fact in your mind, you cannot learn; your mind at the moment of learning has to be a *tabula rasa*. If there is a preconception there, if there is any fixation, if there is an attachment, if there is anything that clings to or binds you, then this imprisons you as someone who can learn, and it imprisons you as an agent because you are always going to act under a fixed idea. Moreover it *karmically* binds you. It binds you because until you have cleared that, while you have that within yourself, you are never going to be free and you are not going to be a free agent of change.

This is a difficult one. I was talking about war and fighting and us being at peace, this is the really important thing, we are at peace. But actually all the stories of war, in the scriptures, in the Bhagavad Gita, even the Islamic conception of *jihad*, the holy war is an inner war, when you are at peace with yourself and only when we are at peace with ourselves will we be at peace with each other. And that peace with ourselves means clearing all the rubbish from ourselves. When we have all cleared the rubbish from ourselves we cut off the supply lines to oppression, servitude and unfreedom. Everything in the social world subsists on our love, our creativity, it could not exist for a moment without them. But oppression is real. These are real structures and real systems but we have the capacity to cut off their supply lines. It is a difficult thing to do but we can do it.

Chapter Twelve

The Limits of Thought*

*T*his is the first gathering to celebrate the opening and expansion of the Kolkata Centre of the Krishnamurti Foundation of India. He was, as you know, a unique and original thinker, preaching a philosophy which articulated what he had in his personal life, what he expressed was a feeling, a perception of light, with a teaching which was universal for man everywhere. And that is that if there is any way to get out of the problems of life he showed us the beginnings. We are very fortunate today to have here with us, Professor Roy Bhaskar, who has agreed to come and participate in this seminar and also agreed to give the inaugural address. Professor Roy Bhaskar is well known to philosophy people all over the world, and so he needs no introduction. Professor Bhaskar lives and works both in India and the UK and his work is widely read throughout the world. Moreover he is well conversant with the philosophy of Krishnamurti, so we are very glad to have him here today to open this centre. I have asked Professor Hui to say a few words to introduce Professor Roy Bhaskar for those students of Krishnamurti's teachings who do not belong to the academic world.

---

* Inaugural address at Krishnamurti Foundation (India), Kolkata Centre, 16 March 2002.

Ladies and gentlemen it is a pleasure to introduce Roy Bhaskar, not that he needs any introduction. He has been gracing the academic circles of the world for the last twenty-five years, since Roy made his initial mark with the publication of his revolutionary book on the philosophy of science, A Realist Theory of Science *in 1975, and he has been developing this philosophy since then. He was born in England on 15 May 1944. His father was Indian and his mother was English and they were theosophists. He went to Oxford, where he studied philosophy, political science and economics. He then went on to teach first economics, then philosophy at the University of Oxford and other universities around the world. In 1995 he became the founding Chair of the Centre for Critical Realism in London, and he remains the patron of this centre. Since then he has developed his philosophy of critical realism into a greater philosophy of universal self-realisation. He believes in the existence of god as a fundamental categorial structure of the world and unconditional love as the cement or binding force of the world. He believes that we are essentially free and godlike. Above all he believes philosophy should exemplify the unity of theory and practice. Now this applies above all to Roy himself. There are many great philosophers, intellectuals, but most of them are not great human beings. And Roy's vision, creative energy and above all his fount of unbounded love is simply breathtaking. When we approached him for this seminar he readily agreed to come to open this study centre. But immediately afterwards he was taken ill with a serious problem, and most of his engagements were cancelled. However he insisted on coming here today to share his talk with us. We are especially privileged because he met Krishnamurti both in India and in England.*

Thank you all very much for coming here today and I should like to thank the previous speakers for their kind remarks (and especially Prabir Hui who made my participation in this seminar possible). Professor Sen has asked me to say a few words before I begin my talk about my personal connection with Krishnamurti. I cannot really say very much more than anyone else knows—that he was a wonderful man, charismatic, striking. I met him in Chennai and I met him in London and even though I was very young, my father, who I should say who was not really an orthodox theosophist, used to read Krishnamurti, among many other things, so I picked up Krishnamurti's books when I was quite young. There are so many things, that I was struck by and that resonated to me as a young person—for instance the idea that the slightest thing, anything reflected something profound. It did not matter particularly what you talked about—you did not have to talk about high philosophical topics, sometimes you could talk about freedom, but you could also talk about anything. For there was freedom, creativity, love, beauty, intelligence in a shoelace, or in the corner of a room—it does not matter what or where. For in anything you will find all the mysteries of the universe enfolded. His was a truly oceanic intelligence, energy, love. So that is all I can say really, and I think the other thing I can say is that although this is all in honour of Krishnamurti, he really would not like me to go on honouring him; he would prefer me to say something in the spirit of him.

I think our primary task is to carry on the work that he began. So what I am going to do is give a talk in the spirit of the work of Krishnamurti on a subject which was very important to him, a talk precisely on the question of thought and the limits of thought. And I will not use, even though I know this is a largely academic audience, academic jargon, I will try to talk very simply and plainly. You all know that Krishnamurti was opposed to—this is the one jargonistic word I will use—heteronomy. That is anything that suppresses the creativity, the love, the unbounded energy that he really believed that human beings had. These aspects of heteronomy consisted of (or were constituted by) among other things, leaders, gurus, systems, religions, orthodoxies, organisations, institutions—and thought. And it is thought that I will concentrate on.

If you read Krishnamurti superficially you might think he is against everything. Now what about this 'being against everything'? I am going to read you a poem from the great Sufi mystic, Jelalalludin Rumi, and there is a little bit of Krishnamurti here:

Not Christian or Jew or Muslim
Not Hindu, Buddhist, Sufi or Zen,
Not any religion or cultural system
I am not from the east or the west

Not out of the ocean or up from the ground
Not natural or ethereal
Not composed of elements at all
I do not exist
Am not an entity in this world or the next
Did not descend from Adam or Eve
Or any origin story
My place is placeless a trace of the traceless
Neither body or soul
I belong to the beloved
Have seen the two worlds as one
And that one call to and know
First last outer inner only that breath breathing
human being

When you do all the negations, when you say no system, no organisation, no leaders, no fixed dogma, no fixed thought, no papal thought, no priestly thought, no spiritual authorities, no fixed emotional make-up, nothing, then what do you get when you have stripped all those things away, what do you get? It is not nothing; it is not only just nothing. When you strip away everything that we impose, everything that, heteronomously, we impose on human beings we get free, creative, loving, spontaneous, energetic, intelligent, right-acting human beings—left to ourselves in what I would call our innermost nature. Technically what I would call our ground state. We are free, creative, loving. We are also right-acting, we will do the right thing and we will love it when we allow it. What gets in the way? This was Krishnamurti's great problem: what gets in the way?

I am going to talk about thought, how thought can get in the way. Let me give you an example. Thought, I want to say, impedes and constrains our creativity, our loving nature, our capacity to act right. Let us think about this. When you have a new idea that never comes from thought, it always comes from a space beyond or behind or between thought. When Newton discovered gravity, he was not thinking; it was when he was going for a walk, when he was not thinking. When he stopped thinking. Of course Newton was unique, he had done all the spade work. If you like, the unknown, the unmanifest, the transcendent, the magical mystery, the boundless energy of the universe was ready there with the answer to pop into his head. But only when he let go, when he stopped thinking. Could he have the idea of gravity without not thinking? No. Not thinking, unthinking, suspending thinking, allowing the move to the null space of unthought was essential to, let us say, the consummation of his thought in gravity. Actually you can show formally that it is impossible to produce a new idea from the orthodox canons that we philosophers have regimented as induction or deduction. Nor can you deduce a new idea by dialectic, nor by the most radical algorithm. A new idea always comes from the unknown, it always comes out of the blue, it always comes from nothing. Obviously we will see what place thought has to play. But to be creative, just in that moment of creativity, you have to stop thinking, to let go. Thought will block that creativity.

Now love, let us talk about love. Normally we just love. A parent will love a child. Or meeting someone you would normally think 'oh she is a lovely person', if I had two apples I would give that person one if he is hungry, I would do that spontaneously. What would stop me doing that? Well I might think, 'is this a good thing?' Then I put a condition on my gesture, then it will not be unconditional, I will not be giving, I will not be loving, I will be taking back by imposing that condition. My thought will impose a condition, 'what is she going to do for me?' What do I get for that apple? That is not love, that is love mixed with a contract, that is love mixed with a condition, that is an exchange, a commercial transaction. We can see that love is stymied, checked, impeded by thought. If we see a little baby crawling into the water, spontaneously we rush to rescue the baby, pull it from the water. We will do that spontaneously; when we do not do it, is when we think. We think, 'oh is this a good thing?', 'will I make a fool of myself?' Suppose the baby was crawling here, 'oh I can't do this in a seminar', 'not in this distinguished gathering'. You see thought will get in the way of our spontaneous right-action.

The way thought impedes our loving, our creative, our spontaneous right-acting nature, it also drains, dissipates, consumes our energy. If you can do something without thinking, what is the point of thinking? You are wasting energy aren't you? It not only drains our energy and prevents us from doing the creative, loving or right thing, it also sets up a repetitive pattern, a syndrome. So Krishnamurti says, and I agree, that the moment you name something, for example the moment you name me as an academic, that sets up an expectation in you. You cannot see the blackboard behind me, but you probably expect me to look to see if you are taking notes, it sets up that repetitive pattern of behaviour. These fixed systems of thought, these syndromes of thinking behaviour, these are terrible things. Thus if someone says 'Islam', or names somebody as a Muslim, that immediately activates, engages, puts into a state of readiness a pattern—and that is just to name someone in a particular way. It was (I do not mean this as a criticism) it was mentioned that my parents were theosophists (whatever else you already knew about me). That is fine, but it immediately sets up the expectation that what you are going to hear today is something close to theosophy, and that is not true. But you see the name, the thought, the label sets up an expectation and this too will tend to trigger an emotional response.

Thinking, naming, judging impedes creativity, loving, right-acting human nature. They drain our energy and they set up repetitive patterns of behaviour. They bind our energy. Really we are bundles of energy. When you have an addiction, say an addiction to smoking, think how much energy you use in keeping that addiction going. You may have an addiction to drinking, or you may have an addiction to reading books or reading a newspaper. Consider how much energy it takes to keep it going, to keep on doing it. Everyday you have to read the Kolkata *Telegraph*, twenty minutes or half an hour gone. In England I know some people who read the *Times*. In the old days they used to start by getting the *Times* ironed! The servants were supposed to iron the *Times*, and it would come nicely ironed and starched and for two solid hours they would read it. Starting with the marriages, births and deaths and going through the sports news and ending up at the world crisis on the back page just before the crossword.

You might suppose that if we can do something with our thought then we should. However the extraordinary thing is that we cannot do anything by thought. Suppose I think there is a glass of water, suppose I think now how do I want to pick it up. Or perhaps I think now I want more than one sip, how shall I do it. At some point I just have to do it, at some point it just has to be spontaneous, at some point I have to stop thinking and do it. You can think about how to do something as long as you like but that thought will never take you to action because, at some point you just have to do it. In any action there is that non-dual, what I would call basic spontaneous component. We cannot do anything without it, we cannot even think without it. What I am saying is that we cannot do anything by thought, or to qualify that a little bit, by thought alone.

We cannot even think by thought. How do you think, who thinks their way into thinking? You just think, you do not do thought, you just have a thought, where does it come from? You do not know, it just comes. Hearing, you do not think about hearing. You either hear or you do not hear, it is simple. Of course if you do not understand, then you think. That is fine but there must be something that you do not understand which immediately you hear, you just perceive. Whenever we do anything in life there must be a level at which we just do it. Moreover, at that level when we just do it, then normally, by and large, we are doing the best thing, the right thing, spontaneously it will be good, it will be creative. When we are doing anything creative it has to be like that: we cannot think our way into creativity, we can prepare the ground for it, but the creativity will just occur like that. Similarly, when we think about doing something loving we are already taking the love away. When we are being loving, we just love. Thinking about loving is putting a condition on it.

Actually this is extraordinary. I am saying we cannot even think about thinking: we just have to think, so thinking is not something we do, thinking is a happening within us. So what we have here is a model which Krishnamurti was very against. The model was of an ego, an I, and an I, moreover, who manipulates, controls the world. So we have the ego, the I in-here and the world out-there and the world out-there includes our thought world, because when we are thinking about thought we think that the ego, the I, the me here is manipulating and in control of my thoughts. But I am not, I do not even know who I am.

Actually the thought is happening of its own accord, so to speak. So this is why it is so important to pay attention to our thoughts. For if we do not pay attention to our thoughts, and we do not understand the limits of thought itself, then we will get stuck into this ideology of thought. This model of an ego and a world, an object world to which the ego is attached which it manipulates, exploits, interferes with, generally in the nicest way you could say it is the model of an individual subject and an object world out-there, which is a world subject to what philosophers call instrumental reasoning, that is means–ends rationality. How will that get me this, or how will it enable me to achieve that objective.

Now Krishnamurti was entirely opposed to this. What he would say now is: unthink, do not think, unthink. But how do you unthink? How do you undo this model. It is very easy. Now you are listening to me, are you listening? Then you are not thinking, you are listening. If you are listening you are not thinking. If you are thinking you are not listening. You cannot do both. You cannot both listen and think. So it is very easy to listen. It is very easy to be, it is very easy to act, it is very easy to be loving. What you cannot do is simultaneously be listening and thinking. Or you cannot think about being creative and be creative.[1] If you are loving, then you cannot be thinking about being loving. Thinking about loving is not loving, but thinking. Similarly if you are thinking about acting right, then your intentionality is split between the thought and the action. Or consider looking, we can look, we look; when we stop looking, when we get distracted then we have lost our focus, then we think. It is well known in the Hindu spiritual traditions that there is an old puzzle that teachers of meditation used to give their pupils. They used to say: meditate, I give you five minutes now to meditate. Then after three minutes the teacher would say, hands up those who are meditating. Fifty per cent of them would put their hands up. 'So you think you are meditating, then go out of the class, you certainly are not meditating: you cannot be meditating, if you <u>think</u>

---

[1] Of course you can creatively think about being creative, but then you are not thinking about your creative thought; you are being creative in thought—you are thinking without thinking about thinking.

you are meditating'. For you cannot both think and meditate. The one precludes the other. Similarly, you cannot be listening to me if you think you are listening to me. For then you are thinking, you are not listening. So it is not difficult to find paradigms of doing things without thought.

Let me just give you a little puzzle, and then we will try and explain it at the end. This is a Zen koan. This is what you are supposed to think about: the wild geese cast their reflections upon the water, but the water has no mind with which to receive them. So a Zen abbot would give his monks or some particular monk that koan to solve. We will come back to that later.

Because we are talking, obviously we know that thought must play some role. Surely Krishnamurti must allow, or I must allow, that thought plays some role in our life. Why were we given a mind if we were not supposed to use it? Why were we given language if we were not supposed to name, classify, describe? So what role does it play, we have to ask. It was Einstein who said 'the world we have created today as a result of the thinking thus far has problems which cannot be solved by thinking the way we thought when we created them'. Yes indeed, but perhaps part of the problem is not just the particular thoughts we have had, but thought, or discursive thought (i.e., thought using or in language) itself, or perhaps the role which we give it. For we are living in a world which is very highly intellectualist, very thought—thought is a big part of our world. We know that thought and mind is irreducible in some way in life, it has tremendous creative power. We are living in a highly technological, technicised world and those technologies and techniques that have been produced are products of thought. There are of course good, beautiful technologies and bad, corrosive technologies, but both alike are the products of our thinking and this is the point that Einstein was making.

So we cannot just dismiss thought, and we know that we all think the whole time. Thoughts play some role in our life, so we have to understand this. We know that we all think directly and intuitively, we cannot help thinking. So even if you set yourself the target of not thinking, unthinking, you cannot force yourself not to think, you have to do something else, you have to listen.

That is why people who meditate use a *mantra*, or if they do it by visioning, they have to contemplate something. Or if they pray or worship then it functions in the same way. But so does listening to music. So extraordinarily enough does watching television. Because when you are watching the television, you are not thinking, you are just following. When you are reading a newspaper you are not thinking.

So the realm of the non-dual, the realm of the spontaneous, the realm of the unthought is basic to human existence. You cannot understand, I cannot communicate with my friend Nirmalya over there, unless at some point he just understands me, no thinking about it. It does not matter, he might not hear my words and say 'Roy could you repeat that', then I would say yes the word is 'recollection', 'ah!'. At some point he must have directly, non-dualistically, unthinkingly understood something even to ask me what he did not understand.

In the same way no-one ever does everything or anything completely wrong. We must get something right or it would not count as an act at all. If you think about it, for anything to count as an act it has to be describable in a certain way. So even if I make a mistake, supposing I knock this tumbler of water over, or upset this chair, that would have to be something which counted as an act, in so far as I was responsible for it. It would still have to be something that I did. Or supposing I introduced Professor Sen as Professor Das or Professor Sengupta then it would be a terrible mistake but at least I would have got the words right.

This is not just the case with action, this is also the case with love. For we would all agree that war is absolutely terrible. But how is a war actually sustained, how? By the soldiers fighting at the front. So what do they do? They show boundless solidarity, that is a manifestation of love for each other, and they will die for their cause. They may be completely wrongheaded but it is a manifestation of love; and war could not keep going for a moment without the love shown by the soldiers at the front and without the support, compassion and solidarity of their sisters, mothers, daughters back home, which sustains them. So war actually depends on love. Similarly you could not have a robbery, a robbery could not be successful, a band of robbers would not hold together, unless the robbers had solidarity. No universe, nothing, no social interaction would be possible without love.

Similarly the most routinised, repetitive systems of thought or systems of production only keep going as a result of our creativity, our creative ingenuity. Everyone knows that you cannot keep a production line going without the people who are operating it stepping in and keeping it going. You cannot even keep a computer going or a fridge going or the electricity going without kicking it, you have to kick the fridge! Human action, spontaneous creativity our ingenuity is necessary to sustain the most repetitive regimes.

Let us see how we can get out of being stuck in this position of thinking that thought is essential. One thing you all know about Krishnamurti is that he asked us always to be watchful, to look, to listen, to notice. This is what I am saying. Now we are talking about being watchful about our thoughts, seeing what we are doing when we are thinking. When we are seeing what we are doing when we are thinking, we are not thinking, remember that. So you have a thought. Suppose your thought is 'what is happening back home', then you are immediately distracted, you are in a non-dual state, you are not understanding, you have a split intentionality, you have a divided mind. You cannot do anything about what is going on back home now. But at the same time you cannot make the best of the situation here and now because you have lost your concentration, your focus. So what we do is we observe. You do not judge, condemn or blame yourself. Instead, you observe. What happens?

There are two ways of being watchful. We can step back from the thought or we can go into the thought. Consider stepping back. Supposing—let us take an emotional case—you are angry. What do you do? You are in a state of angry consciousness, you are absolutely mad. Krishnamurti tells you watch, observe, do not judge, do not say I should not be mad, do not put your thoughts and preconceived opinions in there, just stop, just watch. Then immediately you will find that something magical happens, you are no longer angry, you are not in angry consciousness, you are in consciousness as an observer of your angry consciousness, you are in consciousness of angry consciousness. And then if you want to double-check, you can look at your observing your angry consciousness, your consciousness of your angry consciousness, then you will say yes, I am no longer angry. Then you can of course step even further back, going further inwards in that direction, that dialectic, because whatever state of consciousness you are in you can always (reflexively) make it the object of your consciousness.

One of the useful things about this inwards retreat from a state of mind or a feeling or anything is that once we have identified it, and see it is there, once we know what it is, we can work on it. We can go into its causes, we can look at the situations under which that thought arises. But actually there is something else even simpler than that because the power of awareness, the power of attention is so great that it will even by itself tend to dissolve the problem, to untangle, unbind the problem, then dissolve the thought (or emotional state) you were in.

Before I go into the other form of the dialectic, which is rather than stepping back from going right into the thought (or emotion), let us ask, if we are talking about the limits of thought, then what is thought being contrasted with, what am I contrasting thought to? I talked about spontaneity, I talked about creativity, I talked about love, but these are not philosophical categories. So what philosophically can we counterpose thought to?

Firstly, consciousness. You can be conscious without thinking, you can just be aware, just observe; you are still conscious but you are not thinking. So that is the first thing, the first contrast, you have consciousness that is distinct from thought. The two are not one-to-one related. Not all consciousness is thought. This is a common mistake in western philosophy and indeed in the west generally. In the Indian tradition it is much clearer because there is a conception of Self and consciousness apart from thought, and moreover thought takes two forms. There is the intellect which is *buddhi* and there is the mind, *manas*.

There is a second thing to which thought can be opposed: this is intuition. So we have the intuitive intellect. Actually most of the things we do, we just do by intuition, we just know. Yesterday I was talking to someone about love, and they were saying that within thirty seconds you know whether you are going to love or like someone. I have found that in my experience of interviewing people for jobs, within thirty seconds or less I know whether they are right. You just intuitively know. Intuitively we just know how to steer our way through life. This is extraordinary. Our intuition is something that is never given credence to by our orthodox philosophy. For instance, just consider, look how many people there are on the streets of Kolkata, on the pavements, how is it that they do not bump into each other, is that not amazing! Why are there not more crashes, why are people not bumping into each other the whole time? Intuition is guiding them, just miraculously. When I was in Edinburgh they set up a department of paranormal psychology. Many of my students were philosophy and psychology students who did their postgraduate dissertations in the context of a research programme involving controlled experiments, which showed such amazing things as that nine out of ten people knew when they were being stared at from behind. How? They do not have eyes in the back of their heads. But they know. Intuitive knowing, synchronicity, telepathy—these are facts of life. In fact when I am talking to you, and you are listening, there is no physical mechanism, you just know.

So we have this sixth sense which is intuition and that is characteristically associated in western physiology and psychology with the right hemisphere of the brain. Everything to do with the right brain is underplayed or devalued by our experience. It is the left brain, the masculine, the controlling, the instrumental side, it is not the intuitive side, the side that already knows. The mother will know when the child needs feeding, she just intuitively knows. And she does not think in a linear, sequential, one-at-a-time punctiform way, she intuitively knows what is happening in the whole household, simultaneously. Actually we all do this, whether we are mothers, fathers, not parents at all, we do this in all aspects of our life. That is how we avoid bumping into each other on the streets of Kolkata. By a holistic intuition. Actually everything we do with the left brain, all our instrumental reasoning is undergirded by our intuition. So in addition to the discursive, the thought thinking intellect, we must allow the intuitive intellect, and in Indian philosophy you can do that because you have *buddhi* and *buddhi* is not *manas*, so you can have intellect and discrimination, choice, selection without thought. However that is not really good enough, because then we want to know what is this intuitive intellect? The intuitive intellect is not self-explanatory; it comes from somewhere else, it comes from something which is beyond intellect itself which you can say is consciousness or whatever. So far we have seen that there are two things that thought can be opposed to—consciousness and intuition.

But then of course thought can also be opposed to just seeing. Just seeing, just perceiving. So when I asked you to just listen, you just listened, when I asked you to look, you just looked, when you are watching television you are just looking. Now actually without this *seeing*, a just seeing which is much more basic than thinking, you cannot learn anything. If I try and teach you something, if (for instance) I try and explain a proof in mathematics or logic on the blackboard, and I say p implies q and p therefore q. Do you understand it? How can I explain that to you? You either understand it or you don't. I can never teach anyone anything. At best I can stimulate something within them which will enable them to say: 'ah, now I see it'. That seeing it, that grasping it, that 'now I get it' that eureka, that's it; that does not mean that we have fully mastered it. Then we have to play with it, shape it, toy with it, appreciate what it can do and how it does it. To understand, say, a law of logic such as *modus ponens*, as logicians call it, or a piece of algebra, or something like calculus, you may indeed have to spend years mastering it. Then suddenly there is a third stage at which it becomes part of you. Then it is no longer external to you, it is not in your mind, your mind is free, clear, you are master of calculus, no one has to remind you of it, you just do it. That is a typical dialectic—first the 'seeing', then the 'exploring' and then the 'in-built knowing', which enables us to do, apply or make things with it.

Now this suggests that there is a more basic level than seeing which was the first step of this process of learning, and that is just being. And this is the fourth thing to which thinking may be counterposed. When your knowledge, your love, your humanity, your concerns are just part of your innermost being, then you do not have to think about or do anything else to do something, you just do it. When the appropriate occasion arises you will know how to solve the equation. If you know Japanese, and you come across a Japanese gentleman, you will immediately know how to introduce someone else. You will not have to think about it, it will just happen. This is a state of being and the ancient Chinese made this an ideal. You should really just be, you do not have to do anything, just be. Some systems of Vedic philosophy say ultimately when we are in our *dharma*, when we are in our innermost essence we just flow, the sun does not try to shine, it just shines; a flower does not try to (or make an effort to, think or fuss about) blossom, it just blossoms; an acorn does not try to grow into an oak, it just grows into an oak. Of course you can, and manipulative humanity does, try to stop these things. You can stop it, you can stop the sun shining, sometimes you cannot see the sun in Kolkata because it is so hazy, sometimes I have great difficulty in seeing the moon and I ask people, is this a dark moon again? When is the full moon coming? Does it ever come anymore in Kolkata?

Now we have got being then as something opposed to consciousness, at least in the form of thought. Actually this is the starting point of the philosophy which was mentioned at the beginning and which I suppose I am famous for, critical realism, which opposed the dominant indeed hegemonic view of western philosophy, which effectively denied being in favour of thought— a move initiated in modern times by Descartes in his cogito 'I think therefore I am' and consolidated into a dogma (which I have called the epistemic fallacy) by Hume and Kant. Critical realism, which is really a process of continual self-transcendence, theorised being as something you could think and talk about as a philosopher, so that you could say being was such and such, that not everything was without thought although being contained thought. And then there are various categories of being: there is enfolded, potential, implicate being; there is being in process, that is becoming; there is being as a totality or a whole; then there is being as transformative praxis, that is agency, and there is being involved in reflexivity, that is the unity of theory and practice. But in addition I have argued that there is another very important category of being which is nothing. This is being as emptiness, being as absence.

One of the things that dialectical critical realism said was that contrary to what the western philosophers since Parmenides had maintained, nothing and absence and negation and negative states generally (and so process and change) exist, and in fact they are prior to the positive states of being. We could not articulate a sentence, we could not read something unless there were spaces, unless there were gaps we could not make out any positive states. Unless there was absence, unless the world contained space, absence, hiatus, pause, silence, there could be nothing positive. There could be no talk, you could not have an atom. If the world just consisted of atoms there would be nowhere they could move (there would be no motion) and moreover nowhere they could even be (there would be no space). You could not tell one atom from another, they would have to be an undifferentiated mass. And then how could you measure an undifferentiated mass, an undifferentiated mass would become a single point. Everything would collapse without absence, without negativity, without the not. So we have the category of absence. This is the fifth thing to which thought can be counterposed.

Let me go back to Krishnamurti's dialectics of watchfulness. Pay attention, pay attention to yourself. Observe your thoughts and the great powers of observation and awareness will immediately take you into a state other than your thought. And you will easily, for that moment at least, get rid of your fixations, get rid of your thoughts, your syndromes, your bound (and constrained) energy, you will get out of your thought trap in which you were stuck. Of course when you are back into the normal routines of life you will start thinking again in the same old routinised way and when you do you will have to work on your thoughts, and for example their emotional, unconscious, social or biographical (geo-historical) basis. But we cannot go into that here. Ultimately this dialectic if you focus, if you go further and further back, it will take you to: where? To emptiness, to nothing. But similarly, and this is the extraordinary thing, if you pursue the dialectic of watchfulness the other way, moving away from yourself, your subjectivity, your thought, your states of consciousness, <u>into</u> something else, into objectivity, be it a thought or an emotion such as fear, or another person or situation or indeed any other object at all; and if you go into it, just observing (without judgment, thought), going into it ever more deeply and fully so that you will eventually become one with it—as even now you are one with my words, it too will eventually turn into emptiness. But this emptiness will be rich, energising, liberating, joyous. Not nugatory. Rather, a state of maximum negentropy—blissful potentiality, something like what the Vedic tradition would call sheer *sat-chit-anand*—bliss consciousness of being, or that emptiness (*sunyata*) which is also the richest suchness (*tathata*)—or to move over to a more Chinese inflection, the Buddha-nature which is, in my terminology, the ground state of everything everywhere.

Indeed absence or emptiness is much maligned, for just consider, how can you learn anything if your mind is not empty, if thought is not absent from it? If you have something in your mind, how can you learn anything? You can only learn something when you have nothing, no knowledge, when you have an empty mind, when you have a clear mind. You see if you carry some knowledge into a learning situation, whether it be a seminar or life (and everything is potentially a teacher), then you will have a preconception, a prejudice, a pre-idea which will deflect your learning, just as it will deflect your action generally. It will not be learning, but split-learning, half-learning. Your focus is going to be split, you are not going to learn. For you will impose on your learning a preconception of what you already know, or rather think you know. It will be like learning mixed with what you already knew, it will be half-learning. But you cannot half-learn calculus: you either know it or you do not know it. You can either drive a car or not, you either know how to work an email or you don't, there are no two ways about it. You know how to change a baby's nappy or you don't, there are no two ways. So knowing nothing is the best advice for a student. Just go into the classroom, be empty, carry nothing in your mind. So what does this mean? Obviously, then, you will discover, learn, find out something. I cannot teach you anything, you already know it. You know it, but you are not conscious of it; it is implicit in, not explicit for you, what I can do is, at some point, awaken, bring out, elicit it (if you are listening and if you are following me). And education just means this bringing out of what you already know. Then you have the 'eureka', 'now I see it'. And then at that point you can say 'I get it'. But, as we have seen, you cannot say you know it then. For at that stage it will be in your mind quite a lot. But as soon as you can make it your own then, when it is part of your being, it is not in your mind, cluttering, draining, prejudicing your capacity to create, enjoy, love, learn and act freely.

Teachers tell their students before the exam, do not revise, you will not be rested, you will cloud your mind, but students always revise. Why? Both are correct. The teacher is correct that you should not revise, the students should know it, it should flow from their innermost essence—as the sun shines from its being. It should not be something he or she has to think about before the exam. He should be beautifully rested. But of course the student has not mastered it, or she is not sure if she has mastered it so she has to check if she has mastered it or she has to try and memorise it, desperately. I may never have got to the point of 'I get it' with calculus, I may just memorise the formula which will allow me to pass the exam, or something like that.

Now this ideal state of emptiness is the state we should all try to be in, as much as we can. This is the state beautifully expressed by the German mystic Eckhart when he said that 'blessed are the poor in spirit' was the most illuminating statement in the Bible—and where the poor man, the blessed man, was the one who, as he put it, 'wants nothing, knows nothing and has nothing'. We have nothing. When we have nothing we are everything; we are maximally free—both maximally free from (constraints) and maximally free (empowered) to do. Then we want nothing. So there is nothing heteronomous outside ourselves, which can bind us, cling to us, limit us. This is of course very familiar to the Indian tradition—we all know we should not have desires, we should not have attachments, but we cannot go into this here. So on to 'know nothing'. What does this mean? What this means is that there should be nothing in our heads, in our minds; *everything we know in our being*. We should not have any knowledge in our heads, we should not be thinking, we should be unthinking. Only then will you have a clear mind. A clear mind is nothing, a translucent mind, an empty mind, a no mind which is also a 'don't know mind'. No mind and no thought. This is unthinking or no thinking. To unthink you have to have no mind so that you then have a clear mind, you have an open mind, you have a flexible mind, that you have a creative mind, an active mind, a mind that can do this, a mind that can love.

Then when you go into the classroom—and remember the classroom is life—what mind do you have? No mind, don't know mind, don't know. You don't know, if you don't know something, you don't know it. You say, I don't know it, not I think; everyone says 'oh I think'. You see our world is full of people who are opinionated, we judge, think, name, everyone has an opinion on this or that. As you probably know I am here in Kolkata to give some lectures on spirituality and comparative religion. Whenever I go to give my lecture I sit in a room where I am given very nice hospitality. There is always a particular lady who comes up to me and assuming—she just assumes—that I will be defending everything to do with religion she treats me to a barrage of questions. These questions come in a string: 'how can you justify. . .' 'I really can't understand why you. . .' And she doesn't pause to listen to my answers, if I had any. She doesn't come to my lectures to listen to what I have to say. She doesn't even ask people what I am saying. She just assumes and opinionates. So yesterday, she paused for a bit and waited for a response and said, come on tell me how you would deal with that; and I said 'by silence'. And you know something, she started to smile and we actually started to talk to each other for a bit. And perhaps the next time I meet her we will make further progress. Silence is a very good response in life. Don't we all feel infuriated when someone just talks and talks endlessly. I have two lovely bodyguard students who look after me and take me everywhere in Kolkata, but I was getting very fed up with having to talk to them the whole time. So I said to them listen, now that we are really good friends, we do not have to talk anymore. We can be silent, we can be relaxed.

Now what does this mean, when you are listening, when you are just doing, when you are just being. Supposing I am talking to you and you are listening to me. Something magical is happening—duality and the ego and thought have all disappeared. Just listening, watching, attending immediately breaks down the model of ego and object. Because there is no thought, there is no subject of the thought, no ego and no object of thought, nothing to manipulate or control, nothing to cling or bind you, to entrap, fixate or 'stick' you. There is no such thought. When you are listening you cannot be thinking, when you are thinking you cannot be listening, if you are listening there is no thought. If you are listening to me then there is no separation between us; there is no ego in me and there is no ego in you, so you have lost your ego and you have lost your thought. Then all you have to do is lose your possessions and your desires, your attachments and aversions. But though this is outside the scope of my talk, you have already made a huge stride in this direction—but as you have no ego there is nothing to attach to or be averse from, nothing to conditionalise or constrain you, nothing to cling to you or bind you. In that moment you are whole and free and are at peace without conflict, at one with yourself—and me, and the rest of the cosmos. And then you will satisfy, at least for this moment, Eckhart's ideal. But I have reached the end because I was only talking about the first loss, the loss of a busy mind.

Chapter Thirteen

Unconditionality in Love[*]

1. The first point to realise is that love is not an action. Love is a motive or ground for actions but not itself an action. And in fact when you act you should not feel emotional, you should not experience any emotion at all, as that will diffuse and split its intentionality. It is for that sort of reason that Krishna told Arjuna that he should stop crying and pull himself together and do his duty, that is his *dharma*, what he is best at doing, namely shooting arrows directly at the target. And he shouldn't even think about his target (which in this case were the hearts of his kinsmen), he should just focus and shoot. Love is therefore not an action but a moment in the morphogenesis of any action. That is to say it corresponds if you like to the domain of the real rather than the actual. And the different moments in the morphogenesis of an action are (as we have discussed elsewhere) the moments of will (or pure intentionality), the moment of creativity, the moment of love and then the moment of action or objectification, that is making or doing something in the world.

---

* Abstracts from Santiniketan workshop for Kolkata housewives, March 2002.

2. Unconditionality is a property both of actions and of emotions and when you do something or feel something unconditionally, then you are very likely to be in a non-dual state. We can't say necessarily certainly; but what we can say is that when you do something conditionally then you are definitely not in a non-dual state, you are in a state of duality. To put a condition on something, whether it be a motive in the genesis of any action or an action in the sequence of one's life during the day (these two will be very closely related of course), when you put a condition on anything, say like love, what you are doing is giving and taking back. In fact you could say that the history of civilisation in a way was initially the history of pure **giving** (in the form of sharing, etc.), including of course giving to yourself; then with the advent of phenomena such as barter and money and exchange,[1] it became **giving and taking**. Now civilisation is such that we are in an epoch of **taking**, just taking without giving.

3. I could go into detail on another occasion to show how non-duality performs three roles in social life:

(a) Non-duality is the basis of the realm or world of duality. That is to say that all of our being, and all the structures in our society are ultimately sustained by a non-dual ground or basis, which I have called our ground states which are inter-connected with each other on what I have called the cosmic envelope. Love is a natural property of the ground state. We do not have to be, as it were, taught to love, love will flow spontaneously from our ground state if we let it. What happens is we put blocks and constraints on the manifestation of the love which we essentially are, which characteristically takes the form of negative emotions, such as fear, pride, jealousy, desire, etc. All these negative emotions take the place of or mix with love and deflect its force and power.

---

[1] The first act of exchange between two formerly self-sufficient communities sets in motion a dialectic or process which almost inevitably leads to money and exploitative relations between the two communities, be they tribes or whatever. On this view, which will be justified elsewhere, it is actually money which lays the basis for exploitative relations, class relations and capitalism, rather than the other way around.

What we need to do then to express love is to let go, let go of all these negative emotions.

Now these negative emotions which replace or deflect love actually themselves depend on love, so in any emotional state, in so far as it is coherent at all, you will find some kind of binding power which is, albeit possibly in a very weak form, a mode of manifestation of love. Actually it would be much simpler if we said that there was no such thing as conditional love; and that all love was unconditional. For nothing which is a ground state quality can be conditional—conditionality can characterise only its manifestation, not the quality itself. Conditional love would then be love mixed with some other quality, such as possessiveness in the case for the demand for reciprocation; or desire or greed, or fear, or whatever. When you let go, and of course this is often not simple at all, you have to work through and work hard to let go of these very stubborn factors in our embodied personalities, then you will just manifest at an emotional level pure unconditional love. This will inform or rather e-motivate your actions in a way which will depend on the specificity of the content of your action.

We have already seen that love is not an action, so you cannot say from identifying the form of action whether or not it is a manifestation of love. For instance if I was to rush out and hug the lady in the second row of the audience, that would probably be regarded at best as either an embarrassing joke or even as some form of assault; whereas we all know that hugging is, in other contexts, quite an appropriate manifestation of love. So the way we express our love always has to be specific to the person to and with we are expressing it, our relationship to that person and the context in which it is being expressed. To give another example, I may be in a relationship with someone and I have finally got to the point where I have got to tell them what I think is a very hard truth about them; perhaps I have tried subtle ways of expressing this, but now I have to speak it straight out and that may hurt them. Similarly, the best way in which I can express my love for someone may be by leaving them, or walking out of an unhappy relationship; and this may be the only thing I could do. Although love is associated with union, not all unities are real and not all 'unities' are expansive.[2] I will come back to this point later. So the thing to remember here is that love is a very natural property of the ground state and will automatically and immediately manifest itself in the appropriate action, if we are clear of all the other constraints and impediments.

(b) The second way in which non-duality manifests itself in our social world is through the way in which our social life and our being is each moment constituted and affected. Thus for you to hear my words, you have to identify with me, you have to be one with them. And this level of non-duality, here what I have called transcendental identification in consciousness, is what one might call a primitive, primeval or elemental form of manifestation of love. For in that understanding, that moment of non-duality, we are one. And this is a primary characteristic of love. So here again this is a way in which unconditional love immediately manifests itself on a daily and hourly basis in our everyday lives. Of course much of the time the non-dual mode of constituting, reproducing or transforming our daily activities has superimposed upon it a superstructure of duality, just as our ground states are blocked or constrained by all the non-dual components in our personality. Nevertheless unless there was that non-dual aspect in our social interactions and in our agency we could not communicate (or even perceive) or act at all. So just as love, and I have argued, unconditional love, is necessarily manifest in any e-motivated action, so in the form of transcendental identification in consciousness it is a necessary constituent of every moment of ordinary life.

---

[2] Nor can the notion of unity be identified with any one topographical form. Thus a relationship of love may be sustained despite spatio-temporal difference and independently of what amount of time, or in what activities, the 'lovers' spend together. In general love depends on respect for the autonomy and self-development of the loved one, as I argue a bit later. It is very important to appreciate that unity, a chief characteristic of love, is not identity; and that on the conception of identity that the philosophy of meta-Reality espouses even identity is not punctiform or simple, but rich, complex, holistic and differentiated. When two such entities feel a strong sense of union, the sort of sense of union, which I would normally characterise as love, they will expand and grow and there will be great reciprocity and mutuality, but one should not expect the elimination of differences.

(c) The third aspect in which non-duality appears as essential in our social existence is possibly slightly more difficult to see, but nevertheless it can easily be demonstrated in your own experience. And that is, if you focus or attend without judgment, thought, or intervening feeling on any state, be it a state of your own body or something in the external world, such as a beautiful flower, but in principle equally it could be a coat or a chair, just attending you will eventually experience a feeling of unity and wholeness with that on which you attend, and (here you should try it on someone you 'hate') you will eventually reach the point that through understanding you find love, and then going deeper through it you find the experience of sheer bliss or joy, what the ancient Vedics called *sat-chit-anand*, the bliss consciousness of being. This aspect of non-duality constitutes if you like the fine structure of the world in which we live. Thus what I am saying is that just focusing on any aspect of the world in which we live, you will find that its fine structure is ultimately constituted by the quality of love, which because you are in a non-dual state must be unconditional love.

So you can see that in these three ways we are all more than familiar with unconditional love. Unconditional love constitutes the fine structure of our universe (in fact it could be said to be the binding, coherent force which makes our universe a universe);[3] it constitutes a central feature of all our social interactions, especially in the form of transcendental identification with other beings, and finally any emotion we express ultimately depends upon the ground state quality of unconditional love.

4. We can say that there are five kinds of objects of love, five which define in a way by their interlocking, radiating circles of love, each of which will be expanding for you, the lover and what it is (at least potentially) that you love, the beloved, which will be mutually healing, cohering and totalising, unifying. In these five circles are the circle of love you have for yourself; the circle of love you may feel for one particular human being, say one with

---

[3] We could say that in so far as there is an ultimate level to the universe, a level which coheres or binds it or makes it one (something which has been traditionally associated with god), then it would be characterised by pure unconditional love.

whom 'you are in love', or there may be many such human beings, with whom you feel particular specific love in varying degrees—this is classically romantic or erotic love. Then the third circle of love is the circle of love in which you feel love for all human beings. The fourth circle of love is that in which you feel love for all beings in the universe (here of course we must make a discrimination, because while you can identify with and experience unity in that phenomenological moment with something in our being or in our world which is destructive, such as a person's jealousy, which we are seeking to understand, then this is only to help eliminate it); and the fifth circle of love is love for god. Probably romantic love and love for the divine are the two forms of love which have been most poeticised, talked and thought about.

However the primary form of love must be self-love. For if you do not love yourself then you cannot love, you do not have the power and the energy and the emotion to love anyone else; so that self-love in a way is primary.

Now probably the main motivating factor for most people when it comes to the topic of love is how to find or improve a relationship; this is to talk about the second circle of love. So there are two ways in which you can do this. Let us suppose you want to find someone to love you. The first route is the route of what I would call **reciprocity**. In a moment I will come to the second route which is that of **autonomy**. So following the first path you might think that you want to find someone who is going to complement you, so together you might complete each other, and this is probably the normal feeling about romantic love. Now going into the constitution of such a love. This presupposes some kind of attunement or attraction between the two people concerned. To get this attunement or attraction, you have to be able to become like them, in the sense that you must in a deep way be able to transcendentally identify with them, so that you can see how it is that you can complement your beloved. This will work then through overt or esoteric relations of reciprocity, which I will go into in the discussion. Eventually there will come a point or moment in which you fall in love or are in love, and you may regard yourself as, more or less in some degree, or even feel totally merged or fused or at one. The problem with the first path is of course that sooner or later you may find that you want to grow or expand in a way which your partner does not like or in a way which takes you away from your partner; and then you have the difficult choice or dilemma either to grow or expand or to stay with or fall in line with or tailor your aspirations to that of your partner.

The second path is far superior. So let us consider now the path of autonomy. We are starting from the same position, that you want to find someone appropriate to be with, to love, and hopefully be loved by. On the path of autonomy, what you do is you shed all the obstacles in your embodied personality, moving closer to your ground state so you become closer and closer to actually being love, that is you become more full of love. Being more full of love, you will naturally attract others to you. But if you are essentially love and you are in your ground state, you will soon find whether there is something in the other, or your putative partner, which is blocking or constraining his love, tendentially oriented towards you; then we have a situation in which you are full of love and he is not.

And you will realise that because of that difference, in order, if you still feel attracted or in some way attached to him, you will have to help him clear what it is that constrains or blocks the free flow of love, the kind of way in which your love flows naturally to him. And if that doesn't work, then eventually you will have to realise that this is not going to be a suitable or appropriate or happy relationship. (Or you will have to sacrifice your autonomy, your own aspirations in life which, we have already seen, powered by the norm of single-pointedness or clarity in pursuit of any objective, must eventually take you to a point where you are in your *dharma*, that is on the path towards self-realisation.) And you can carry on in your own way, growing and expanding, becoming more and more full of love and sooner or later you will find an appropriate object of love. In fact if you set out just to find someone to be with, then, as is well known, this will block or inhibit your growth or expansion and be rather counter-productive; you will be living a very limited existence.

A far better thing would be just to go straight into your *dharma*, what is naturally, effortlessly, spontaneously you, then you will find someone who is in their *dharma*, who will resonate harmoniously with you in the sort of relationship of love which you both want. And then you can grow for a time or in principle forever in a relationship of what I will call **co-autonomy**.

You will all perhaps be familiar with the two most typical modes in which people link up with each other in India today—these are the institutions of arranged marriage and the love marriage, or sometimes just the love affair. The arranged marriage presupposes that in some way the parents (and this is the justification they would give) have some sort of insight into your ground state or your *dharma* in terms of which they can match you with someone else, irrespective of your choice or feeling. Of course this choice makes a huge presupposition, namely that you will have to feel that the people who are making the choice for you have an insight into your ground state, which you may feel is not justified by their insights (or rather probably, you will feel their lack of insights) into other features of life. The love marriage or relationship or affair, as it typically occurs in India today, is just a simple route on the path of reciprocity, that is striving for completion by an act of transcendental identification or attunement with the other, and we have seen this is inherently inhibited if you or the other is unable to be at one with their ground state. Only if someone is at one with their ground state in a way which will not inhibit your growth and expansion. So basically both the preferred institutions in contemporary India fall a long way short of the path of autonomy, which I would call co-autonomy, which I have been mapping here.

5. Turning now to the other circles of love, the five it will be remembered are love for oneself; love for a particular or group of 'significant others'; love for your fellow human beings, love for all beings; and love for god. I have already argued that self-love is a necessary condition for any form of love. And further, that if you go for romantic love, the second kind of love, the best way to get it is along the path of self-realisation; that is the best way of achieving romantic success is by moving into your ground state and then you will find a partner who won't inhibit your expansion and development in life. So self-realisation would seem to be what is necessary for the second form of love. The universali-

sation of self-realisation, to collective human self-realisation, is obviously what is implied by the third form of love, because clearly your love is going to be somewhat short if you love yourself fully enough to achieve self-realisation, but you do not love your fellow human being to help them achieve their own freedom, fulfilment and realisation. The fourth form of love, by an extension of the previous argument, namely for all other beings whether they are human or not, suggests a goal of universal self-realisation. And in fact it is not difficult to show there is no dialectical unity between the goals of self-realisation and universal self-realisation, in that as you approach your ground state you will immediately become a better and more loving (as well as creative, energised and right-acting) person, thus spontaneously aiding the processes leading to universal self-realisation.

This then leaves the question of love for god. Where does god come into it? Ultimately we would have to say that god, if he exists, would be the totality, something like the cosmic envelope, or if you like the ground or creator of the cosmic envelope. All love is characterised by the conatus or impulse to union or unity, which is not of course the same as (though we can incorporate aspects of) identity with the beloved. In fact the easiest way to define god is in terms of the conception of what is ultimate, the coherent binding force in the universe which I have called the cosmic envelope, or, if you like, the ground of that cosmic envelope (if they are not one and the same). The chief defining feature of the cosmic envelope, that is the totality that binds ground states, would be pure, unbounded love. Therefore any love will tend to take you towards, via your ground state, to the cosmic envelope, it will always have this spin-off or side-effect; but a pure love for god will take the form of the love for the totality, that is all the ground states of all beings in the cosmos; and the more you experience that love, the more you will become one with that totality. Now if you suppose, as I have argued elsewhere, that the totality is in fact enfolded within you as an implicit potential in your ground state, then the more you experience love for the totality, the more elements within that implicit enfolded totality co-present in you will be awakened or brought into a state of readiness. And the more you will tend to become one with that totality.

So to love god then is to love the totality (or the ground of that totality) and at its limit the love for god would take the form of an objective which went beyond self-realisation, beyond universal self-realisation, which is the realisation of all beings in and for themselves, to the objective of 'god-realisation', that is unity with the totality. This means that at this point you would become one, at least in significant aspects of your being, become the totality, not just be at one with the totality, or exist in a totality which was a harmonious whole, as in the case of universal self-realisation. Becoming the totality would be the ultimate end of love for god. And this in fact we find in the spiritual literature as the goal of what is variously called *fana*, in Islam, the annihilation or replacement of oneself by god. In Sufi literature, one dies to oneself become one with god, but given the particular interpretation of god within Islam, this means that you do literally die, are annihilated, your existence is not preserved, you are replaced by god. Of course it might be said this is just a state of mind reached in ecstasy, but let us not go into that here. Alternatively, we might take a tradition coming from the Vedas, namely the Buddhist tradition. The ultimate goal would be that of *nirvana*, which is a kind of becoming one with god in which you lose not just your sense of separateness from the rest of being (as in the loss of ego in self-realisation), but your very identity. The difference is this that to lose your ego is to lose your feeling that you are separate from other beings, to seek for their realisation as much as, and to realise that it is ultimately the condition of your own. And this I have argued elsewhere is an implication of virtually all emancipatory projects when you go deeply enough into them, but it is very explicit in the ideal of the Bodhisattva of Mahayana Buddhism or Marx's vision of a communist society in which the free development of each is a precondition of the free development of all. This then is the state of universal self-realisation.

The state of *nirvana* or *fana* is rather a state in which you have no identity or existence apart from god. One way of looking at this is that you literally cease to exist and are in a sort of way replaced by god. Another way is suggested by Jesus' talk about going to join his father in heaven, and the metaphor used was of sitting on his throne, a kind of retirement of engagement from struggles on earth. This then would be achieving unity in consciousness and being with god, and in this state of *nirvana*, on this interpretation, then surely no-one in their right mind would prefer to have only their own powers and consciousness (as it was constituted in a way independent of the totality) rather than the powers and consciousness of the totality itself (or its ground).

It would be as silly to take an example I used in another context—that of Hume saying he really could not decide whether to prefer the destruction of his little finger to the rest of the world. What is wrong with his statement is obviously that (detotalising himself, or his little finger) he does not realise that the destruction of the world would entail the destruction of his little finger too. So clearly he should prefer only the destruction of his little finger. So that if you were given the choice just to be you, or to be you and everything else, would it not be supremely irrational to go for the former? So becoming one with the totality, you could still be, in the sense of having the powers and consciousness of you, at the highest point of your realisation and development before you became one with the totality, i.e., as an independent individual; but now you would have in addition the capacity to become one with the powers and consciousness of everything else that existed. So it would be quite irrational (as irrational as Hume) not to prefer to lose your own identity in that of god, wouldn't it?

6. So what I have sketched out is a natural dialectic in terms of whatever object you love, and remember that whatever your emotion or feeling is (and remember also that you can never not have an emotion or feeling, since emotions and feelings are necessary constituents of all human being and activity), that emotion or feeling ultimately depends on love. And I have argued that all love depends ultimately on unconditional love. We have seen that whatever your initial object of love might be and this in principle includes objects I have not included here, such as a love for architecture or a dog or a particular brand of coffee, that will eventually take you on a dialectic on which you will need to move through the stages of self-realisation, universal self-realisation, and that unity or rather fusion with the totality or the ground of the totality which I have called god-realisation (however far removed from

purview this is now). Indeed I would argue this is a goal which is implicit in all being, since the totality is enfolded in principle within every being which exists, a feature which does not remove the distinctiveness of those beings, while the totality is as yet unfolded within them as so it is with them. So any form of love will set you on this dialectic, in which the first step, a step that most of us (at least those of us who are even aware of it) are struggling very hard on, namely the path of self-realisation, is the best way of achieving any feeling or emotional objective you have. The best way to love and be loved is to become self-realised; and this means you will immediately be working for the self-realisation of all other beings, i.e., the totality of all beings, which, in a way, you are increasingly identifying with and therefore becoming one with.

7. Then can we say anything about *what* you should love? In fact *only* if your love is for the ground state of your lover will your love succeed. Because if you love anything else but that, then there are two possibilities—either what you love about him is consistent with his ground state, but then his embodied personality may well develop in a way also consistent with his ground state but one which you do not love; or it is even possible that if there is no direct connection he will develop a quality that is not consistent with his ground state in his own journey in life. So this then is the second possibility, that what you love about him is inconsistent with his ground state, that is, it involves some heteronomy or block or constraint on the love that he can express or reflect back to you, and of course this will not only impede his love for you, but will block and drag back that directness of union of unions which is love loving love, which would otherwise occur if it was you from your ground state loving him from his ground state, and in that situation you can indeed lose, in the sense that your love, that is the love which is you, your ground state, may grow less, be less full, than it would have been if you had chosen some other object of love.

In fact there is only *one* object that you can really love, and that is the *divine ingredient* in the ground state of the one you love, a divine ingredient which may well and indeed will be normally different from that divine ingredient which is your love. So when you realise that what you really love is the divine or immanent god in your beloved, then you will soon appreciate that you only love *god*, and that *god is actually the only thing you can love*. Because ultimately the love at the ground state of the thing or being that you love is or must be that most ultimate and basic ingredient which is most full of love which will be precisely at the level of the cosmic envelope which is the totality. So do you think you have another love besides god? If this argument is correct you mis-identify your love if you think in loving a being that you can love something other than god. However, if you think you can love god without loving the totality of other beings then you are equally mistaken. For there is no god that you can love which is not ingredient or does not depend on the ground state of the totality of all other beings. So love itself embodies a drive to totality, that means you must ultimately, once you love anything, be set on a dialectic in which you must unconditionally love the totality of all beings, albeit in ways which are specific to the concrete singularity of the relationship you have to them, which does not qualify the unconditionality of your love, but merely qualifies the form in which you express it, i.e., your behaviour.

The drive to totality is not just on the traditional path of devotion, but on the other paths as well. Because if you follow the path of knowledge then the norm is truth and if you seek anything other than the whole truth, you will be in error, because leaving something out will inevitably generate a contradiction which will sooner or later become apparent. Similarly on the path of action, unless your work is dedicated to the totality of all beings, then you will err in your practice (of yoga which of course means union), again yielding an incompleteness in your love or practice and failure in what you strive for. A single person in a society founded on eudaimonistic principles as the free development of each is a condition of the free development of all can undermine that society completely. There is one further point to notice about the relationships of these great norms of truth, love, service.[4] So being full of love on the cosmic envelope, how can

---

[4] Similarly, in the case of the path of Hatha Yoga, full embodiment of the principle of love must be practiced because if you do not love any aspect of your embodiment you will go out of balance and become ill. This is true in terms of

you tell whether someone else is full of love? Well you give love and you experience the quality that you feel when you have given the love. If what you get back is an insult or a lie, then of course it may be unintended and you test it further. Eventually a lie or a neglect will expose itself to you in the absence of the peace and wholeness that you should feel as a being of pure unbounded love. If every time you put your hand in the fire you feel pain then sooner or later you know something is wrong. In fact no heteronomy whether it be cognitive, emotional or practical can withstand the scrutiny and power of love. On a final note, it is important to see the connection between love, which unifies all the virtues, and strength. Because actually nothing is stronger than love, love is not soppy or sentimental at all, of course these may be manifestations of a strong love in a particular context. But in its essence love is as the cohesive force in the universe and in your ground state, that which makes you strong.

    8. The ultimate end or this goal, the totality, is not just something which is there implicit in love, in fact in any form of desire, it is implicit in all the constituents of our being. Thus if you take the three traditional paths, the path of truth or wisdom, that is Jnana Yoga, union through wisdom or knowledge or truth, Bhakti Yoga, or the path of devotion, or Karma Yoga, or the path of action or service, we can see that they all aspire to union, union which ultimately must be the totality. Thus the path of wisdom is the path of remedying incompletenesses and absences in the way I have sketched elsewhere as the process of dialectic until you

---

the relationship between the qualities that define these paths macroscopically. Thus if you are extremely creative but do not allow yourself to express love then you can end up being an enormously successful villain. Or if you are very loving, and indeed also loving to yourself, a necessary condition for any love at all, because you are only as strong as the love that constitutes you, even if you are full of love and you are extremely boring or uncreative then you will not be able to expand your love because you will not be acting in ways which exploit the natural variety and opportunities of the environment to express your love. You will be a monological lover, knowing only one way to love you will not increase the love that you are at the rate you would be if you were creative.

reach a theoretical totality, the whole truth.[5] The path of Karma Yoga proceeds in exactly the same way until you have a practical totality, ultimately this will be something like a eudaimonistic society, in four-planar social being, which can be extended to the cosmos as a whole. Bridging these two, the theoretical and practical totalities, we have the path of Bhakti Yoga, the path of love, in exactly the same way aspire to the whole. In fact love must ultimately strive for the whole, to leave anything out is inconsistent with the unifying, totalising binding force of love which, to stress, does not mean the engulfment, differentiation, of the different species and individuals in creation—for the more beings there are in their *dharma* the more they flower in a unique, empowered way.

So it might seem that if one has to prioritise these three paths one can say that it is ultimately the path of love which binds and sustains each of these paths, love is the expanding totalising force whether in the theoretical field of knowledge or in the practical field of action; and love is of course the defining quality of Bhakti Yoga. So if there is a supreme value in the universe (or some particular aspect of it, or piece of our life) then we are going to have to say it is love. So if you wanted to ask what was the totality, or the universe, or god, then the best answer you could give would just be the source or fount of union with all possible union, that is pure unbounded love, irrespective of the particular forms of its manifestation. For to recapitulate the beginning of

---

[5] The whole truth is something which will always have to be relativised to context; the whole truth is what will be relevant and significant for the matter at hand; and you will have to be one with it, and this means that merely you know the central principles in terms of which you can access any particular truths. And there would be no such thing as the whole truth, independently of some particular interest or issue. In this respect there are always practical questions, which will include in the world of duality strategic questions about the truth and its communication, which I will not go into here. In a parallel way in the domain of emotional life on the path of Bhakti Yoga we have seen that the goal often and indeed normally requires fighting and splitting, alienating yourself from elements of the totality you want to heal. You do not stay in a bad relationship, you get out so that you can struggle the better to put an end to a condition in which people slip into bad relationships.

this talk, I argued that love is not an action, but the ground or motive for action. In the same way love is not knowledge, but a ground or motive for knowledge. And now what I have just said that it is love which binds the cosmos together and is the ultimate source of value, and moreover, that if one wanted to know what god was then the only thing you could say would be pure unconditional love.

Actually, however, on close inspection these three paths are not at all distinct. For the defining characteristic of knowledge is identification; which is also at the level of intuition of alethic truths, the actual becoming one with that which you know. This becoming one is an active process, an action, a creative action on your part. And this becoming one is a form or moment of unity between you and what it is that you know, which you have become, and in becoming one, you love; because you cannot know something in this way without becoming one with it, and you cannot become one with it without loving it. On the other hand, if you love something enough, you become one with it, and then you are it, and you know it, so the paths of knowledge, love and action all reduce to one.

9. We have seen that any sustained act of attention, some awareness, in a non-dual mode, without the intervention of judgment, classification, thought, emotion, or physical feeling, will ultimately result in an experience of first understanding that which we have identified with, then feeling love for it, and finally experiencing that pure joy or bliss, which is suchness, emptiness, the Buddha nature or whatever, but an experience characteristic of pure consciousness at the level of the ground state. So when you focus on something evil, some moment of heteronomy, you will first understand it—this is the first moment in the dialectic of attention or awareness. You will then, understanding it, and the more you become one with it in your consciousness, the more fully you will understand it, then be in a position, retreating from that non-dual mode of identification, to fight and eliminate it. However if your attention or awareness is sufficiently strong, because all the elements of the universe are ultimately constituted by or depend on or can be seen under the aspect of implicit consciousness, and all the elements of the universe are ultimately sustained by the cosmic force of love, then your awareness itself will dissolve it. That is to say your awareness will eliminate the heteronomy or evil you have identified, whether it is within you or outside you. Let us see how this would happen. You would go into it, and then you would find that that element of heteronomy, definitionally being inconsistent with a ground state, would nevertheless depend on a ground state, feed off the energy of the cosmic envelope or love. You would eventually by attending to it, by being aware of it, be able to trace it back to that ground state that it was feeding off, dissolving it in a soup of cosmic love so to speak.

Tracing back the heteronomous element, the illusory or demi-real aspect of being which you have identified will ultimately be dissolved in this way, at the level of the 'Buddha-nature', or ground state it feeds off, which sustains it. When you get to that point, it cannot be part of the universe any more, because it must *either become one* with the ground state it is draining, and so lose its identity or cease to exist (Thus the capitalists would have to become one with the workers, or the aspect of a human being who was a master would have to become one with the aspect of a human being who was a slave, and it is easy to see that the system of master–slave relationships, or the oppressive nature would be no more). So in dealing with elements of heteronomy, what would loosely be called evil, or unfreedom, oppression (including self-oppression), dualistic duality, alienation and contradiction, recognising that all these things are ultimately sustained by the energy and the attributes of the ground states of beings, once you cut off their supply lines, they must either collapse into the sea of cosmic love and become one, lose their identity in the ground state they were feeding off or draining, or they will just exist no more, not be one with the universe which is bound by the force of cosmic love.

As such beings constituted by heteronomy depend on love and the other qualities of the ground state, the more you suffuse and overwhelm them with love, the more those aspects within those entities which are contrary or inconsistent with love will be outweighed and dissipated, until the point at which they become virtually extinct. You can see this tactic of love, this tactic or strategy of defeating the enemy via love, as being one in which you drive it back to the ground state which sustains it, then it must either collapse to love and the other qualities of the ground state or lose its independent identity. This actually defines a path of fighting oppression and evil by love. Actually, once you realise that love is an emotion, not an action, it does not necessarily have any specific implications for how you do it. At the same time once you realise that what is really important is to be clear about what it is in the being that you love, then you will see that you cannot love something that is opposing or oppressing the flourishing of the ground state qualities of that being. So inevitably love will tend to destroy the heteronomous and oppressive elements within what it loves. And as the most basic power or level of the universe is just the power of that form of awareness or consciousness which is pure unbounded love which keeps the whole universe together, then ultimately by being at that level, focusing on that object from that level, that object must, in so far as it has love, come to you, and in so far as it has not got love, it will no longer be part of the universe. This is the true meaning of 'the turning of the other cheek', or the path of non-violence.

10. I have been arguing that whatever objective you seek in life, the norm of clarity and the insistent intentionality of your ground state will eventually force you into a position, that is, set you on a process, whereby you will strive to be only consistent with your ground state, that is self-realised. And this goes for love in all its forms, including romantic love. The mechanism is very simple: that so long as you have an objective in life or a strong attachment to something which is inconsistent with the flourishing of your ground state qualities, then because those qualities and their intentionality (which we will call your *dharma*) will be manifesting themselves anyway, you will not be able to achieve your objective; the only objectives that you will be able to achieve (any objective or goal in life, depending clearly on a clarity, a single-pointedness in the direction of that objective), or the only set of objectives you will be able to achieve will be those consistent with your ground state. Because whatever happens, whatever you do in life, the intentionality and the qualities of your ground state will always be there. And so long as you have objectives or heteronomies or emotions contrary to your ground

state, then your intentionality in life will be split and necessarily unfulfilled. So the first step inevitably is towards self-realisation.

But the next step is equally clear, and happens at each point on the first path, the path to self-realisation. This is a commitment, or even just a way of acting, which will necessarily flow from your being clearer in your being as you move towards your ground state, you will spontaneously act in a way which maximises the possibilities of the self-realisation of all beings. In fact we have already seen that there is no way that you can be fulfilled or even truly free, so long as there are heteronomies or beings which are unrealised outside you, because in so far as you are all interconnected, their heteronomies, constraints will actually preclude you from expressing or fulfilling your *dharma*. For instance if you want to be a musician, you have to presuppose that you are going to be able to have instruments with which to play your music, people to play it with, and people to play it to. If any of these conditions are not realised then you will not be fulfilling your *dharma*. This is another way of explicating what I have earlier called the fifth theorem of action. This is that whatever you do, even though you do it necessarily yourself (because it is your action), you will inevitably be affecting in principle all other beings in the universe; and at any rate immediately having an effect on nature, on social interactions with others and at the level of the social structure. Certainly self-realisation in the sense of enlightenment, in the sense of having no heteronomies within yourself is an attainable objective. But even when you are realised you will not be free until all other beings are free. And as you are on the path to realisation, you will be automatically and spontaneously acting so as to liberate, that is to maximise, the possibilities of self-realisation of all other beings.

So we have seen that there is a natural dialectic from any objective you set yourself in life to consistency with your ground state, i.e. self-realisation. And then that this will automatically lead you to a commitment, whether you realise it theoretically or not, to the self-realisation of all other beings. But as you develop, the more you will experience identification, whether in the form of knowledge, love or action (traditionally known as service) with other beings, until eventually you reach a point which that totality, which is the whole cosmic envelope, which is implicit within you, enfolded within you, becomes explicit and at that point it is plausible to say that you are one with the cosmic totality. You have ceased to be just your ground state but you have actually be-come one with the cosmic envelope. And this is to put a secular interpretation on what is known as 'god-realisation'.

11. Now we have seen that the condition of possibility of accessing a transcendent other, whether it be a piece of knowledge, the alethic truth of another being in the cosmos, or whether it be the divine, in the form of an epistemically transcendent but ontologically immanent god; or even whether it be interpreted or take the form of a transcendent god, is that you have the possibility of identifying becoming one with that which you strive for. Let me put this very concretely. If you believe that god or the divine is transcendent, ontologically, as in the traditional monotheistic religions of Judaism, arguably Christianity, and formally Islam, then you believe that the most fundamental feature or thing about you is your capacity, which defines in our terms your ground state essence, of conforming to god's will. God's will for you is the most basic feature about you. And this dialectic that we have already seen will take you back to a position in which you can see that any objective that you have set yourself, which is inconsistent with that most fundamental defining parameter will not be attainable, or sustainable. Now what is this condition of possibility of being one with god's will—there must be something inside you which enables you to become one with god's will. And therefore a transcendent god automatically entails an immanent god, or if you like an immanent divine, a potential that you have to conform with the will of god, a potential which you can actualise, and then you **are**, that is actually instantiating god's will. So the idea of the completely transcendent divine, which is nevertheless accessible or can play a role in human lives, is not a tenable one. What we are doing when we are seeking to observe god's will is to realise that aspect within ourselves which is in conformity with god's will for us; and in the same way we will be seeking to act in such a way that all other beings in the universe realise god's will for them. In other words the dialectic of self-realisation and univer-sal self-realisation applies here too. When you are totally

at one with god's will, then we have a position which is tanta-
mount again to 'god-realisation', that is to say you will be totally
at one with the will of god for the universe. So the dialectic of
self-realisation, universal self-realisation and god-realisation
applies to transcendent as well as to immanent interpretations of
the divine. In both cases what we are concerned with in our
human lives is to realise some aspect within ourselves, and clearly
that is all we can do. There is no point telling someone to realise
an aspect in a cosmos or a universe that he cannot access.

So whatever it is that we want in life, whatever it is we want
to do, become, know or love, it will always be a case of ourselves
becoming one with that which we want to be or know or love.
Let us take the simplest case of knowledge. You are seeking very
hard to discover what it is that explains apples falling to the ground,
or iron filings being attracted to a magnet or whatever. You are
getting nowhere; and you take a break or you stop thinking, you
unthink and then suddenly 'eureka', you get it. At that moment
there is an identification, something within you has been elicited
by a transcendent outside you and/or what has already been awakened within you is allowed to express itself in your consciousness. Whatever happens that truth was, or is at the point of
'eureka', something that was implicit within you. If it was not
implicit within you there is no way you could know it. So this is
the basis for saying that all knowledge is enfolded within you,
and only has to be awakened. In this moment of knowledge you
become what it is that you know, you are one with it, just a heightened accentuation of that transcendental identification we must
necessarily experience with each other in order to communicate
anything at all. In this becoming one with the other, you are the
other, and at the level of your ground states we have, so to speak,
one bundle of love becoming one with another bundle of love.
So essentially it is *love loving love*. To seek to aspire to become one
with the cosmic totality is to seek union with the source of all
union and this will inevitably set you on a dialectic at which you
will feel you need to become one with all. Or which is grounded
in the cosmos, which is one with its ground state. And this will
not be a merely passive mode of relating to the world. Elsewhere
we have seen that perception and action at the level of the ground

state are not easily differentiable, if at all. Be that as it may you will be an active agent in the world, so that once again we have the tri-unity of these three paths of knowledge, of love and of action. And in whatever way your *dharma* or own particular ground state qualities are inflected, this drive to universal self-realisation that you experienced on the path to self-realisation will inevitably take you on a drive to union with the alethic truths of all those beings on the cosmic envelope in which you are grounded. Inevitably you will be set on a path to union with the totality, which will be the unfolding of what is already enfolded within you. And so the goal of god-realisation or union with the totality is one which is also implicit like universal realisation or any desire or objective you have in life.

From the point of view of the cosmo-theogony of creation what does this mean? If the only logical way of making sense of a source origin or ultimate ground of the universe is the idea of an ultimatum (or a goal), which must be self-created out of nothing, for if there was something out of which that god was created, then it would not be ultimate. So the beginning or ultimate ground must be self-creation out of nothing. What then is the end or goal state? It must be the becoming one of all, that is the god-realisation of all beings on the cosmic envelope, that is the becoming one with the totality of all elements of the totality. Then of course there would be no duality at all.

12. Let us be a little bit more specific about what this actually entails for human practices. The world of duality is underpinned and sustained by the realm of non-duality. As we become non-dual beings, or approximate or strive towards it, then we still have to perform dualistic actions in the world which is characterised by physical constraints, the world of relativity; and more so because that relative world, the world of duality, the world in which our embodied personalities live and grow and develop, is a world which is dominated not just by duality, but dualism, alienation, contradiction, split, that is oppositional duality, taking the form of all kinds of heteronomies or unfreedoms, constraints on the realisation of beings and on the freedom of realised beings alike. This is the world of the demi-real. Universal self-realisation, or more concretely the construction of a eudaimonistic

society which satisfies the kinds of ideals of Marxian 'communism', namely a society in which the free development of each was the condition of the free development of all, or Mahayana Buddhism, in which no being could be realised, or at least ultimately free, until all beings were; ideals which we have seen are implicit in all emancipatory projects and universalising systems of ethics, involves the dialectic of disemergence, the shedding of all those constraints both inside and outside you. When a society of universally self-realised beings is constructed, then we will have, so to speak, heaven on earth: demi-reality, master–slave relationships, the totality of constraints on the development of human powers and potentialities will be eliminated. This would be the ushering in of such a society which would mark the end of prehistory, and the beginning of a real history. We would now be living in a world in which the zone of non-duality had expanded and was continuing to expand, this would be the beginning of real development and flourishing, unconstrained by blocks which resulted from split human intentionality and any other constraints or sources of heteronomy in being.

13. At this point we would have the disemergence of co-presence, the elimination of heteronomy and the realm of the demi-real. This then would be the level of universal self-realisation, there would still be a world of duality, still be a relative reality, underpinned by the ground state and the cosmic envelope and the realm of non-duality, but that realm of a relative reality, the realm constituted by our physically embodied personalities would grow and expand and develop in an unconstrained way. This is the dream of all utopias. This is what Jesus probably meant when he talked about the establishment of the kingdom of heaven on earth. This was one inflection I gave to the term 'god-realisation' in my book *From East to West*.

The other inflection I gave to that term was the actual goal of an individual being, at the level of its ground state or inconsistency with its ground state becoming one with the totality. This would be god-realisation in another sense. This corresponds presumably to what Jesus meant when he told his disciples that he was going to leave them and join his father, that is become one with god. We have seen that this ideal of becoming one with the totality is not only a plausible one, but one which is initiated and sustained by the same conatus that takes us to the goal of universal self-realisation. So it cannot be dismissed. If each being in its ground state becomes one with the totality, then we have a false state of affairs. Not only individual god-realisation and universal self-realisation manifested in the realm of duality, we also have a state of universal god-realisation. What this would mean is the elimination of relative reality, that is the elimination of duality, and not just dualism and split. What this realm of non-duality alone would be we cannot imagine. For all the models that we have for imaging it would be taken from the realm of relative reality. What we could say is that it would be one of intensely rich blissful experience and unlimited potentiality not even constrained by physical parameters or laws. The world of physical embodiment as we know it would cease to exist. We have then four stages in a dialectic:

[1] Individual self-realisation
[2] Universal self-realisation
[3] Individual god-realisation
[4] Universal god-realisation

Now we can put this perspective in a logically coherent way in the form of what must have been the case in the beginning or if we take time out of it, at the ultimate ground of being, the level of the ultimate. The first moment in this process of creation would be:

(1) Self-creation out of nothing
(2) The generation of a world of duality
(3) The generation of a world of demi-reality, of dualism and split (inevitably proliferating out of this realm of duality.

Then the return or reverse dialectic:

(4) Individual self-realisation

We have seen this to be implicit in any objective you set yourself. We have also seen this to entail a commitment to:

(5) Universal self-realisation.

At this point the dialectic of disemergence, of shedding, of emancipation would usher in the eudaimonistic society and unconstrained flourishing within the realm of duality, of relative reality, a realm bound by constraints of the purely natural and physical parameters of the world.

But we have seen that the drive to union or unity or oneness, or the loss of a sense of separateness from other beings would eventually result whether you conceptualised your activity within the realm of duality cognitively or emotionally or agentively, on the paths of knowledge, love or action; it would inevitably result in the becoming one with the totality, in which your own individuality would go; and we have seen that it would not be a reasonable thing to retain your own individuality if you could have the individuality and powers, that is possibilities of the totality. Who would remain in their ground state if they could be in every ground state. But as every ground state is enfolded within any one ground state, as a being grows and develops, the cosmic totality enfolded within that being will be explicated, a process continuing until it is fully explicated when he or she or it will be one with it. That is:

(6) individual god-realisation

Exactly the same conatus will apply to every being, until the point of:

(7) Universal god-realisation.

At that point, of universal god-realisation, there would be no more duality, relative reality as we know it would have ceased to exist. And it would be very difficult to differentiate that stage from the initial stage in the dialectic of creation about namely (1)—or rather we could imagine that whatever happened at (7) would eventually result in the renaissance of another act of our auto-poesis out of nothing. If the seventh stage saw the extinction of the realm of duality, then we can imagine that eventually there would be another initial stage, a self-creation out of nothing, corresponding to the big bang. And then the seventh stage might be given a secular interpretation such as the black hole. Fortunately my time is running out and I will leave these speculations to the cosmologists of the future.

Index